D1588993

£10
1ST
EDITION

Fleetwood Mac

40 Years of Creative Chaos

Donald Brackett

 PRAEGER

Westport, Connecticut
London

Library of Congress Cataloging-in-Publication Data

Brackett, Donald, 1951–
   Fleetwood Mac : 40 years of creative chaos / Donald Brackett.
      p. cm.
   Includes bibliographical references and index.
   ISBN-13: 978–0–275–99338-2 (alk. paper)
   ISBN-10: 0–275–99338–8 (alk. paper)
   1. Fleetwood Mac (Musical group) 2. Rock musicians—Biography. I. Title.
ML421.F57B73   2007
782.42166092'2—dc22   2007020592

British Library Cataloguing in Publication Data is available.

Library of Congress Catalog Card Number: 2007020592
ISBN-10: 0–275–99338–8
ISBN-13: 978–0–275–99338–2

First published in 2007

Praeger Publishers, 88 Post Road West, Westport, CT 06881
An imprint of Greenwood Publishing Group, Inc.
www.praeger.com

Printed in the United States of America

In memory of my father, and in appreciation of my mother, for letting me be...

This book is dedicated to my wonderful partner
Mimi Gellman, who knows all the reasons why...
To my old friends Gerry Watson and Peter Moss, who may or may not.
To my fellow writer Kevin Courrier, who shares the struggle.
And to Bob Welch, master of the spooky transition.

Contents

A photo essay follows page 94.

Introduction: Plugging in

"If Music be the Food of Love, play on..."

—Shakespeare

How do you celebrate the 40th anniversary of a perfect marriage made in hell? Perhaps by counting your lucky stars—or even better, maybe by counting your money.

Imagine two old geezers. Nothing can come between them. You can see them, Mick Fleetwood and John McVie, both bald with snowy white patriarchal beards, sitting on the massive terraces of their country estates, where they often visit each other for high tea and ponder how it is they are still together after all these years. One of the old lads may turn to the other and quote John Lennon, in between sips of Earl Grey: "Life is what happens to you while you're busy making other plans." "Indeed it is, mate."

Fleetwood turns 60 this year, and McVie is already a crusty 62. Both are still crazy after all these years and tears. They are bona fide rock royalty, no matter what your musical taste. Back in 1992, when Mick was celebrating the mere 25th anniversary of his little experiment in musical mayhem, he produced a lovely pictorial book with a text by Stephen Davis. It opens with a touching and surprisingly tender observation in his dedication of the book to his musical partner, McVie: "To John, from the first until this, the brother I never had, you have been to me. My God, I swear we deserve each other. I love you very much, Mick"

Not exactly the sentiment one might expect from a grizzled rock beast, and yet his tender side is there for all to see. That was 15 long years ago, and now here we are celebrating the 40th anniversary of the band's founding in swinging England. They are still at it, or at least still talking about being at it.

Indeed, if the level of market penetration is one of the things that determines a legend, then Fleetwood Mac certainly qualifies, even though many listeners and critics alike may cast aspersions on their amazing grasp of the gold record contest. Commercial success often creates a musical allergy that is undeserved, and in the case of Fleetwood Mac, their three successive careers qualify them as legends of a sort, even though most people tend to take their lofty British peers, The Beatles, far more seriously.

Few groups have moved from the status of legend to myth, and then from myth to brand, quite as seamlessly and mysteriously as these masters of both disclosure and concealment. And yet, it goes without saying that Mac lasted a full five times as long as their illustrious forbearers for some simple reasons: Lennon and McCartney began to manifest music as a kind of self-development therapy through the fleeing of all limits, while Fleetwood and McVie always saw music as a form of entertainment celebrating the acceptance of limits.

For example, we can imagine the different message received by aliens if instead of discovering a copy of *Revolver* in our Voyager time capsule ashes, they discovered *Rumours;* one shudders. Like The Beatles, they experienced the reality of John Updike's admonition that "Celebrity is a mask that eats into the face." But they did not turn or run away from it; instead, they chose to wear the mask proudly. They even went so far as to title one of their later efforts, *Behind the Mask*. While both groups did use their art as a "pain machine" for the healing, transformation, and transcendence of suffering, only Fleetwood Mac maintained a firm grip on their roots in the blues (even when their blues was covered in the shiny varnish of their later-phase pop music). More importantly, they also maintained their inseparable link as creative partners joined at the hip.

Theirs is a truly unique and fruitful collaborative partnership, despite all the style shifts and personnel changes in their eponymous musical group. The following pages serve to explore the nature of their highly charged creative connection, which predates even the beginning of their own band and therefore has to be referred to as the prehistoric period of Fleetwood Mac. They are among the few rock dinosaurs who did not become extinct as a result of the perpetual climate changes in pop music, and they survived the way all evolutionary survival occurs: by adapting to reality.

This long history of Fleetwood Mac's chameleon-like adaptation, while still holding on to their early blues roots and middle psychedelic phase, has often been overshadowed by the sheer scale of their later success. But that early dynamic of creative chaos made the later triumph possible. This history clearly indicates how they cleverly shifted gears from blues to rock to pop, and especially how they simply turned those blues into purple, forms the core of this book. Their story is a wild ride, and those of us who are "of an age" often feel it was our ride, since this band seemed to echo and express so many of the issues, ideas, and even disappointments of the post-1960s era.

Along the way, the ride contains some perhaps surprising connections that may help us understand how Fleetwood Mac ever existed in the first place, let alone how they managed to subsist in the face of self-scrutiny, one another, and the rapid changes of an entertainment industry that seldom sees or prizes their kind of longevity. There are also several insights that help explain the success of their creative chaos—most importantly, perhaps, the unusual concept put forward by the psychologist Mihaly Csikszentmihalyi. His notion of "flow," the psychology of optimal experience, clarifies how the creative state required to make any art successfully, but especially music, requires an absorption in the present moment where all else disappears, a single pointed form of concentration that allows the artist to achieve the work.

Most alarming for some artists however, especially those combative crews such as Fleetwood Mac, is the ironic fact that in certain special cases that state of "flow" is only possible while in the company of certain collaborators. These collaborators, not surprisingly, are seldom the ones we really get along with; quite the opposite in fact. imagine the curse of being able to achieve that state of "flow" out of which great art or music originates, but *only* in the company of someone we really do not like at all.

What if your mortal enemy is your best friend, and the only one in the entire world who can make your magic possible? In the strange world of celebrity companions, held in the sway of the forces of crowds and power, it happens more often than you might think. Recently, the *New York Times* culture critic Holland Cotter made a telling remark about our attempts to chronicle the past and fit it somehow neatly into our own present, not to mention the folly of trying to anticipate the future based upon it. Cotter suggested that histories get lost, implying that that is just the way life is; and then, perhaps when the time is right, those same histories are found once again. Our subplot here could therefore quite rightly be entitled, "Finding the Fleetwood Mac Muse." That is precisely the purpose of this book: to reclaim some of Fleetwood Mac's "lost histories" and tie together the meandering threads that have kept them on the pop music scene for almost half a century.

By giving up, or sharing, creative control with Christine McVie and later, Stevie Nicks, the original core of the group, Mick Fleetwood and John McVie—a blasted bassist and dazed drummer—were able to remain behind the scenes and capitalize on the truly unique direction that this feminine dimension opened up for them. Part of that distinctive quality is what made this group's sound irreproducible: they have a chemistry that cannot be copied. Their sound could not be imitated quite as easily as that of many of their equally famous peers.

To this we attribute their magnificently improbable balancing act, one powered by internal conflicts and bizarre chemistry. This is more than merely the infamous intraband heartaches (John and Christine McVie, Lindsey Buckingham and Stevie Nicks, and Mick Fleetwood and his wife all ended their relationships prior to and during the making of their blockbuster *Rumours* album), and even more than their massive collective drug and champagne intake.

And yet ironically, all this hubris was not new at all: the template for their self-destructive band behavior had long ago been established by the group's founder, Peter Green, in the late 1960s; and temporarily assuaged by the group's savior, Bob Welch, in the early 1970s. There is more than one history of this group, not only because there is more than one group (there are indeed three separate but overlapping lineups to be chronicled here) but also because each phase of its overall history has its own fetishistic adherents, its own passionate fans, and its own unique qualifications for musical greatness.

The bond between Fleetwood and McVie is stronger than some marriages, even their own. But a secret exists in the core of this group. The same secret propels and perpetuates the most notorious soap opera in pop music. It animates and explains the star-crossed and storm-tossed romances within the group and its surprisingly effective governing dynamics. The same secret fuels the ongoing animus between the surviving members, who stay together in order to transform the common base metal of everyday life into the gold of scintillating pop songs with striking poetic power, and also to transmute the less lustrous fool's gold which emerges from a pathological love affair played out on the world stage.

Certain things resist easy and straightforward telling, and Fleetwood Mac's survival is one of them. Some things cannot be spoken of and can only be communicated through music itself. Contemporary songwriter Elvis Costello has even complained that writing about music is like dancing about architecture. Perhaps, but some architecture needs dancing about and some music needs writing about.

Forty years of Fleetwood Mac? That question mark is very important. How was it possible? Two reasons, perhaps: first, time flies when you are having frenzied fun; and second, nothing succeeds like excess. These two underpinning elements make what has been called the longest running soap opera in rock music continue to fascinate and entertain us. But it is the actual, real, and yet operatic overtones to the band, its musical and its personal history, that captivate us.

Continuity is hard to come by in pop music, yet this group manages to not only survive but thrive as a result of its continuing commitment to expressing artistically one of the key ingredients in their own lives, and in the lives of all their diverse listeners: the anguish of personal relationships. Especially the kind where your incendiary partnership fuels both joy and agony simultaneously, and where the pain of pursuing, captivating, breaking up, and reuniting again forms the hub and axis around which your creative wheels revolve.

This book, by charting Fleetwood Mac's continuity as a whole, is a critical reassessment (an "anti-exposé") of the supergroup, researched and timed to coincide with this year's 40th anniversary of their founding. It is also intended as an anniversary appreciation of their place in our shared musical history. It is a chance for fans of their sound, and of their highly personal brand of creative chaos, to realize that they are even more innovative, and way more clever, than even you may have thought. For others, it may be a shock to their system of assumptions about the supergroup and its ongoing thematic reincarnations. Fleetwood Mac's three major transformations were evolutionary leaps of sorts: their brand of creative chaos thrives on multiple styles in collision, and these leaps resulted in three distinctly different musical entities that somehow managed to perpetuate a permanent state of disruption and discontinuity.

The story of Fleetwood Mac, and their long-lasting survival and success against all odds, is the story of lurching from one creative moment to the next, from one personnel lineup to the next, from one record to the next. This band engaged in the dangerous method of charting their course without the aid of a compass, known as point-to-point navigation, and that is still the best way to appreciate their accomplishments. This book attempts to clearly identify and capture the musical spirit of the ongoing Mac metamorphosis: from drunken blues hounds, to psychedelic art rockers, to cocaine-influenced chart champions. And finally, to two blissed-out geezers sipping tea, contemplating the chains that bind them together.

So let's look at that chain, link by painful link.

The question you will want to ask yourself, especially if you are already an acknowledged fan of their music, is this: Was the self-titled album they released in 1975 (called by some their "white album") their first arrival on the pop music scene? Or was it only the first time the group suddenly loomed large on the radar of contemporary entertainment? Obviously this is a trick question of sorts. It was, in fact, their 12th record release, to be followed in 1977 by *Rumours,* which is still one of the top-selling records in industry history.

The band that drummer Fleetwood and bassist McVie started way back in 1967, under the leadership of the gifted but troubled British blues guitar genius Peter Green, has gone through more personnel changes and stylistic innovations than any other pop group in our cultural history. And the reason no amount of personal calamity or professional madness can derail them is simply this: perpetual change is what they have always been about. Thus, transition is their middle name, and indeed, some of their most impressive music was produced during transitions from one group lineup to the next.

They managed to accept the existence of irreconcilable differences between them, rather than using those differences, as The Beatles did, to allow their work to implode and die a premature death. Instead, and as a result, they manufactured a supernaturally prolonged life for themselves.

In 1960, T.S. Eliot pointed out, in his essay on "Tradition and Individual Talent," that the existing order is complete before the new work arrives and that then, the whole existing order must be altered ever so slightly. So the relative proportions of each work of art to the whole are constantly being adjusted. This is what he called the continuity between old and new, and ironically, few artists display it as fitfully and fruitfully as Fleetwood Mac.

Those who have approved this "new idea of order" will not find it preposterous that *the past should be altered by the present just as much as the present is directed by the past.* That was the task here: to readjust the proportions of Fleetwood and McVie's musical partnership, and to examine how their historical past is altered ever so slightly but significantly by their present—by our present.

I have followed Fleetwood Mac's music for forty years—as long as they have been making music, in fact, and long before they morphed into the blockbuster pop group they are today: commencing with their original blues lineups within the senior bands of their gifted mentor, John Mayall in 1963–65, and later launching their own incendiary brand of psychedelic British blues as Fleetwood Mac, featuring the brilliant and equally doomed guitarists Peter Green, Danny Kirwan and Jeremy Spencer in 1967–69.

Were it not for two teenaged pals who came to North America from England with their families in the early 1960s, I too may have been blissfully unaware that the three phases of Mac's fabulous career maintained a powerful creative grip, and equally unaware of how the three parts fit, almost neatly, into an amazing musical jigsaw puzzle lasting four decades. It was my old friend Gerry Watson who forced me to listen to their music more closely, as well as to all their fellow "limey blues" mentors (he could say this since he was himself an Englishman). He also deserves credit in this book for first alerting me to the almost alarming continuity contained in their musical history as it evolved through its three major phases, showing me that they were not as distinct as first imagined.

Thus we listened, first with blues ears, then with Californian rock ears, and finally with shiny pop music ears. And it was another British expatriate high school chum, Peter Moss, himself a gifted blues musician, who steered me towards the blues in the first place. Without him, I may have found myself only listening to the music that those other well-known British geniuses evolved *out of* the blues. Moss's Blues Band was recently slated to accompany the mythical Cream on their well-intentioned world reunion tour. But most of us felt that Eric Clapton's difficult collaborators, Bruce and Baker, would surely sabotage it with their bickering. And of course, they did.

Moss was and is a living archive of blues in particular and music in general. Like the great guitarist Mike Bloomfield, he has the whole history of blues in his head. Unlike Bloomfield, however, he is still alive to share it with us.

Looking back now, it seems all but inevitable that I would try to chronicle Fleetwood Mac's ongoing rise and fall and rise again to the heights of pop music fame and fortune. This group possesses a radical form of personal continuity, which somehow flourishes through apparent discontinuity. My theory is that as a musical continuum, Fleetwood and McVie managed to subvert multiple standards simultaneously. They also forged an inconceivably strong bond while playing (and living) the blues. As the word "continuum" suggests, this bond enabled them to perfect a partnership together which musically explored the link between two things, or a continuous series of things, that blend into each other so gradually and seamlessly that it is impossible to say where one becomes the next. The link of their continuum is The Blues, and what it means to have them.

Other cultures, some of them very old, have a major context for transformations. Our relatively young culture does not. Our music and record industries have occasional trouble with the concurrent existences enacted by its more exotic and successful performing and recording properties. Yet these concurrent existences are crucial to the creative life of the singer/songwriter. Fortune was the most difficult trial for the early bandmates to withstand. It was the 1960s, after all, and some of them felt almost guilty about achieving such early and astronomical success by simply interpreting the black delta American blues that had so inspired them to play music in the first place

By 1970, acid meltdowns had claimed Green, by 1973 Kirwan had imploded, and a strange religious cult had claimed Spencer. But Mick Fleetwood and John McVie, the spine and soul of the group, were only just getting started on their meteoric rise to fame and fortune. Two other personnel changes ensued: the addition of Christine McVie from the legendary band Chicken Shack, and Bob Welch, who remained with the band for at least four highly engaging and experimental records from 1971–74. But it was not until hearing a little-known 1973 record, by the incredibly young Lindsey Buckingham and Stevie Nicks, that Mick Fleetwood heard the true future sound and pop potential of his own group. Throughout these changes, Fleetwood and McVie remained masters of their insane domain. One was the sail and the other was the wind, but it is hard to determine which was which.

By 1975, the dynamic duo of Buckingham and Nicks had joined the group, and the rest as they say, is history (or rather, histories). It resulted in the "first" recognizable "Mac" sound, which then quickly triumphed in the 1977 record *Rumours. Rumours* launched them into the commercial stratosphere. This was followed by a raft of massively successful hits—even recently, with the reunion tour *The Dance* in 1997, and their contemporary recent release *Say You Will* in 2003. And all along the way, their own dysfunctional relationships have informed both their professional successes and their personal downfalls. These serve as raw material from which they, as creative collaborators, can produce their art.

As part of our shared cultural and commercial memory, we can clearly witness the dynamics of supremely successful collaborations, such as that of Fleetwood and McVie, and also examine the exotic extremes of the highly charged emotional and creative collaborations between Stevie Nicks and Lindsey Buckingham and, of course, Christine McVie and husband John. Such is the irony of either saints or devils meeting that we can begin to see the outlines of a remarkably creative "disequilibrium chemistry" at play. While this does not help all artists, it certainly seems to have helped Fleetwood Mac, perhaps by helping all of its members to fully realize and appreciate their own unique solution to the collaborative contest itself. Fleetwood and McVie, in particular, are like the left-handed and right-handed crystals found in amino acids: they are mirror images that cannot be superimposed, yet they cannot be fully effective when separated either.

There is indeed a curious star-crossed element to the encounter between any two great creative partners, nearly to the point of a synchronistic destiny best summed up by that astute observer of human nature, the surrealist Andre Breton, when he declared that in all our lives, what at first appears to be coincidence is later revealed to be merely "desire reaching its quarry."

When Mick Fleetwood met John McVie and Peter Green while in John Mayall's Bluesbreakers, and later when Fleetwood and McVie met Lindsey Buckingham and Stevie Nicks, it was a supreme case of "desire reaching its quarry". Few people now remember the haunting lines of a pre-Fleetwood Mac Buckingham-Nicks song from 1973, but they certainly apply here: "If you go forward, I'll meet you there." Only a slight alteration of its title makes it even more spookily applicable to the saga of the whole Mac juggernaut: They are the "Long Distance Winners." In other words, certain creative equations involving certain artistic individuals seem nearly inevitable, or at least hard to imagine otherwise, whether or not the collaboration in question is a heavenly or a hellish one.

While trying to explain the constant angst of the group, I was especially taken by the fact that the many musical ventures they created together were far more compelling, and more entertaining in their exotic way, than the music any of them made independent of each other. Suddenly, and almost without realizing it, I began exploring the odd fact that so often the best artistic work in our culture (modern and postmodern Europe and North America that is) is produced in partnership by polar opposites who can barely tolerate each other, but who remain partners because no one else seems able to spark their creative magic as well as their most intimate enemy, their mortal friend.

Fleetwood Mac are exemplars of this peculiar creative trait: partners who brought out the best and worst in each other. After a while, I began to see this subject as a study of artistic marriages made in hell, an ironically entertaining subject for the rest of us, as it turns out: we the consumers of the diverting and riveting cultural side-effects of all their artistic suffering.

But just look around our entertainment forest, and consider the sheer volume of these lightning-blasted and towering artistic "trees" that so often come in pairs, and whose branches are so intertwined as to threaten the survival of both. I could not help but think of that overly sentimental 1961 Neil Sedaka song, "Breaking Up is Hard to Do," as an odd emblem. Many such partners desperately want to be independent of their teammates and yet realize, if they are clever enough to do so, that they alone hold the secret to whatever creative and artistic alchemy blesses their work together.

Exactly what is happening here? What does all of this mean? According to Vera John-Steiner, in her book *Creative Collaboration* published by Oxford University Press, all of us have been held in the thrall of an illusory cultural assumption.

> Rodin's famous sculpture, "The Thinker", dominates our collective imagination as the purest representation of human inquiry...the lone, stoic thinker. Yet while the western belief in individualism romanticizes this perception of the solitary creative process, the reality is that artistic forms usually emerge from the joint thinking, passionate conversations, emotional connections and shared struggles common in all meaningful relationships.[1]

John-Steiner offers a rare and fascinating glimpse into the dynamic alliances from which some of our most important ideas and art-forms are born, focusing on the creative process unfolding in the intimate relationships of such luminaries. "Many of these collaborators complemented each other in major ways, meshing different backgrounds and forms into fresh styles of thinking, while others completely transformed their respective fields."[2] And many of them simply loathed working together.

This study was something of an archeological dig. There is an odd term in archaeology that sums it up quite nicely: anastylosis, or the reassembly of ruined monuments from fallen or decayed fragments. One of the key methods of doing this in the case of a pop giant like Fleetwood Mac is by a careful examination of something called the "interregnum"—the transitional pauses or interruptions of continuity. For that is where their secret creative glue can be found and explored. Fleetwood Mac had three interregnums, in 1970, 1975, and 1979. For all we know, they may yet have another.

One of their early recordings of alternates, *Pious Bird of Good Omen*, seems to sum up the paradox at the heart of the group itself. That pious bird is, of course, the legendary albatross. Originally a good luck herald for mariners, it later morphed into a weight that we might have to carry, usually around the neck. The notion also conveys the burden of the astronomical success that always threatened to destroy the group, as well as the strange irony of the fact that what made them most appealing to the musical public was the personal nature of the dysfunction they wrote so lyrically about as composers. The "albatross" which haunts this supergroup, apart from the decline and fall of several of their earliest and most creative members, is the very fact that what breaks them apart is also what keeps them together, by writing and singing about it and by transforming their dark relationship dilemmas into glittering entertainment for the rest of us.

In this respect they are quite similar to those other exemplars of creative projection, The Beatles—except of course that Fleetwood Mac have found the secret of not just surviving but thriving, by managing to control the very hubris and collaborative demons that perpetually threatened them. They discovered how to carry on creating "for the sake of the music" and by agreeing that neither creative combatant would prevail over the other. Thus they have become a living "brand" rather than a wistful memory, such as their other British peers. They somehow realized that they had to stay together, since no one else but them could produce the music that resulted from their own stormy teamwork.

John-Steiner has well illustrated that the creative mind, rather than thriving on solitude, is clearly dependent upon the reflection, renewal and trust inherent in sustained human and professional relationships. Such compelling depictions demonstrate the key associations that nurture our most talented artists and thinkers. While compelling, the creative alliances she studied are generally synchronized and synergistic, where supportive compromise reigns. What motivates such extended collaboration is generally some deep compatibility, though what is equally intriguing is the coupling of certain successful creative "ensembles" who are woefully, utterly, and entertainingly incompatible. The teams for whom the creative discord itself is the key to success—these are the ones who compel our attention.

And so this glimpse into the geography of the imagination triggers one of our most puzzling cultural questions: why is it that much of our great art is so often produced by creative partners who cannot stand the sight of each other? Significant works of art in all media, but particularly in music, are often cocreated by teams of "significant others" who blend together personally like oil and water, but who professionally manage to reach great artistic heights that they may not have been able to reach alone or with another partner.

Whether they are intimate life-partners, or solely creative collaborators, or both, these tormented teams somehow succeed in producing cultural artifacts of lasting value, but frequently they themselves are trapped in a mutual muse vortex. This is more than a question of conflicts between mere gender and creativity being played out in partnership, since some of the collaborative teams are intimate partners and some are not, while some of the same-gender teams seem to encounter an intimacy even more harrowing than that of their "married" artistic peers.

The crucial concept of interest here is that of creative and artistic self-expression in pairs, not the personal struggle for self-expression that engages all of us. And the key dynamic we need to clarify is that of creativity within the boundaries of a collaborative professional partnership. Fleetwood Mac's sublimely creative chaos is a perfect example. We need to unearth the "quantum level" of their creative partnership, and that means finding the basic level at which all these different sets of creative partners intersect, and where all their shared compulsions meet.

Sorting out the complex balancing act between such mutual muses also provides a way of separating creative myth from actual artistic practice, of disentangling the image of the partners from the lives of the players, and most importantly, of appreciating what Bernard Benstock, in *Creativity and Intimate Partnership,* referred to as the uniquely singular achievement of the collaborative process itself. An equally important question is posed by the apparent success of certain creative collaborators who seem to connect with a large audience and thrive, despite the fact that they reserve a special and significant contempt for the very person who shares their gifts most intimately.

Among these ironic survivors are the titanic creative teams propelling Fleetwood Mac, each of which has become a current corporate entity, a "brand" name that soldiers on regardless of the heated hubris of their leaders. It also helps that the creative partnerships of the couples in Fleetwood Mac each make for a great dramatic story in their own right. Seldom has comedy melted into tragedy, and back again, so seamlessly as in these iconic couples.

The turbulence of their private interactions both enriches and afflicts the end product of their artistic collaboration, so that while we are often entertained—and even edified in some cases—by their frenzied pursuit of happiness and immortality, they themselves are usually trapped in a mesmerizing soap opera of staggering proportions.

And, of course, it goes without saying that their intimate suffering in public entertains us all the more, especially since the souvenirs of that suffering, exceptional musical artifacts left behind for the rest of us, are frequently so universal in their meaning that we learn from their lessons of darkness. Even if they cannot learn from those lessons themselves. We the audience, while appreciating and consuming these cultural artifacts, also begin to accept and even celebrate the unique "brands" among these marriages in mayhem. After a while, it is their brand, in the form of the image and identity of the shared art they produce, which we ourselves use to identify and expand our own personal sensibilities.

Their joint brand together however, is that of romantic love, and the kind of passionate or even compulsive attraction which transcends all obstacles, or at least so goes their shared mythology. They have succeeded in becoming emblematic names and symbols, whether they like it or not.

Such is Fleetwood Mac's insight, seemingly beyond—or below, or above —the personal level of shared animosity, that they succeed in recognizing their own brand together and even elevate it to a corporate status worthy of maintenance, no matter what the personal cost. Such teams as this realize that working together, as distressing as it might be, is the only means to reaching that obscure magic which is only available by "looking through" their partner's eyes. And for all of us—the beneficiaries of these uniquely tortured teams—there remains the mysterious source of their harrowing creativity. We are fortunate enough to witness it all, from a safe distance, and to thus observe one of the most ironic aspects of human nature.

Once they establish a bond that unites them creatively, and especially if they achieve a huge degree of success, wealth, and recognition, breaking up is not only hard to do, as Neil Sedaka crooned, it is often impossible. The amazing paradox of Fleetwood Mac and their ongoing popularity is a perfect lens through which the strange dynamics of creative collaborations can be viewed most clearly, since they magnify the dangers of incompatible creative opposites so outrageously, so sadly, and yet so triumphantly in the end.

One of the most obvious but often overlooked reasons for the long-term survival of such a group of self-destructive team players is childhood and the dynamics of young friendships. Through studying this band and its history, it became clear that the tortured teams who managed to survive together were generally the ones who had known each other, personally and intimately, for the longest time—some of them, quite literally, since their very beginnings. After all, Simon and Garfunkel met each other when they were 11; Pete Townshend and Roger Daltrey met when they were 14; Mick Jagger and Keith Richards initially met when they seven; Frank Zappa and Don Van Vliet met when they were 15; Lennon and McCartney met when they were 15; Lindsey Buckingham and Stevie Nicks met when they were 18; and Mick Fleetwood and John McVie knew each other from their early teenaged years, and are still creative playmates as geezers today!

The creative and chaotic crew formed their initial bonds while they were still practically children—before they had even fully formed their own characters and identities—in alliance together against adult society. They accepted their differences in order to achieve success together, especially once they discovered that it was only through that particular relationship that success would be possible. They thus accidentally applied one of the great discoveries of interactive creative dynamics made famous by the mathematician John Nash, who won a Nobel Peace Prize for his subtle cognitive concept of "governing dynamics" as applied to game theory. Simply put, governing dynamics involves the resolution of two competing forces in noncooperative games in a manner where neither side prevails over the other, where no one is the winner and no one is the loser. Or put more accurately, by agreeing that neither will win or lose, both parties win, by being able to soldier on with their work—in this case the work of composing and selling mountains of records to an adoring public.

So however harrowing their personal relationships, a team such as Fleetwood Mac desperately does not want to say goodbye. They simply cannot say goodbye because we won't let them, even though for most of them it has been a hard day's life indeed! Vicente Todoli once described the creative collaboration between artists Richard Hamilton and Dieter Roth in terms that apply across the board here: "The surprising thing about their partnership was their contradictory personalities, a meeting of opposites. As in physics, poles of the same charge repel each other and those of the opposite attract each other."[3]

Since others have aptly documented the where and when, this book asks and answers the questions of how and why. In 1968, commenting on his famous partner's liaison with Yoko Ono, Paul McCartney himself sarcastically remarked, "When two great Saints meet, it is a humbling experience." I can almost appropriate this observation intact, changing only the details, in that, "When two great Devils meet, it is a harrowing experience."

Fleetwood Mac's survival secret lies in what their official Web site calls a "griffin-like hybrid of pop traditions." The surprising part of all this, I hope, is the odd fact that they are *still* a blues group. But to appreciate that fact, we have to go back to before the beginning.

British Blues in the 1960s: The Musical Roots of Fleetwood Mac

1

"It was like a Crusade..."
—Eric Clapton, on the British Blues movement in the sixties

It is an error of judgment to claim, as too many others have done elsewhere, that Fleetwood Mac had its "meager beginnings" in the raw, rough, and ready sound they cultivated upon first forming in 1967. This sound has often been characterized, especially by fans of their later phase, as a somewhat primitive sound which cannot be favorably compared to the scintillating pop of their golden age. The roots of Fleetwood Mac are deep—so deep, in fact, that few of their current fans may fully realize how far back they actually go.

In order to fully appreciate those roots, and to absorb the amazing trajectory that Mac took through and away from them, it is essential to appreciate the blues as an imported cultural phenomenon floating over and influencing postwar Britain. After playing its role, along with rhythm/blues, country and skiffle, in the foundations of early American rock 'n' roll, the blues was imported in its unvarnished and original Delta format to Britain and caused a hugely sensational "revival" among English music lovers. More importantly, both blues and rock 'n' roll were cleverly improved upon and perfected by their erstwhile English inheritors.

The word *meager* suggests something deficient in quantity or quality; lacking in fullness or richness, poor, scanty, or inadequate. But no careful listening to the masterful music of Fleetwood Mac's mentors, Alexis Korner and John Mayall, or especially to the first three masterpieces by the Peter Green era–Mac, provides any support for such a claim. If anything, their early output was more like a diamond still covered by its coal clothing. Talk about a musical pedigree: thoroughbred Fleetwood Mac has one of the finest.

What some have called meager is merely the feeling of a live, in-studio recording technique, which consciously eschews the use of overdubs or any technical polishing. This is how they made a record in three days, rather than the two years it would sometimes take once Fleetwood Mac became a super pop-group. And meager is also merely the mentality of postwar British culture: vulnerable, fragile, shell-shocked, poor, and desperate to overcome their inherent limits, both material and musical.

The question of why such an exotic sound as the black folk music of Mississippi and Chicago would find fertile ground in the postwar poverty of London streets is a tantalizing one. The answer, if there is one, might be twofold: firstly, the lack of American racial tensions that prevented the black blues masters from gaining a professional foothold in their homeland. After all, Muddy Waters often could not stay in the hotels attached to the American clubs in which he played, nor in some cases even enter through the front door. Whereas Europe, especially England, embraced him wildly on his triumphant 1958 tour, as they did the other advanced music brought over to England by the emancipating American GIs.

Secondly, and perhaps most importantly, young British people climbing up out of the bomb shelters after the war genuinely had "the blues." They were ready to hear the core message embedded in its dark charms. This was particularly true in the case of Peter Green, the insecure genius and progenitor of Fleetwood Mac, whose ability to channel an authentic spirit of burden and hurt shocked even the black blues masters with whom he jammed in Chicago. He was nearly able to erase the raw racial line that carves the blues itself out of oppression.

* * * * * * * * * *

One of the advantages of writing a comprehensive history of Fleetwood Mac, from its inception in 1967 until today, is that we don't have to search for facts or establish a trajectory. The facts are never in question, and the mountain of documentation on one of the most famous groups in history is exemplary, even compulsive to some degree. The more important role here is to interpret those facts and properly present a coherent meditation on their meaning.

There have been books aplenty at each stage of Fleetwood Mac's career, which, most observers always assumed, was about to end. Indeed, the constant process of ending and resurrection is part of their essence. The other advantage of this present vantage point is that we get to comment on the books of other authors who also approached the subject, although only from the angles of their own time and of Mac's own perpetually fleeting incarnations.

Two of the most important and valuable volumes come from a vital voice, still surprisingly clear after all these years, Mick Fleetwood, with his own weighing in on the subject. He is after all, half of that unique subject. *My*

Twenty-five Years in Fleetwood Mac, a great pictorial essay, and *My Life and Adventures in Fleetwood Mac,* both with the help of Steven Davis, are excellent encounters with a reality that only he can convey. It is telling that Fleetwood dedicated his own life story to his early troubled idol, Peter Greenbaum.

In addition to actually playing with the group and knowing all the other players on the scene, Bob Brunning's *Fleetwood Mac, The First Thirty Years* has the added charm of seemingly expecting another 30 years, and also in the way it embraces and accepts the ongoing transitions of the band's continuum. He quotes early guitarist Jeremy Spencer on the subject: "There are some places where we play, where if we don't play blues, we get shouted down. But good audiences will listen to anything you do, if you do it well. 'Albatross' [the first big hit for the band] hasn't made any real difference in where we play, only in the number of people who come to hear us."[1] Little did poor Jeremy know how prophetic those words would become.

Only ten years later, when a post-Mac Spencer would still be playing the role of mesmerized "religious" cult member living in a virtual limbo, his former bandmates ascended the glittering staircase of an international cash register of vast proportions. He was saved but dazed, while they were dazed yet wealthy.

One of the best chronicles of this exhilarating roller coaster ride was also presented by Bob Brunning in 1986, in his excellent study of the period *Blues: The British Connection,* which charts the course of the English absorption of American blues idioms from a bird's-eye view. It has the added bonus of his own historic involvement with the Mac band, albeit briefly, as their temporary bass player prior to the imminent arrival of John McVie. Brunning then went on to play with another phenomenally good white blues channeling group, Savoy Brown. His words have weight.

> There is a long, substantial and consistent history of blues music as a performing art in Britain. Fuelled by loyal enthusiasts, both in their role as performers and consumers since the early 1950's, the music has never lost its appeal to the largely underground audiences which have always supported the singers and bands who have kept faith with the blues. The deceptively easy structure of the genre, with its reliance on the simple twelve bar formula, has allowed musicians everywhere to express their feelings through the songs, which return again and again to the themes of oppression, sadness, poverty and emotional deprivation.[2]

The puzzle as to how these extremely white kids, the baby boomers descended from the British families who climbed out of those bomb shelters, came to embrace and embellish such heavy sentiments is definitely worth exploring. Mac would emerge at the perfect time to supply the ideal amount of angst for those baby boomers, though the prosperity attached with the postwar boom would be somewhat slower coming to England that to America.

* * * * * * * * * *

When the boom arrived, it synchronized these dark sentiments just in time for what we now so wistfully refer to as the "swinging sixties." And no one anywhere swung quite like Fleetwood Mac did. But long before England swung "like a pendulum do," it was still recovering from the collective nervous breakdown known as World War II, and a glimpse into the dark days immediately following that conflagration goes a long way toward clarifying the appeal for the blues that existed amongst Britain's youthful inheritors of the victory celebration, which would last almost until the 1970s. It is not that the Blues themselves as an expressive living art form are inherently nihilistic; only that a nihilistic state of mind searching for meaning in a world without much of it left inherently turns towards the Blues for consolation, solace, and an outlet for abstract anger. The postwar youth, or at least some of them in enormous numbers, all found shelter in this imported musical style.

Stewart Harcourt has done a masterful job of depicting and recreating postwar London in a suitably gritty film noir style for his recent series *Jericho*. As reviewer Marilyn Stasio characterizes it, we are "drawn into a London weary of wartime deprivation but also weary of losing its social constraints: a city not quite ready for the hedonistic liberties of the 1960's."[3] Harcourt himself provides a clear picture of the prescene we are studying here, "I thought it was an exciting time because it was a period when everything was about to explode in Britain. In terms of race and social class you could feel the tectonic plates shifting under people."[4]

Well, to those of us who were listening to Fleetwood Mac back then, we could certainly hear those very plates shifting and crashing together and apart. "After the war, we still had rationing, and the stores were always empty. In 1958, it all went wrong and there was rioting in the streets."[5]

* * * * * * * * * *

Coincidentally, that same year the black blues master Muddy Waters, from whom the Rolling Stones would take their group name, arrived in England with an electrically amplified guitar that simply blew the minds of youngsters such as Brian Jones, Eric Clapton, and Peter Green, who were so utterly ready to have their minds blown. Stasio states that, "The racially mixed music scene suggests another cultural change." And Harcourt concludes that, "People like The Beatles were just around the corner, it was the first time that working class lads could become really rich and move up the British social scale. Because our parents had lived through the war, endured such terrible things and witnessed such horrors, they only wanted to protect us. Until the 1960's, when people started rebelling, we were so cosseted."[6]

But being so protected, and eventually so prosperous, also contributed to the nihilism essential to both understanding and producing the blues. The critic Greil Marcus has a great grasp of that basic British nihilism: "Nihilism is the belief in nothing and the wish to become nothing: oblivion is its ruling passion. Nihilism can find a voice in art, but never satisfaction. The nihilist is always a solipsist: no one exists but the actor and only the actor's motives are real."[7] And solipsism is the one key tempting danger to which the blues is often prey.

Marcus also provides a fine insight into the relationships between current trends and past creative movements which helps to elucidate the bond and marriage between white punks on dope and black masters of an exotic folk music format.

> The question of ancestry in culture is spurious. Every new manifestation in culture rewrites the past, changes old maudits into new heroes, old heroes into those who should never have been born. New actors scavenge the past for ancestors, because ancestry is legitimacy and novelty is doubt—but in all times, forgotten actors emerge from the past not as ancestors but as familiars. In the rock and roll 1960's it was the Mississippi bluesman, Robert Johnson of the 1930's.[8]

As Fleetwood Mac would later sing in their middle phase, "Heroes are hard to find."

In England, the search for new heroes would lead some musically minded children of both poverty and privilege back to the basic roots of rock and roll, the blues. As defined by Brunning: "The roots of blues and its danceable offspring rhythm and blues are entwined with the very beginning of jazz, and the two kinds of music exist as complementary elements of the same broad section of largely improvised, creative music."[9] In other words, you didn't necessarily have to know anything technical about musical theory or history in order to be able to crank out a 12-bar blues song that revealed the deepest basement of your feelings. You just had to listen, learn, and play. The blues sound is as infinitely creative as it is mostly because it is spontaneous, nonarranged and hyper-performance oriented, even though its basic structure remains constant and unchanged.

This is the confluence of links that made the blues so accessible to young British "lay-abouts" and art school dropouts such as the members of many of the most important mid-1960s bands, including The Beatles (though they altered its origins unrecognizeably with their own astronomically brilliant talents), Mick Jagger and Keith Richards, Pete Townshend of the Who, Ray Davies of the Kinks, Roy Wood of the Move, Eric Clapton of the Yardbirds (then later, with Mayall's Bluesbreakers and his own Cream), Jeff Beck, Jimmy Page, and many more.

The late Ian Macdonald attributed the high-level invention and articulation of the British bluesters to what he called the "Anarchic-individualistic art-school ethos of British pop...ensuring that when its forms ceased evolving, it can still ring changes in presentation and interpretation which provide the appearance of something new. It was their art school backgrounds which allowed them to introduce the concept of "concept" into pop, along with other postmodern motifs such as eclecticism, self-referentiality, parody and pastiche"[10]

Such was the distinction between America's appetites and those of Britain at the time: a gulf of distrust apparently existed between "instinctual" rock and "intellectual" art, a divide that Macdonald has stressed as being less noticeable in England. This is largely due, he claimed, to the art school tradition that collides so marvelously with the English music hall tradition. "The result of this mismatch of sensibilities has been a transatlantic translation problem which has occasioned much amusement on both sides. A study of the contrast between American naturalism and British artifice in pop music (and life in general) would make a fascinating book. A comprehensive history of Sixties culture and counterculture is likewise long overdue. Meanwhile there is scope for several 'special area' investigations within this period."[11] This book is precisely just such a "special area" investigation of how a rough-and-tumble, but not-ready-for-prime-time, little British blues band with a fanatical following somehow managed to merge their own progressive musical fantasy with American West coast sensibility and proceed to sell more of their records than almost anyone else—at least, that is, until the later arrival of Michael Jackson.

What Bob Brunning refers to as the "rich and bottomless well of talent," providing inspiration for British blues enthusiasts from the American side, did indeed create the initial swell of a blues muse, and still does to this day. And it was the British fans, as well as the rest of Europe, that howled the loudest when Fleetwood Mac appeared to leave the blues behind. The British simply always loved and still do love their blues. But why? The two-part question is not as naïve as Brunning suggested, but it is definitely as controversial as he implied: can white musicians play the blues authentically? And, what makes the English audience so receptive to this exotic and deceptively simple musical format? Brunning partially suggests that the question needs to be put aside in favor of a larger challenge. Would it not be better, he proposes, to support the music as a live and living entity by attending its ongoing performance in the real and changing world, rather than keep the music enshrined as a "sterile academic branch of American culture"?

Yes, it is. And that is exactly why it is necessary to follow the twists and turns of the Mac "river" as it flows forward, through the blues and beyond the blue horizon where they first began. Blues musician Robert Cray concurs:

Those guys, Howlin' Wolf, Robert Johnson, BB King, all had their own styles, rhythms and songs.

Try to do your own thing. It doesn't mean the blues have to go away—if you fall in love tomorrow and break up the next day, you're gonna have the blues. Anybody can sing the blues, you don't have to be black. I like to sing this music because it's about real life situations.[12]

You do not have to be black, but you certainly have to have a special sensibility and sensitivity to human suffering, whatever your skin color, in order to do the art form justice—contrary to the Tubes' satirical sarcasm when they sang about "white punks on dope." And with Fleetwood Mac, perhaps the ultimate collection of white punks on dope, they not only had the blues in its raw and valid form, they were able to communicate it to a mass audience, something that white-dominated society would not allow black musicians to achieve. However, the success in doing so would exact a terrible toll on the band's three principal front men, who carried a burden of guilt, perhaps unnecessarily, for managing to do nothing more criminal than to truly communicate with its audience. Each of the key guitarists, in turn—Peter Green, Jeremy Spencer, and Danny Kirwan, in that order—would implode under the imagined weight of their guilt for "stealing the black man's music," as Kirwan once lamented.

They would have done well to listen to one of their own musical gods, Riley "Blues Boy" King, when he tearfully answered journalists' probing about appropriation charges with a heartfelt thank you to the young white musicians who processed the music so masterfully, while also providing an entire second career and living, via royalties, to many black musicians who were literally starving. King is certainly correct when he says that far fewer people would know the names of Robert Johnson or Willie Dixon if adoring and "zonked" white punks like Eric Clapton and Peter Green had not sent their sounds swirling out across the sea of writhing white bodies at festival concerts.

> Indeed, there is a strong, almost overwhelming argument to be made in support of the oft-aired theory that the huge influx of white r 'n b bands into the States in the 1960's and 1970's actually directed the American audiences attention towards their own rich black culture, of which many white (and black!) Americans were quite unaware.
>
> British bands like the Rolling Stones, Cream, Ten Years After, The Yardbirds, Fleetwood Mac, Savoy Brown and John Mayall toured the States with their exciting stage shows, which were dominated by their fervent and energetic interpretation of the black rhythm and blues material upon which they all relied.[13]

Far from stealing the sound and spirit of the culture from which they borrowed, these young musicians, especially in the case of Fleetwood Mac, were eager to promote interest in and awareness of the primal power of the music that so moved them personally. They *wanted* their fellow "stoners" to fully appreciate the origins of the sounds that were transporting them so far and so effectively. Brunning believes that there is no doubt that the power of the blues itself is the insurance that it can cross all boundaries and cultures with an ease unknown to other forms of musical expression.

He is right, of course. "Whatever else, blues music is here to enjoy, respect and celebrate, and the door is open to all. Open it wide!"[14] And in the case of Fleetwood Mac, they did not simply open the door wide and peer out or in—they genuinely kicked the door right off its hinges and invited everyone in the world in for a party with the blues. For a time in the late 1960s, their party was so popular that they briefly outsold The Beatles and the Rolling Stones. Much later, of course, after they camouflaged their blues in a pop music overcoat, they were outselling practically everybody.

But before we arrive at the lads that kicked down the door, let us take a closer look at the older gentlemen who preceeded them and who were the architects of the building which they were lucky enough to invade and occupy. Among these luminaries are legendary names such as Ken Colyer, Humphrey Lyttelton, Chris Barber, Cyril Davies, and the late lamented Alexis Korner, a down-to-earth mentor who once claimed that the real test of whether you can work with someone is whether you can face them across the breakfast table in the morning. These proved to be telling words for the future Fleetwood Mac.

* * * * * * * * * *

No history of the blues in England, or anywhere else for that matter, can properly commence without an appreciative nod to John Mayall. Mayall was born on November 29, 1933, in a small village near the industrial center of Manchester. After a musically supportive childhood, he taught himself to play piano on a neighbor's instrument. Like so many of the greats, his is a truly innate ability. A product of the English Art College mentality, which shaped so many of the great British blues and rock performers, he established early on his own set of innovative attitudes towards both art and music. A stint in the army during the Korean War provided him with that other integral aspect of musical growth, the contemporary blues and pop records conveyed by American GIs throughout Europe during their visits.

When Alexis Korner's Blues Incorporated kicked off the beginning of the British Blues Revival, Korner strongly encouraged Mayall as a mentor, perhaps also giving him an early taste of how important learning from a supportive master can be to one's own evolution. Once Mayall moved to London, and while under the sway of Korner, his popularity as a live club performer spread. Very soon thereafter, he launched his own unit, John Mayall's Bluesbreakers, an ever-shifting lineup of the great and near-great who immediately stepped into history.

In the first of what would be many mentoring roles, Mayall took in the fledgling Eric Clapton, who had achieved pop fame as a Yardbird but was itching to leave behind what he then perceived as the hollowness of that fame. That partnership, and their first recordings together, would make them both legends. But both Clapton's allergy to rock fame and his allegiance to "pure" blues seemed to take a back seat when he left Mayall's group, along with bassist Jack Bruce, to form Cream—perhaps the best of the heavy blues-rock bands to emerge from this period. Clapton's replacement was the then-unknown young guitarist Peter Green, hovering in a holding pattern until he was ready to break out on his own. Mayall's other alumni, John McVie and Mick Fleetwood, were only too happy to oblige, once they fully realized that the three of them had captured lightning in the proverbial bottle.

Mayall remains a legend to this day, not only for accidentally bringing together three-fifths of Fleetwood Mac, but also for serving as a unique kind of teacher. Similar to Miles Davis in the jazz idiom, Mayall not only brings out the best in his young sidemen but also provides a key ingredient to their own musical evolution. He, like Davis, was and still is a creative catalyst par excellence. And like Fleetwood Mac, Mayall has surfed creative chaos for over four decades.

* * * * * * * * * *

Back in the early 1960s, when the entire fledgling blues revival was in its infancy, the avuncular Mayall provided the inspiration for a veritable army of gifted musicians who would go on to their own stellar careers—especially the most important among them, Fleetwood Mac.

As anyone who lived through it will testify, the 1960s was a period of accelerated change. Such change affected Fleetwood Mac so rapidly that, in a few short years, it would morph from gritty blues band to polished pop group in the apparent blink of an eye. Naturally there was a great deal of living, interaction, and suffering in that long blink. But in retrospect, it seemed they would magically shift in an amazingly canny way that captured the spirit of several successive periods, from blues to psychedelic rock to slick pop, all without ever looking back long enough to ask themselves how it was all possible. They managed to break the very mold than gave birth to them.

But that breaking open and apart would not happen until the very end of the 1960s. Before then, anything was possible, especially in the hands of the gifted, angry young white men who embraced the blues and its message of transcendence. Fleetwood and his fellow "sixties slackers" were the classic cases of the art school type: an academic misfit who could more or less draw and was otherwise consumed by a chaotic creativity in need of channeling. As Ian Macdonald argued: "Already a crucible for creative fusion, art school as a result became the secret ingredient in the most imaginative pop-rock."[15]

But although the music of groups such as The Beatles, Rolling Stones, Who, and Fleetwood Mac has now been enshrined in popular history and counterculture folklore, the values inherent in the historic period of the 1960s which both produced and reflected their aggressive genius are still quite controversial. This is largely because one is bound to believe either that this period fostered the expansion of freedoms and liberties for all concerned, and for all future generations, or that it began a slow slide into the entropy of values that fostered today's social chaos. Take your pick, depending on your perspective. For Macdonald, and for many others,

> The fact that the debate continues to rumble on is in itself a tribute to the momentousness of the Sixties. But if blaming the shameless greed of the Reagan-Thatcher Era on the sociable and morally concerned We Generation is transparently silly, it would be just as fatuous to pretend that the Sixties did not harbor its own complement of idiots, demagogues and outright criminals. Much counter cultural rhetoric—notably its airy notion of a money-free share-all society, of post-scarcity anarchism—was adolescent nonsense.

> Many undergound leaders were either sociopaths in love with disruption for its own sake or self-dramatizing opportunists on their way to careers in Wall Street and Madison Avenue. Yet in spite of all this, the sense then of being on the verge of a breakthrough into a different kind of society was vivid and widely felt.

> Attitudes formed in this potent atmosphere were lasting, the glimpse of something better, however elusive, permanently changing the outlooks of millions. Why?[16]

Surely some of the best questions are those that we all know are without answers. Yet we ask them all the same, since not to ask them is to surrender to a slumber worse than the disillusionment of having no answers. This is precisely why in order to fully comprehend, or at least appreciate, the 1960s, it is essential to understand the 1950s and, for that matter, the first boom of the 1920s. Each decade in isolation means little or nothing, while all three together mean something quite special indeed: the momentum of collective desire and the magic of crowds and power.

Ian Macdonald has remarked on the fact that much of the contradictory nature of the 1960s stems from the unexpected interactions between the many parallel developments in the era, as well as its immediate inheritance of the Beat culture ethos from the 1950s, and thus the utter lack of any homogeneous unity associated with an ironic generation so fixated on its own wholeness.

> The mostly middle class Beats were visionary hobos alienated from society, 'on the road', both literally and metaphorically. American cousins of the Existentialists—whose enigmatic chic drew Lennon and McCartney to Paris in 1961, and, in the form of Germany's Exis, fascinated them in Hamburg—they were less preoccupied with the integrity of the self than with transcending personal limits, reaching out to something beyond the range of everyday experience. Since they did not know precisely where they were going, they defined themselves instead by what they were for or against. Seeking self-realization through "hipness" and paradox, the Beats were the authentic religious voice of the Atomic Age.[17]

Macdonald also stresses the apparent cyclical nature of change occurring in decadelong clumps. "As a rebellion of free essence against the restraints of outmoded form, the Sixties began with a flood of youthful energy bursting through the psychic dam of the Fifties. The driving force of this rebellion resided in The Beatles, in their capacity—then suspected by no one, least of all themselves—as unacknowledged legislators of populist revolt."[18]

And while neatly packaged decades are not the only way that radical change chooses to manifest itself, it is the way we, as passengers along for the ride, tend to quantify our cultural forward motion and to manage its often unruly momentum. In Bob Dylan's brilliant "Ballad of a Thin Man," he snarled, and some would say sneered, about an average person's plight when faced with the countercultural revolution, or even just rapid change in general, and how such an extra-normal individual must be struggling with the seemingly invisible meaning of the times in which they lived.

* * * * * * * * * *

At the very beginning of that overly hopeful decade, John F. Kennedy expressed a whole nation's combined excitement and trepidation: "We stand on the edge of a new frontier—the frontier of the 1960's—a frontier of unknown opportunities and perils, a frontier of unfulfilled hopes and of threats." In retrospect, he might just have easily described it as a frontier of unknown perils and threats, period, so momentous were the changes in the air.

These changes were also the same reality-in-flux that so perplexed Dylan's Mr. Jones. But as the British novelist and essayist Hanif Kureishi expressed so well in his editing of the *Faber Book of Pop,* the reason he and they could not figure out what was happening was more straightforward that we might assume. Not just that the social or cultural changes were so wild as to be unacceptable, which they were; but also because the average observers "were snobs who imagined they were part of an intelligentsia," and the intelligentsia always had contempt for the unruly forces of popular culture.

The tensions between high and low culture were anxieties that further stretched the definitions of high and low to a significant breaking point. In that sudden gap, all sorts of "cultural outsiders" such as Fleetwood Mac, and especially young people fueled by optimistic desires, were able to design and launch whole new forms and systems of communication.

This is almost certainly because pop, as Greil Marcus has often pointed out, is "an argument where anyone can join in." But what exactly is that pop argument about, exactly?

Considering how deceptively simple and supposedly disposable it is, pop culture and its artifacts, not to mention the elegant beings whose personal taste crafted the culture's appetites, are obviously far deeper and broader than the cursory glance or listen we so often ascribe to them. Looking twice, and listening more carefully, provides a dizzying window onto the wider world of so-called high culture, but reflected and refracted.

This was a historical period in which the customary vertical hierarchies of the serious art and music worlds were being tilted severely sideways until they became horizontal hierarchies, merging serious with frivolous, high with low, in a reckless abandon that eventually gave birth to what we now know as the "anything goes" mentality of postmodernism.

Raymond Williams clarifies it this way:

> Popular culture was not identified by the people but by others, and it still carries two older senses: inferior kinds of work, popular press as distinguished from quality press; and work deliberately setting out to win favour, popular journalism or entertainment; as well as the more modern sense of being liked by many people. The mass is always seen as fickle, threatening and uncontrollable.[19]

Pop artist Richard Hamilton coined a series of ideal descriptions of pop as early as 1957, before such a thing as "pop art" even existed. Pop art, he liked to claim with tongue in cheek, was "popular," meaning it was designed for a mass audience, transient, a short-term solution, expendable, easily forgotten, low cost, mass produced, young and aimed at youth, witty, sexy, gimmicky, glamorous, and clearly designed for big business. But for pop culture critic Jon Savage, that summed it up perfectly, as indeed it did.

> This is what The Beatles embodied in the mid-Sixties, before everyone realized that pop had done its job too well: it was too good to be transient and expendable.
>
> 1966 was the high point of British pop art and with top three hits like the Who's "Substitute," The Yardbirds' "Shape of Things," and The Beatles' "Paperback Writer," there was an incredible compression of ideas and emotions about the mass media, consumption, perception and gender, all poured into the three minute long forty-five r.p.m. record.[20]

Obviously Fleetwood Mac would inherit an artistic template that was just right for them to subvert into a strangely twisted combination of musical styles, some of which are still hard to define to this day. Like every other musical group in our age, they capitalized on what The Beatles had wrought, but they also perfected that format in a way their forefathers could never have dreamed possible.

* * * * * * * * * *

Suddenly, the single pop record, and later the concept-based full length pop album, became the ideal vehicle for expressing the dislocation, disaffection, and disinterest of postwar youth in Britain and especially in America. The British writer Rodney Garland distilled it quite effectively in his 1953 essay "The Heart in Exile": "The young were living mostly in exile, but exile gave them possibilities of which they had seldom dreamed before. Nearly all of them, willingly or unwillingly, became creatures of the moment, the past had vanished, the future was uncertain."[21]

As true as it may have been that the future was uncertain, one thing was very certain indeed: whatever that future was to be, The Beatles expressed it personally and manifested it musically, more clearly and articulately than anyone else, before or since. Except of course for the fact that Fleetwood Mac are still expressing it four decades later. Jon Savage characterized the moment of crystallization aptly when he remarked that the arrival of The Beatles marks the moment when the postwar baby boomers claim their time. (Indeed, it still is their time, even though their youth is no longer its banner.) The Beatles themselves, as a new cultural brand, had evoked such energy in a personal manner when they quipped, "Youth is on our side, and it's youth that matters right now."

This is oddly reminiscent of George Melly's take on youth in his 1970 work, *Revolt into Style:* "For the adolescent with sufficient potential pop talent in any field, pop culture offers the only key to the instant golden life, the passport to the country of "Now," where everyone is beautiful and nobody grows old."[22] The Beatles were clearly the principal ambassadors representing this impressive new country called "Now." But strangely obsessive blues bands like Fleetwood Mac would become immediate citizens of such a country and remain there still to this day, perhaps incongruously to their many critics, but naturally to their many fans.

Soon enough, much of the world's youth would enthusiastically apply for citizenship. This new country without a past was one to which anyone, or almost anyone, could emigrate if they had the inclination: it was anticipated as a glistening utopia where the hierarchies of history had been demolished and a freshly minted tribal fairness was to prevail. Technical mastery was not required to gain access.

In fact, The Beatles themselves were immune to professional training of any kind, eschewing the academic feeling of actual musical study and preferring instead the immediate impact of raw intuition. For them, of course, it worked, since they were primitive geniuses led by a Byronic sage, John Lennon, who never could figure out exactly how he did what he did, and perhaps did not really ever want to know the mechanics of his magic.

Obviously the 1960s were about breaking the rules, and to some extent, they were about breaking rules without even knowing what the rules were. But while change was a palpable presence that would eventually seep into every nook and cranny of the culture, its effects were often ambiguous and occurred in a mesmerizing slow-motion effect.

For culture critics like Macdonald, "The sexual repression of the past all but vanished from the world of the newly classless metropolitan young, but it took another decade to begin to disappear elsewhere; and while censorship was rolled back, homosexuality legalized, and women given the benefit of the pill and abortion on demand, the loosening of over-restrictive divorce laws inevitably created the conditions for the replacement of marriage by 'relationships' in the Seventies and a widespread collapse of the nuclear family during the Eighties."[23]

Clearly, Fleetwood Mac is a major celebrant of such dysfunctional relationships, especially by the 1970s and 1980s, having made an entire career out of chronicling their own turmoils. By then, the 1960s dream had turned into a nightmare from which only large sums of money would allow you to awake. Alas.

As always, there was far more concrete continuity between cultural generations than there appeared to be on the surface. As Macdonald wrote:

> The emphasis on informal and immediate fun that was the hallmark of Swinging Britain during pop's peak years of 1965–67 was less evident abroad, particularly in America, where two other socio-cultural movements were unfolding. Inherited from the Beat generation of the late Fifties, the first of these took the form of a radical "counterculture" which, springing up in opposition to the materialism of mainstream society, arose in California with a special concentration in and around San Francisco. Though framed in terms of sexual liberation and scaffolded by religious ideas imported from the Orient, the central shaft of the counter-culture was drugs, and one drug above all: lisurgic acid diethylamide 25, or LSD.[24]

The Beatles, being among the cultural and social elite of the time, were among the very first, after Aldous Huxley a full decade earlier, and Timothy Leary along with the Beat poet Allen Ginsberg, to gain access to and sample a brave new world of psychological and spiritual exploration. It would prove to be the undoing of many—including and especially John Lennon, whose fragile personality buckled under the weight of drastic consciousness expansion, and whose identity was literally burned away under the constant torrent of acid he poured into his gifted brain.

Unfortunately, some sensibilities should simply never have ventured down that chemical highway. The obvious and famous ones include household names like Lennon himself, Syd Barrett of Pink Floyd, Skip Spence of Jefferson Airplane, Brian Wilson of the Beach Boys, Brian Jones of the Rolling Stones, Keith Moon of the Who, and Jim Morrison of the Doors. These were all fragile manic depressive people with preexisting nervous conditions leading to inevitable breakdowns. Nonetheless, we love to watch them climb and fall. (Perhaps the science fiction author Philip Dick was right when he suggested that a thing that burns twice as bright only lasts half as long!)

Then there are the lesser-known, "backyard" names who are known to that lesser cult crowd. Among those names are three key members of the early phase of Fleetwood Mac: Green, Spencer, and Kirwan. Certain doomed personalities require enablers, and all of us together perform the role of supportive consumers of their darkness. And since we live in a future that was partially visualized and personified by the work of these many gifted but troubled teams, in a curious sense all of us become their collaborators, too.

We collaborate with them by deciding who becomes enshrined in history and exactly what it is for which they will be remembered. After all, our collective memory is a museum of their dreams, whether delightful, demented, drug induced, or otherwise.

But only in the case of a band with the creative chaos and musical invention such as Fleetwood Mac would it be possible to explore three different stages of three different bands, all coordinated and conducted under the magnificent mayhem of Mick Fleetwood and John McVie, the most gifted rhythm section in rock music.

* * * * * * * * * *

Still, the question remains: if this explosive era of accelerated change and social evolution was so fixated on the new and the now, how was it possible that so many of the leading musical luminaries of the age were turning back to the historical past of black blues music and playing with its semitraditional forms, mutating them into progressive rock idioms?

Firstly, the blues rapidly became a cult status symbol, and the blues cult satisfied a certain appetite for the outsider-outlaw sensibility ingrained in the American ethos which so inspired these young white Brits. I can still recall the disdain with which my friends and I viewed the early Beatles and their pop skin, preferring instead the gritty realism of their blues rivals and especially the raw incendiary power of the great white blues guitarists, compared to which The Beatles were little more than the easy-listening soundtrack to the movie called "the Revolution."

Much to my own embarrassment, as a dismissive teenager I can even recall giving a special gift to a Beatle fanatic friend: a copy of *Sgt. Pepper,* smashed to pieces with a hammer and covered in red paint. Naturally, we later woke up from this snobbish judgment and accepted the enthusiastic orgy of late-Beatlemania playing itself out across a global stage. But we still reserved a special place in our listening hearts for the incredible innovations of blues bands such as Chicken Shack, Savoy Brown, Cream, Ten Years After—and, of course, the Fleetwood Mac boys, and later its girls.

Secondly, contemporary blues was a sound rooted in the urban struggle and its connected battle, the romantic struggle, something they and we all shared, and the new format that was discovered in the electrified volume of its angry sorrows was just what the doctor ordered. And the psychic vitamins used to achieve ever higher degrees of raw blues innovation, just like the West coast's subculture in America, only further cemented their tribal cult-like status as outsiders, as a blues tribe, far beyond the cute cage of commercial "pop."

Steve Clarke seems to agree with the classification of British blues fans as a cult following.

Since the Fifties, British musicians such as Alexis Korner and Cyril Davies had attempted to build up and audience for blues in Britain but, faced with the competition of rock, it was an uphill struggle. Rock and Roll was custom built for teenagers. Blues had a history that went back to the first decade of the twentieth century, and post-war adolescents didn't care that the records they bought would never have been made without the blues pioneers of the first half of the century. Part of the appeal of blues was its cult status.

Like folk music, blues had a purity and a folk poetry that convinced those disillusioned with the rapid commercialization of rock. The commitment and dedication that blues inspired was taken up as a kind of crusade by musicians like Clapton and Mayall.[25]

And Bob Brunning, the musician who was there from before the beginning, clarifies the yearning for this transcendent "folk poetry":

Since the early 1950's in the United Kingdom, there have been many blues musicians who hold their heads high in any company. The British blues instrumentalists who have worked convincingly in the blues scene constitutes a list too long to even begin to reproduce: they are to be found all through the musical narrative.

It is my firm belief, shared by many of the black American performers with whom it has been a special pleasure to work, that here in the British Isles we can look back at three decades of a convincing and significant contribution to the world-wide blues scenes, as can our European musician colleagues who are carrying the blues flag equally proudly.[26]

But to properly appreciate that pride, and to get the clearest picture of the history of white blues, we must again return to John Mayall, one of the biggest, best, and brightest flag bearers for the blues, and the man synonymous with both its early history and the early history of Fleetwood Mac.

"A good portrait" said Baudelaire, "resembles a dramatized biography." The portrait of the blues being presented here is definitely that of a soul, and thus is psychological in the widest sense of the word, especially once the inherent psychological difficulties of the first three Fleetwood Mac guitarists become clear. This new kind of "folk music from hell" is in itself basically also a portrait of the many gifted performers who either sold their soul, or gave it away, or lost it entirely, in their frantic search for the new electric roots to an old tree. Standing close by that tree, as if protecting it from the axes of commercialism, was John Mayall. Nearby were the great white blues singers and songwriters of our era—many of whom, just like Fleetwood Mac, had learned their craft from Mayall. The most important among those names, intertwined with Fleetwood Mac's own destiny, was Eric Clapton—in my view, the second-greatest guitarist in the world, and—perhaps after Mac—the most effective purveyor of mind-altered white blues to a world audience.

Clapton, was born on March 30, 1945, in Surrey, England. Understandably mistaken for a divinity by some of his more ardent fans, he gained instant credibility for rejecting the perceived softness of his own Yardbirds' new pop direction as exemplified by their hit "For Your Love."

While his fans were confusing him with God, "Slowhand" Clapton concentrated on what he did best, burning up the air with his brilliantly incendiary guitar style. His watershed year was 1965, during which a dazzling round of sizzling club dates, as well as the Mayall Bluesbreakers' masterpiece recording, garnered him worldwide recognition. Only a twisted visionary at the sublime level of a Peter Green could ever hope to surpass the standards Clapton set with Mayall, and that of course is exactly what happened.

Clapton was definitely not God, but he was really more like John the Baptist heralding the coming good news. Because when it comes to the blues guitar played by an angry young white man, Peter Green is as close to God as talent and madness allows.

And while all this testosterone-drenched posturing was going on, hidden in the shadows, and often overlooked, was a remarkable British blues group called Chicken Shack, most notable for the unique presence of a female singer/songwriter named Christine Perfect. She was and still is one of the best-kept secrets in rock music, a brilliant writer and vocalist at par with any male performer in the business. She would eventually become the partner of Mac's bass player John McVie, and as Chrtistine McVie, she would revolutionize their early sound, evolving it into something truly unique and drastically distinct from the rest of the mostly macho mentality associated with both blues and rock music.

The white-hot nuclear core of Fleetwood Mac has always had the most impeccable of blues pedigrees, a result of their early and historic interactions with many of Britain's premier white blues groups, especially John Mayall's Bluesbreakers. In addition, that rhythmic core was eventually even accepted by the classic black blues bosses in Chicago. While The Beatles and the Stones managed to mutate the volatile imported mix of black blues, rhythm and blues, country, and skiffle, into their own masterful and visionary brews of brilliant rock 'n' roll, Fleetwood and McVie were visionary in quite a different way. They maintained a hardcore and rugged blues spirit in their astonishing "white boy on dope" renditions of the classics, and in their own incendiary original compositions, most of which moved far afield from anything remotely like the traditional 12 bars that had so captivated them as young men.

Their long-term vision, however, unfolded in slow motion—so slowly, in fact, that many people are unaware of their magnificent middle period. Their creative trajectory was so distinctively innovative precisely because of this long-delayed production of their own uniquely personal style. Unlike their ambitious peers, who seemed to arrive full blown on the musical scene, it took Fleetwood Mac another 10 years (plus a great deal of tragedy) before they would deliver the shiny baby of their later pop phase. But it was well worth the wait. Whether it was well worth the personal pain is best left up to them to decide.

BLUESBREAKERS: JOHN MAYALL WITH ERIC CLAPTON: RELEASED 1966, LONDON RECORDS

Clearly the greatest exponent of pure white blues prior to the arrival of Fleetwood Mac on the world stage, Mayall's Bluesbreakers, featuring the young firebrand Eric Clapton, were especially effective in live performance, where the power and danger of their interpretive blues appetite was most keenly felt. Neil Slaven has commented that playing the blues is such a complex business, involving so many personal and external conditions, that it is never certain how well you are going to play until the first number of the evening is over. When Slaven watched the Bluesbreakers perform live, he reported that he was immediately aware of their intense search for new ways in which to interpret their classic material.

But sometimes a record can capture that essential fire, and this one succeeded in enshrining many of the songs the band delivered during their blistering live shows. People who were curious about why Clapton left the Yardbirds just as they were breaking the big time need only listen to this record for their answer: the sheer joy and rage of blues improvisation as its best.

In the new context of Mayall's setup, Clapton's technique evolved at a mind-boggling rate, with Slaven noting that he had the ability to "make time stand still." The solo on "Have You Heard" is a perfect example, as are his superbly crafted instrumental cuts "Hideaway" and "Steppin' Out." Also making this outing significant was the first hearing of Clapton's musky voice on record, rendering his idol Robert Johnson's "Ramblin' on My Mind" with exquisite devotion to detail. One of the special and unique abilities of the Mayall organization was their skill at breathing a zesty new life into classic and even dusty old blues tunes, injecting a bold urban grit into the familiarity of cuts such as "What'd I Say." Some critics feel this natural expressive range makes his versions even more vital than the originals, and they are right to acclaim the purity of Mayall and Clapton's shared compulsion to channel something truly transcendental.

The music magazine *Mojo*'s collection of top albums called them "the commercial breakthrough of British blues" and that is just about right. The rapid ascent of Clapton to star status can be characterized best by the man himself: "I was arrogant, and I had an accelerator going." But he is still naturally gracious enough to characterize his mentor Mayall as "a real father figure, I grew a hell of a lot in a short time with his help."[27] The *Mojo* editors came up with the best description I've heard for his playing: "a radically new sound, distorted, creamy and sustained."[28] Clapton himself said he wanted "some kind of thickness that would be a compilation of all the guitarists I'd heard, plus the sustain of a slide guitar."

It is the sheer power and clarity of love in the playing which places this band in a permanent pantheon of the greats, and why, as Slaven pointed out in his label notes of 41 years ago, their capabilities make them "the only group in Britain today whose music closely parallels that being produced by a Chicago blues band."[29] Or at least they were, until Fleetwood Mac came along.

The *Mojo* editors pointed out the irony of his great accomplishment: Before the album ended its 17-week stay in the British charts, Eric Clapton had already left to form Cream, and Mayall had lined up the ideal replacement in Peter Green. Neither party would ever look back.

Other significant record releases of 1966: Aftermath by the Rolling Stones; *Pet Sounds* by the Beach Boys; *Blonde on Blonde* by Bob Dylan; *Revolver* by The Beatles.

JOHN MAYALL WITH PETER GREEN, *A HARD ROAD:* RELEASED 1967, LONDON RECORDS

Mayall himself best characterized the challenge faced by the young and strapping Peter Green when he assumed the mantle of the great one.

> I think most people will realize what a tough time lay ahead in the way of comparison and criticism for any guitarist in the country faced with replacing the acknowledged master of blues guitar, Eric Clapton, in my band. However, Green took over the job and managed to brave out the storm. Within weeks he developed his own ideas and the technique to express them, until now it is obvious that both Eric and Peter have improved beyond recognition but in totally different directions.

> Peter is featured as lead singer on "You Don't Love Me" and on his own composition, "The Same Way". His guitar playing is well exposed on "The Stumble" and particularly on "The Supernatural, which he wrote specially for inclusion on this LP.

> I consider this one of the most meaningful instrumentals I've heard and it certainly stands as one of the high-spots on the record. Blues in its true form is a reflection of a man's life and has to stem from personal experiences, good and bad.[30]

The only thing better than Mayall supported by the brilliant Eric Clapton was Mayall supported by the supernaturally gifted Peter Green. The result was spine-tingling white blues that erased the color spectrum altogether. One of my favorite pieces of accidental art in the real world was the appearance of that famous graffiti around English side streets declaring "Clapton is God." In one ironic photograph of just such a scrawled site, below the scribbled message, a mangy dog lifts his leg to relieve himself against the same wall. It is the same kind of ragged-looking street dog that appears sniffing around the garbage cans on the cover of the first Fleetwood Mac album. Nothing beats life's own serendipity!

The most important elements of the Hard Road recording, apart from the fact of merging the musical spirits of bassist John McVie with the future inventor of his own great band, Peter Green, are the two Green-composed cuts, "The Same Way" and "The Supernatural." These songs are a clear indication, a clarion call almost, that a new force had suddenly arrived on the electric horizon of contemporary blues and rock music.

When Green croons, "don't want no evil woman....she's so sweet, she's my honeybee...and she feels the same way about me," he is already forecasting a theme that would haunt his brief but fiery Fleetwood Mac days: the odd feeling that evil is somehow pursuing him with the intention of crushing his willpower. While in the strange instrumental piece, "The Supernatural," all the stylistic pieces are in place for the later masterpiece "Black Magic Woman." But all on its own, "The Supernatural" has some of the most exquisite and sustained high, squealing guitar riffs which would make him an instant fetish object for so many of us. What is the ostensible subject matter of "The Supernatural"? It is impossible to know, but when he slowly grinds down the tones into silence at its end, you realize you've just heard something from the future, an echo of the distressing and downtrodden electric future which would both push Green to the top of his field and yet also drag him down to the darkest bottom of himself.

This almost perfect blues record was produced by Mike Vernon, who would of course go on to found Blue Horizon Records and unleash Fleetwood Mac on an unsuspecting musical world. Vernon's other additional claim to fame, as if capturing the genius of Green's Mac wasn't enough, was producing the band Chicken Shack, Christine Perfect's group before she herself joined her husband McVie and Fleetwood. To my mind, and ears, Chicken Shack is nearly as sublime as Mac, but in a wholly different way, a way that sadly became rapidly overshadowed by their more newsworthy label mates. But hearing the pre-Mac Christine Perfect sing her breathy blues is still a thrill.

Other significant record releases of 1967: The Doors by the Doors; *Sgt. Pepper's Lonely Hearts Club Band* by The Beatles; *The Velvet Underground, with Nico* by Velvet Underground; *We're Only In It For the Money* by the Mothers of Invention; *Are You Experienced?* by the Jimi Hendrix Experience; *Piper at the Gates of Dawn* by Pink Floyd; *Disraeli Gears* by Cream.

The Original Peter Green's Fleetwood Mac

2

"These times were short lived, and yet spawned a musical freedom within Fleetwood Mac that became an anthem which to my mind has led to the very survival of the band..."

—Mick Fleetwood[1]

It was 1967, the so-called summer of love, though I have always preferred to think of it as the summer of hope. That year, Peter Green dramatically left Mayall's group, bringing with him its rhythm section of Fleetwood and McVie, and after loudly complaining about the constraints of Mayall's new "jazzy" direction. The addition of horns to that group was apparently all it took for Green, ever the fanatical purist, to believe that Mayall was somehow selling out to popular trends. Green hated trends, even though he was about to start one of the longest lasting trends in musical history.

The year 1967 was, of course, fabled for many different reasons, with the emphasis on the word "fable." The Beatles were recording their last master-piece, *Sgt. Pepper,* before descending into the paranoia, addiction, and hubris that would badly affect their famous follow-up *White Album* and lead to the implosive and rancor-filled disaster *Let it Be,* and the brief but brilliant light of *Abbey Road*. But the atmosphere of 1967 was still drenched in hopeful happiness—not to mention somewhat clouded by the new recreational sub-stances that abounded then and that made music all the more serious an art form (at least until the effects wore off).

Of that time, Mick Fleetwood himself commented that, "The London that welcomed me was a city coming alive after the re-building postwar years.

It was an incredible time to be alive and working as an artist in London. One of those lost eras when Art reigned supreme and a new generation was being hatched."[2]

In 1967, Cream, a penultimate collision of white blues, electricity, drugs and amplification, was launching its debut, *Fresh Cream,* on which Clapton, taking another Mayall student, the superb bassist Jack Bruce with him, left no ambiguity about where he was traveling after Mayall's mentoring.

And Peter Green, late of the Mayall Bluesbreakers and rivaling the medical achievement of Dr. Christian Barnard, is busy performing a little heart transplant of his own: the creation of Fleetwood Mac. But early the following year, when my English chum crunched the needle down on the vinyl pressing of the first actual Fleetwood Mac record, entitled "Peter Green's Fleetwood Mac (featuring Jeremy Spencer)", we knew that we were in for a whole new ball game. "This is the blackest blues I've ever heard!" I remember commenting in a guitar-induced stupor. "How is it possible?" I asked my equally incredulous friend. I spoke to him recently, 40 years later, and we still do not have an answer. Some questions in life do not have answers, and Fleetwood Mac is one of them.

Enigma becomes these men and their shared blues roots, and myth was quick to follow. Mac chronicler Mark Trauernicht has stated that their fateful encounter in 1967 "formed the spark that ignited Fleetwood Mac." That description sounds spontaneous, and it was. But it was to be a chain formed link by link, in a blistering furnace of chaotic and dangerous brilliance.

* * * * * * * * * *

Everything naturally begins with the drummer: Michael Fleetwood was born on June 24, 1947, in Redruth, England. Like many of the most accomplished musicians under discussion, he started playing at a very early age, teaching himself to drum while listening to imported American recordings. A pivotal meeting with Peter Bardens permitted him an early gig in his band, but it was meeting the 18-year-old John McVie that triggered a sense of his mission as a Bluesbreaker. Bardens again recruited him to drum for his next band, Peter B's Looners, where a historic meeting with Peter Green cemented his desire to play intimate music on a grand scale. Also during this particular period of his well-spent youth, he encountered, fell in love with, and soon married Jenny Boyd, the sister of iconic girlfriend Patti, consort of George Harrison. This brought Fleetwood deliriously within sight of the court of rock music royalty, very early on.

By 1966, the Peter B's band added two singers, Rod Stewart and Beryl Marsden, and changed its name to Shotgun Express. Peter Green had left the group to join John Mayall as Eric Clapton's replacement, and the Express shut down in 1967. Once Aynsley Dunbar left Mayall in 1967, Fleetwood was approached to join the Bluesbreakers, but due to his penchant for extreme drunkenness, a trait he was to share with McVie for the next few decades, he was sent packing. By that time however, the chemical compound of Green, McVie, and Fleetwood had already begun to coalesce, and they got a taste of the peculiar magic that tended to erupt whenever they were playing together. When Green decided to form his own band, it was obvious to him who his rhythm section should be, and equally obvious what the new band's name should signify.

A chain with two links: John McVie was born on November 26, 1946, in Ealing, West London. He was asked to join Mayall's crusade devoted to pure white blues at the tender age of 17. He quickly became a solid fixture with the Bluesbreakers, despite the fact that he was perpetually being fired for overindulging in alcohol. Eventually, he logged five golden years with the group, contributing to some of Mayall's greatest recorded achievements and proving himself to be a subtle bassist who was clearly the equal of several of the greatest bass players in history, Paul McCartney, John Entwistle, and Bill Wyman.

After deciding, along with Green, that Mayall was moving way too close to the jazz territory and appearing to abandon classical blues, he was ready to join his drinking buddies and step into the pages of history, almost overnight, as one-half of the most perfectly oiled rhythm machine in rock music.

A chain with three links: Peter Greenbaum was born on October 29, 1946, seemingly with the innate ability to both play electric guitar as well as hauntingly channel his idols, Muddy Waters and B.B. King. By the time he was 15, he had made two major commitments: dropping the "baum" from his name and devoting himself to the exotic field of contemporary urban blues.

His status as a legend was cemented early on by somehow upstaging and surpassing Clapton within the Mayall enterprise. Mayall commented that "his emerging voice aspired to say as much as possible in a few well-chosen notes, delivered with a haunting, sweet yet melancholy tone."[3] Sadly, no one really knew the extent of this inherent melancholy, or that it was far more than a musical affectation. For Green, it was a means of survival.

A chain with four links: Jeremy Spencer was born on July 4, 1948, seemingly the immediate incarnation of the great blues charger Elmore James. His abilities, though limited, earned him a special place as an original member of Peter Green's Fleetwood Mac, and it was his obsession for straight-up 12-bar blues that helped catapult the group to the uppermost peaks of the British boom period.

He was however, equally absorbed by early rock and roll and was capable of pulling off extraordinary evocations of the precursors: doo-wop, Elvis, and lovesick rave-ups. Perhaps cursed early on with a dark spiritual sense of crisis, he carefully crafted an obscene, irreverent, and hysterical stage presence in order to conceal his own fragile sense of himself. Drenched in self-doubt, his vulnerability was hidden under layers of sarcasm and misogyny—a John

Lennon–style method of self-defense. The little Bible he kept concealed in the lining of his jacket while on the road was a very early warning signal that he was ripe fodder for the wide menu of 1960s spiritual cults.

A chain with five links: Danny Kirwan was born in South London on May 13, 1950. At an incredibly young age he was discovered by Green and Fleetwood in a less-than-memorable band called Boilerhouse. His sublime playing however, was enough to ignite the interest of Green, who was searching for an alternative to the perceived Eric Clapton Guitar-stud dead end. His solution was radical and revolutionary, just like everything else Green did: expand the guitar foundation of the band to three players, allowing him to step back and suffer more silently in the shadows.

The revolving door of Mac continued turning, no matter what.

* * * * * * * * * *

Even before the beginning, this band seemed inevitable, especially once the musical paths of Green, McVie, and Fleetwood crossed through John Mayall. Mayall's morphing lineup was in many ways parallel to that of the innovative jazz master Miles Davis. Like Davis, Mayall had a special talent for surrounding himself with brilliant young players he could mentor, applying their talents to create music, and then watching them move on to form major careers of their own. Even the avuncular and professorial Mayall, however, couldn't keep the reins on the three champion racers that fate had delivered on his doorstep.

All Mayall could do was to capitalize on the impeccable bass time of McVie for four amazing years, from 1963 to 1967, thrive on Green's furious guitar for barely three months, and groove on Fleewood's fine and underrated drum time for barely three weeks. Fleetwood was fired for excessive drinking. Green decamped after a heated difference in musical philosophy, and McVie followed suit shortly afterward. McVie shared some fascinating insight about his experience with Mayall:

> I've only ever played in two groups in my life: John Mayall's Bluesbreakers and Fleetwood Mac. I joined Mayall in January 1963 when he moved down to London from Manchester where he'd been flogging around for years. I had been in a Shadow's style group and I knew nothing about blues music. Mayall just gave me a stack of records and asked me to listen to them to see if I could grasp the style and feeling. Over the months I began to learn what the blues was about.[4]

It is rather stunning to hear that one of blues/rock's greatest bassists felt he lacked knowledge of the blues, but this indicates the incredibly quiet, inherent genius of McVie.

Imagine the tenacity it took, the year The Beatles were crooning their earliest love ditties, for McVie to turn away from pop's oncoming locomotive train and seek the shelter of painful and plaintive sounds derived from Muddy Waters and others—sounds that no one back then, least of all him, ever expected to become quite as popular as they did. Yet McVie's British tenacity was shared by that ever-growing cult of blues enthusiasts, and once Jeremy Spencer was introduced into the mix by early producer Mike Vernon (who deserves a huge amount of credit for starting Mac on its way to stardom), the die was cast. As Vernon tells it,

> You know how sometimes you can tell when the writing's on the wall? Well, it was a bit like that with the relationship between Mayall and Green. John really rated Peter's playing as well as his vocal prowess. Peter kept telling me he was fed up with the Bluesbreakers set up and wanted to put his own unit together. When he recorded that instrumental (self titled) and told me to put "Fleetwood Mac" on the box, I knew something was afoot. During the next couple of weeks he kept dropping hints with regard to my label Blue Horizon (home of the first three Mac records). Need I say more?[5]

Vernon acted as house producer for Decca and worked on many of Mayall's early ventures. He was running Purdah, a small independent blues label, then along with his brother Richard, launched Blue Horizon in 1967. Not a bad opening act for a budding producer to find.

Fleetwood's memory regarding this period is somehow still miraculously intact:

> A few weeks after I'd been ejected from the Bluesbreakers, Peter Green gave in his notice...he'd had enough. His initial plans didn't involve forming a new band, but his agency persuaded him, and he came round to see me, and between us, we got Fleetwood Mac together. At the time we had no manager, so we did everything ourselves, and Peter did all the negotiations with Blue Horizon. In fact it was Mike Vernon who suggested Jeremy Spencer...Peter went up to Birmingham and asked him to join us...whereupon we started rehearsing for our debut.[6]

The addition of a second lead guitarist would be only the first of many innovations that Peter Green, owing to a severe aversion to his growing adulation as a male rock-god, would devise for his new band. He would outdo himself yet again by bringing an unheard-of third lead guitarist, Kirwan, into the group, thus sealing their experimental fate forever. On the subject of Green, whom he still refers to as "The Green God," Fleetwood is also still hugely emotional, even after 40 years. "Peter Green, my leader and mentor, indeed the founder of Fleetwood Mac. He's never far away, to this day, my favourite guitar player!"[7]

Fans of the darkly melancholy and unpredictable Green, who would later be capsized by the very storm he had helped to create and be left apparently without an intact identity, would not be surprised by the gigantic scale of his healthy ego at this early stage. Fleetwood later characterized him as "very ambitious when he started, maybe overly so. He was intent on making it... he had this "I'll show you" thing, which I could never understand."[8]

Some have suggested that Green was not at all certain about his future after quitting Mayall. He weighed several options, including going to Chicago to perform and record with the black blues musicians who had inspired him to play in the first place. In the end, he would do it all: he would "make it" big, start a hugely successful band, and return to Chicago to record with the Chess masters.

Early producer Vernon, however, believes that Green, together with the "rhythm section," had been planning a departure from Mayall for some time. And more than enough evidence exists for the possibility that Mayall himself may have instigated the trio's liberation. One legend even has it that as a present for Green, celebrating his 21st birthday at the time, Mayall paid for some studio time and this trio lineup recorded a unique instrumental. Titled "Fleetwood Mac" by Green, after his favorite rhythm kings, the instrumental remained unissued for four years (ironically, not until after the actual demise of the personnel who had recorded it, but during the formative year of the group we now know as Fleetwood Mac).

* * * * * * * * * *

The world first heard the uniquely edgy sounds of the infant Fleetwood Mac at their debut performance during a three-day event, the Windsor Jazz and Blues Festival on August 13, 1967, as part of a stellar lineup headlined by Clapton's new blues based supergroup Cream, as well as their main mentor, John Mayall's Bluesbreakers. They played a nervous 20-minute set before 30,000 rapt listeners who would already have projected saintly status on the leader, Peter Green.

September saw them record their first sessions at the Decca studios under the guidance of Mike Vernon, both tracks eventually becoming b-sides for their debut record releases. These two sessions were the sole appearance of Bob Brunning on bass. By the end of September, McVie was finally coaxed into leaving the security of Mayall's paycheck for the uncharted waters of co-leading his own band, a decision one doubts he ever regretted. (Although he went on to play with great bands like Savoy Brown, Brunning must have had some of the wistful feelings of loss that attend such figures as Peter Best, who was almost a real Beatle. But at least he did play a major role in this historic band's inception, and over the years he has become a stalwart documenter of the British blues he obviously still loves deeply.)

For the rest of Mac, it was off to the races, beginning a wild roller coaster ride that would take them to unimagined heights of popularity, even when they were still a "traditional" blues band. It was their own little corner of the massive Anglomania sweeping over the pop world at the time. They immediately began recording unofficially live sessions, which was always their best format, such as the September 15, 1967, appearance at the Marquee Club, a famed cathedral of experimental British music.

The very air must have been crackling at the Windsor Festival, with a lineup strong enough to make the young Mac lads more than a little self-conscious, especially the insecure Peter Green, who was already then being lauded as a figure capable of eclipsing the cosmic Clapton. And the astute Mike Vernon realized that his best bet of capturing the band's fiery essence was to try to record them as if they were playing a live gig. As he tells it, "There was an air of excitement and expectancy and thankfully never one of felling under any pressure. Everyone did what they felt as and when they felt it. We knew we needed to make an album that would represent the band "Live" and we felt at that time we achieved just that. All in all it was an album to be proud of."[9] A lovely understatement, indeed.

Considering how remarkably crisp and emotionally intact their first sessions for the first album, *Peter Green's Fleetwood Mac*, still sound 40 years later, it is rather amazing that they were engineered (by Mike Ross) onto a four-track machine, over three slim days, completely live, including vocals, with no overdubbing whatsoever. This alone places them in stark contrast to their other famous British peers, who were by then making experimental music that could not be performed live at all, thus beginning an alienation from their audience that would corrosively affect their creativity in the long run. In fact, for those famous peers, there would not even be a long run.

It was during this rough-and-ready period that Fleetwood Mac also became the "house band" at Blue Horizon Records, which was also signing up many other little-known British blues cult bands. Most important among these, of course, was Chicken Shack, with its unique female pianist/singer/songwriter, Christine Perfect (later McVie). At this early stage, Mac also performed as an in-house backing group for many other notable figures, including Duster Bennett, Eddie Boyd, and the great Otis Spann. All in all, it was a fantastic learning experience for a gifted group, which used the early opportunity to perfect its special sound and feel.

* * * * * * * * * *

But almost immediately, Peter Green would serve notice that he was intending to "break the blues" in a far more radical manner that his former band, Mayall's Bluesbreakers, ever dreamed possible. By January 25, 1968, he was creating the masterful "Black Magic Woman," a blues song disguised as a Latin-flavored rock anthem which would take the newly passionate Mac audience into uncharted musical territory. Considering Green was labeled a "purist," it is ironic that almost everything he ever composed was a move away from blues formats and towards something purely "Other."

Indeed, as Leah Furman, author of *Rumours Exposed*, has said, "By virtue of sound alone, the Fleetwood Mac of today could never be mistaken for the Fleetwood Mac of 1967. Fans of the pop super-group would be hard pressed to identify the scrappy gang of guys who took their first bows under the moniker. In fact, few people knew what to make of the band the night they astounded their maiden audience."[10]

Fleetwood himself has since commented on that intense, historic early period and on their "meager" beginnings: "These were times that rang of innocent energy. A sense of music that one by one we all became part of. That power would be led by Peter's hands in those early days. Looking back, it was to all of us a dream come true. Most certainly for myself to this day, it is the first and last lesson in life and music: less is more and more is less."[11]

That same ironic devotion to simplicity, so paradoxical considering the band's future heights of technical overindulgence, is summed up nicely in one of Fleetwood's own musical dictums, surprising only for its apparent modesty: "I want the effect of my playing to be that people feel the emotion I'm trying to create with rhythms. For me the point of the craft is to complement your fellow players and not get frustrated, the drummer's malady: wanting to get noticed."[12]

Who would ever have suspected that such laid-back self-effacement would still result in his playing being globally applauded? But it also sums up the secret for success that Fleetwood shared with bassist McVie for four decades: let's produce the rhythm this band needs to move forward, regardless of who the frontline "stars" are. Despite this deceptive modesty—particularly since it also shelters a massive ego at the same time—Fleetwood is definitely one of the top rock drummers in history. Only the superb Charlie Watts of the Rolling Stones, and the sublime Ringo Starr, the most underrated drummer in history from that *other* group, come close to Fleetwood's permanent grasp of pure musical timekeeping.

* * * * * * * * * *

Suddenly the Mac legacy was launched, and soon everything would be moving so fast it made the heads of the three main guitarists spin. Unfortunately, their heads were spinning in different directions. Luckily no one in the band noticed, and they just plunged forward, the only direction available to them. And somehow, against all odds, they became an almost instant hit.

In fact they had a "fistful of hits." *Peter Green's Fleetwood Mac* was released in late February 1968 and became a smash on the British charts for the remainder of the summer. Incredibly, the following year, a crucial watershed year for the band, they sold more records in Britain than The Beatles or the Stones. Their success, ironic considering that blues had never before achieved such high popularity, was fueled by Green's highly experimental yet somehow still pop-oriented "songs," the likes of which had never before been heard. I call this success ironic because prior to this point, the blues had been a series cult, but a cult nonetheless. Now, owing to the wildly eclectic music tastes of the 1960s (in which African or Indian music might be heard on the same festival bill as blues, jazz, pop, folk, and psychedelic sounds) blues contained something that suddenly appealed to the antiauthoritarian countercultural stage of history which had recently commenced.

Green biographer Martin Celmins has observed some of this irony in action himself when he chronicled the fact that Green was "living out the lore of 'Rambling Pony,' that primitive blues he wailed onto acetate during the summer of love. Around the time that he cut this Robert Johnson–inspired track, blues music had seriously captured the imaginations of young English white boys cosseted in the cockroach-free comfort of mother and father's home in some safe part of town." Celmins continued:

> From there, these obsessives who stalked Peter Green backstage would get off on what amounted to stud imagery from dark and bygone days Stateside. Images of the blues musician's low life were of wild whores, bootleg liquor and violence. A blues man was a real man—a homicidal roustabout banged in the penitentiary along with his guitar playing prowess. And the glamour of raw, black blues was its danger: it was music for closet outlaws. There was really only one guy on the British music scene in the late 1960s who could disinter all of that remote afro-American slave culture and bring it back to life before their very eyes. He was, of all things, a chirpy Jewish cockney![13]

Curiously enough, it would actually be the grandly decadent Rolling Stones who fully lived out the whoredom and violence issues, while closet outlaws like Peter Green would bend and break under the strain of success. After all, he reasoned (in his own unreasonable way) how could an outlaw become so wealthy and influential and still remain an outlaw. He could not, and he did not. Even though by the time of their second record release, *Mr. Wonderful*—recorded in an equally raw style designed to channel the authentic feel of the classic American Chess studios in the 1940s—the founding Mac man had since been enshrined in the public's imagination as the "guitar hero extraordinaire."

The growing youth culture, especially helpful expanding the horizons of those no longer young, was now exploding. Heady days followed. The Beatles' *Sgt. Pepper* had created a new watermark for studio creativity, and the mysterious death of Rolling Stone Brian Jones had, in the minds of many bands and producers, permitted them a drastic return to their own roots.

A kind of "get back" feeling ensued across the musical board, inevitably influenced by the sudden resurgence and the unexpected popular success of the old-fashioned blues format. Companies scrambled to do what they do best, capitalize on realities happening too fast for them to predict effectively. Suddenly, blues bands were competing with pop bands for the affection and wallets of young listeners; and some of these bands were quite talented, such as Chicken Shack, Savoy Brown, Ten Years After, and Free. Even Jethro Tull started out as a pseudo-blues band. Meanwhile, the American blues roots were being further tilled by extraordinary talents such as Paul Butterfield,

Canned Heat, and the Blues Project, featuring the incendiary guitarist Mike Bloomfield.

But Green was a purist, which was why he left the erstwhile Mayall in the first place. "There were a million groups making a mockery of the blues. And a million guitarists playing as fast as they could and calling it blues. I didn't want the music messed about. I was possessive about it," he lamented. And Fleetwood himself, always a Green worshipper, indicated that it was all merely structure: "I think the musical rules of the blues only appealed to Peter as an avenue to other things he could express himself through."[14]

Mr. Wonderful, while still maintaining a hold on the traditional, recognizably bluesy 12-bar format, also pointed ahead toward some very unconventional directions. The first of these was the rather radical inclusion of female singer-songwriter pianist Christine Perfect as an uncredited but immediately influential band member. This act alone, having a "girl" performing the otherwise ruggedly macho blues format, along with the soon-to-be lauded addition of extra lead guitars, was a prime indicator that Mac was not a run-of-the-mill blues band. The band moved even further from the middle ground through its release in rapid succession of Green's newest and most daring departures into the musical unknown, singular singles such as "Albatross," "Black Magic Woman," and "Man of the World."

This band's classic "identity crisis," the fuel that would feed all their upcoming and greatest hits, was being felt almost instantly after only a year of incipient existence. The addition of 18-year-old Danny Kirwan would prove to be the creative cement that would both produce some of Mac's loveliest music and some of its most manic and distressing mayhem. Apparently they just couldn't have one without the other.

Of these early experimental blues hybrids producer Vernon would remark, "'Albatross' was a departure from what the band had been doing but in a way it pre-empted what they were going to do, because 'Man of the World' was just as much of a departure."[15] Far from being only a departure, "Man of the World" is also notable as the first sign of cracks appearing in the dream. It is saturated by a kind of disenchantment with fame, unheard of until Lennon's "primal" record two years later. And it is an important precursor to perhaps the most volatile rejection by an artist of his audience that the music world has ever heard, Green's wickedly unhappy "Oh Well, Parts One and Two." Yet strangely, even "Oh Well," the ultimate repudiation of fame and a statement of disregard for listeners seldom equaled since, unaccountably became a hit. His bandmates had even bet him that it could not sell, but it did, and in a big way.

Whether he liked it or not, and he certainly did not, Peter Green had a golden touch when it came to parceling out his pain in such gorgeous packages that his adoring public simply could not get enough. But very soon, Green would reveal that he himself had had enough. What began as a liberating feeling of expressing shared sadness eventually overtook him and became the keynote for his creative tragedy, bringing him face to face with a sadness that simply could not be shared. Once the sharing was gone, the implosion began. One particular track on *Mr. Wonderful*, "Trying So Hard to Forget" finds him trying to both mourn and eliminate the childhood during which he was "nothing but a downtrodden kid." Speaking of his affinity for the black blues he commented, "When you're Jewish you can create a lot of feel of your own. I was always a sad person, I don't know why, and I suppose I felt a deep sadness with my heritage."[16]

Whatever the sources of his sadness, it was so profound that what began as a magic ability to express his feelings, in a way that instantly connected with his audience, quickly turned into an inability to express any feelings at all—except, of course, for the towering rage, sorrow, and ultimate retreat for which he became just as famous as for his brilliant writing and playing. Alas, for the temperamental Green, that emblematic phrase used as a title by Booker T. Jones for his classic blues piece, "Born Under a Bad Sign" would have to be changed to born under a mad sign. Badness will get your far in the blues, but madness will lead you nowhere.

$$* \quad * \quad * \quad * \quad * \quad * \quad * \quad * \quad * \quad *$$

Yet Fleetwood Mac, and Green, would soldier on, albeit briefly, for their third record release. The first on a big splashy label, Warner Brothers/Reprise, it was the first record to fully launch Mac's music out of the blues ghetto and into the wild world of psychedelic rock. It was also the last clarion call for the rapidly downward-spiraling founder of the band.

While such classics as *Fleetwood Mac* and *Rumours* were waiting to be born in 1975 and 1977, back in the Summer of Love (and the two-year hangover that followed) the band had a wild old time exploring the furthest edges of the blues, including a breathtaking record of their encounter with their own old black idols in Chicago. They also explored the furthest edges of sanity, and beyond, through a unique kind of hybrid drug-rock/blues, and then they explored a form of music made by Peter Green which has yet to be adequately defined. From 1967–70 they pursued a furiously edgy style in both their music and, especially, their personal lives. The music on the records is healthy evidence of that, but then so is the combination of mental hospitals, religious cults, addictions, angst, and anger.

The cultural environment in which the early records were conceived and created was one of extreme artistic, social, and personal experimentation. This context is what made the 1960s what they are, which is essential for assessing all that the later third version of Fleetwood Mac would eventually attain in the world of global pop music. It is sometimes amazing to contemplate their origins, as well as from what exotic and chaotic roots the mature and commercially sophisticated popsters would later become the gods (and goddesses) of the 1980s musical cash register.

At the early threshold of actual fame and fortune, their founder Green would have shuddered in horror if he had been given a glimpse of the future of his band without him in it. His early success, from which he could not fully recover or endure, was a merely a tiny dinner bell compared to the roaring tidal wave of wealth that was yet to come. But to get to hear that roaring wave, they would first have to survive. As it turns out, this was much easier said than done.

* * * * * * * * * *

The group that had begun by channeling, however accurately, the gritty sound of urban black blues, had almost immediately morphed into a difficult-to-describe entity by their third album. The singles that issued from Peter Green's feverish imagination were a clear indication that regardless of his allegiances, he was first and foremost a groundbreaking innovator. He also discovered, much to his apparent horror, that he had a superb ability to write chart-busting hit single songs, despite the fact that they were actually harrowing confessions of his own sense of inadequacy and shame. Success has a strange effect on some gentle souls.

But paradoxically, while plunging full steam ahead into uncharted musical territories largely fueled by LSD intake, Green and his band were still romantically committed to memorializing the sounds they grew up loving. So in the late fall of 1968, while beginning to cook up some of the strange brew that would alarm many British blues purists, they simultaneously took part in two historically important recording sessions in America organized by producers Mike Vernon and the blues magnate Marshall Chess of legendary Chess Records.

Known as both Fleetwood Mac in Chicago and Blues Jam at Chess, these encounters would both seal the pedigree of Fleetwood Mac as legitimate heirs to a classic American songwriting style, while at the same time propel them further away from their roots. This kind of back-and-forth by Green's fragile and conflicted sensibilities is the first and most glaring indication that he was operating from a somewhat bipolar point of view. Later on it would become abundantly clear to his bandmates that, far from being merely temperamental, he was in fact a full-fledged basket case, insisting that they give away all their hard-earned wealth in a binge of guilt and misplaced charitable paranoia.

By the time *Blues Jam in Chicago* was released in 1969, the band had already moved so far from the roots they were heard to be celebrating that it was mostly an instant antique conveying authentic nostalgia in its plaintive mixing of music beyond racial boundaries. Though the encounter with many of their boyhood heroes, Otis Spann, Willie Dixon, Buddy Guy, and Walter "Shakey" Horton among them, was inspiring and rewarding, it was also a bit of what John McVie identified as "a drag, because most of the black cats had the typical opinion of Whitey playing the blues. Look at my pictures on the cover and you'll known exactly how I felt."[17] For Green, however, that did not seem to matter, recalling that, "I didn't so much as want to play *with* the bluesmen as to hear *them* play. But once we got going, I didn't care what they thought of me. I was just happy to be playing."[18]

The Chess sessions were followed by a masterful encounter between McVie, Kirwan, Green, and drummer S.P. Leary. In a colossal celebration of what it meant to have the blues, however sadly for some, these lofty meetings were also the band's last ventures into classic blues material. They were already past this original style by the time the records came out, and well into the exotic and radical mixture of musical traditions (some of them not even invented yet) that came to be explored on their third (and last) recording together, *Then Play On*. Since that record had no "old-fashioned" formats to groove to, Jeremy Spencer had no real role to play and was not to be heard at all. Danny Kirwan was now the official guitar partner and foil for Green's brilliant forays into personal darkness, a high-pressure creative position that would eventually cause him to crack at the seams as well, though his inevitable breakdown due to personality and psychological problems had been a long time coming.

The highly disturbing and iconic single "Man of the World" would be the first harbinger of the darkness to come. It was Green's personal version of Lennon's "Nowhere Man," and it was almost too sad, too downtrodden, and too blue, to even be enjoyed as a song, let alone a blues song. "Guess I've got everything I need, I wouldn't ask for more. And there's no one I'd rather be, but I just wish that I had never been born," sang the deeply confused Green in this harrowing revelation of his anger and angst. Yet his friends, his bandmates, and the public seemed blissfully unaware of his true suffering, in exactly the same way that many other geniuses can deceive us into being entertained by their pain rather than enlightened by their message. Just as no one paid attention to Lennon when he was sinking into his dark period, no one noticed Green's descent into a dark night of the soul that would prevent even his gifted artistic vision from either emerging as music or stemming the tide that was about to wash him away.

"Man of the World" was the first song to appear away from the home that Blue Horizon and Mike Vernon had provided in their early days. It was released on the Immediate label founded by the Rolling Stones' mercurial entrepreneur, Andrew Loog Oldham. Around this same time, in early 1969, it was widely rumored that Mac would sign with The Beatles' new label, Apple Records—a partnership that, in retrospect, would have been disastrous for them both creatively and financially.Instead, they would sign with Warner Brothers/Reprise Records, their label to this day. Though it would have its ups and downs, like all relationships between creative musical artists and voracious businessmen, this commercial collaboration would make them all wealthy beyond their wildest dreams, and certainly beyond Green's worst nightmares.

Their first Warner record, *Then Play On,* remains one of their best, and one of the best experiments in hybrid blues-rock ever conceived. "The blues was the first and last music Fleetwood Mac played that relied repeatedly on certain structural restrictions and stock changes. After *Albatross,* things were wide open, and the group simply played whatever songs the various writers had that seemed suitable, whatever felt right, whether it was bluesy or not."[19] They became, in Fleetwood's words, not just a blues band, but a musical band. Of *Then Play On,* Fleetwood says, "We knew we couldn't just make an album like the others. We didn't have an exact concept of what we were going to do, but we knew what we weren't going to do, and that was put out another album of Jeremy singing Elmore James. We just went in and made the album—Pete knew pretty much what he wanted to do."[20]

But though he may have known what he wanted to do, Green's acid intake and the emergence of his inherent depressive nature made it an angst- and guilt-ridden project. He was skeptical about shifting from the little independent pure blues label Blue Horizon, and the producer who had nurtured their early talents, Mike Vernon, to the big-business machinery of Warner Brothers. "I was the last to agree to leave Blue Horizon. I was quite happy there, and I didn't like leaving just for more money. I said to the rest of the guys, Watch out, there'll be a comeback from this."[21] Considering that he himself was already leaving the blues far behind in his highly intelligent and experimental personal forays into abstraction and rock music, it seems all the more paradoxical that Green would have had these fears, since he himself was leading the charge toward a new form of rock. Either way, the heavy blues feeling was about to be diminished in favor of a different sort of heaviness, as would the original "live in the studio atmospheric recordings" By now, the band was producing their own work, and for the first time, they were experimenting, like so many other talented rock units of the period, with the magic of overdubbing.

For the nominal leader of the group, Mick Fleetwood, this would be but the first of multiple incarnations through which he and McVie would weather any and all storms. His take was that the changes were part of a personal and a personnel evolution that had its reasons in the music, and he never questioned the music. It runs like this: "Musically, Fleetwood Mac grew to a five piece band, that for the most part would set a precedent of having three performer songwriters within its ranks for many years to come. Another way of saying the above would be as Shakespeare said, 'If Music be the Food of Love, Then Play On.'"[22] Few things give me more pleasure than when severely dyslexic rock stars quote Shakespeare. But Fleetwood was right, of course. He always is when it comes to this historic band and its meteoric rise, although he could just as easily have said that "if madness be the food of love, then play on," because that is just the way it played out in the end.

* * * * * * * * * *

Like all "good" managers, Clifford Davis was always ecstatic when he could wrest control of talent from someone else and get a better deal for everybody concerned. This managerial coup was no exception.

> I think the biggest coup I ever pulled off for Fleetwood Mac was getting them out of their Blue Horizon recording contract. The deal Peter Green had struck with Mike Vernon prior to me coming on the scene as the band's manager was simple. One year's recording contract followed by two one year options on Blue Horizon's side, to be taken up only if they wanted the band. I just sat praying that Richard (Vernon's brother) wouldn't notice the renewal date coming up. And he didn't. I notified Blue Horizon the following day that they had failed to take up the option, and therefore Fleetwood Mac were free from any further contractual obligations.[23]

But like all "good" managers, Davis was also a voracious control freak who wanted as much as possible out of the talent, regardless of their own needs and desires. This would become abundantly clear a few years later, when Davis, believing his potential gold mine was being panned out, attempted to put together a "faux" Fleetwood Mac and put them on the road. Even he was aware early on that Mac was a living brand as well as a band, and in his quest for more of the same, he didn't hesitate to assemble a bogus version of the group, claiming that he himself owned the creative property of his music makers.

Davis's true colors would emerge in 1973 during an angry presentation in New York, when the audience began to notice that this was a surrogate Mac put together by their manager, and not the real thing. His explanation, incredible as it may seem, was along the lines of "Don't worry I *am* Fleetwood Mac!" He imagined that he himself had put the band together, that he owned the name itself, and that if he wanted to call a band by that name, it was his right to do so.

So in the end, which in reality was far from near, maybe Green had been correct about certain portions of the business side of the music business that had so irked him that it melted away his ability to play at all. But for now, in 1969, it was the best of times and the worst of times, at the same time. And music had to be made, and played on, and so it was. But for Green by then, to quote his idol B.B. King, the thrill was gone.

Green was more than restless—he was coming apart at the seams. It seemed that no matter what he did, he could not help but produce hit records, thus expanding around himself the kind of attention and adulation that he had so dreaded after replacing Clapton in Mayall's band. What would have made any other young blues-rocker in his place ecstatic was instead the culmination of Green's worst fears. It, along with the acid he was consuming, wore him down, and eventually his fear, guilt, depression, and paranoia would sink him. Even something as powerful as LSD cannot be fairly blamed for his downward spiral, though that has been the mythology around him, the foundations of which will be explored in the next chapter. It just happened to be the drug that provided the catalyst for an inevitable descent.

After the second tour of America, during which the band played an incendiary show at the Boston Tea Party (still one of the best live blues recordings ever made) and during which their fateful encounter with the Grateful Dead would lead to the LSD connection forming part of the Green myth, the band returned to England in a triumphant wave of Mac-mania. They had clearly established themselves in America, no mean feat, and they had a number-one hit in the wistful instrumental "Albatross," a haunting melody that became so influential that it even inspired The Beatles to create a song called "Sun King," as a tribute to Green, on their brilliant *Abbey Road* album.

By this time, Mac was astonished to discover that they were outselling both The Beatles and the Rolling Stones. They released a compilation record called *English Rose,* which though filled with earlier songs also contained the formlessly floating "Albatross," as well as four new, innovative songs by Danny Kirwan. They had laid the groundwork for a full departure from their blues roots, much to the horror of their stalwart British fan base, and would launch themselves full force into the new "free form rock" format of the equally new FM radio stations just then popping up across America.

As Stephen Davis has pointed out astutely in his collaborative book with Mick Fleetwood, the FM format came along at the perfect time to accommodate Mac's new musical spirit, and its more commercial middle-of-the-road appetites would provide Mac with its new core fan and audience base. These new fans would form the entire basis for the band's upcoming rise to the top of the musical mountain. But alas, not all the band members would make that perilous climb all the way.

There was at least one other encouraging accolade for the band, in addition to the irony of outselling The Beatles without selling out. John McVie's wife Christine, still the fiery woman behind Chicken Shack, was voted the UK's "best female vocalist." For this writer, she still is.

* * * * * * * * * *

By early 1970, Mac was touring Europe in their usual exhausting mode, mostly performing the hybrid sounds on *Then Play On.* But Kirwan was becoming more insecure about Green's incredible generosity in trusting him to create half that record and to perform on an equal basis with him on stage. He was beginning to exhibit some of the neurosis that would soon explode into full-blown psychosis. Spencer was also starting to fray at the edges, under the weight of both relentless touring plus his own inherent musical limits. According to Brunning, "Peter Green's personal problems were coming to a head. He was becoming more confused, taking less interest in the band, and surrounding himself with a lot of eccentric people who were certainly having a bad influence on him....His religious feelings were developing dangerously close to paranoia, and his state of mind was not helped by copious amounts of LSD."[24]

And again, like good managers do (especially the kind with ulterior motives hiding inside them), Clifford Davis had a gift for drastic oversimplification:

> The truth about Peter Green and about how he ended up how he did is very simple. We were touring Europe in late 1969...Peter told me he was invited to a party and I understand from him that he and Danny Kirwan took what turned out to be some very bad, impure LSD, and so did plenty of other people. He was *never* the same again. Later I talked to Peter, he told me he had taken the drug again in this country. He once told me that he thought he was Jesus, and he thought everyone was greedy, and that's why he gave all his money away to charity. I've read a lot of articles saying that Peter Green is a religious fanatic. I'm afraid the truth of the matter is different. Sadly, he was suffering from drug-induced delusions.[25]

But I too am afraid the truth of the matter is different. In fact, the truth is never quite as black and white as managers seem to think. After all, John Lennon, the most famous acid casualty in pop culture history (along with Brian Wilson and Syd Barrett, of course) once convened a business meeting at Apple Records with his bandmates and seriously announced to them that *he* was Jesus Christ. In those days, lots of people thought they were Jesus. But none of them gave away all their own hard-earned wealth and urge their mates to do the same—not even Lennon. Fleetwood himself recollects the following: "I think there is certainly some credence given to the idea that Peter's condition could in some way be blamed on a bad acid trip he had in Germany. We called the group who held the party the 'Munich Jet Set.' They were basically a bunch of very rich brats who were living in a commune, and they sort of whisked him away, and I don't think it did him much good."[26]

The usually quiet Green commented on the touchy subject of his own sanity in an interview with Trevor Dann in 1988, a full two decades after he first encountered LSD on the West Coast of the States: "I'm at present recuperating from treatment for taking drugs. I was a sucker for taking drugs. It was drugs that influenced me a lot. I took more than I intended to. The effect of that stuff lasts so long, twelve or twenty four hours. I wanted to give away all my money, if we ever earned any big money. I went kind of holy....no, not holy, religious. I was kind of religious. So I thought I could do it. I thought I was all right on drugs. My failing!"[27]

Unfortunately, this gentle and fragile soul, with such dark melancholic edges, was unable to weather the storm that he himself had largely created and choreographed. The going of Green is one of the greatest and saddest losses in musical history, at par with the early departure of Charlie Parker in jazz circles. And yet strangely enough, without his departure, Fleetwood

Mac would not have evolved into the musical institution they quickly became and remain to this day.

PETER GREEN'S FLEETWOOD MAC: RELEASED 1968, BLUE HORIZON RECORDS

This album was recorded during the period November 22–December 11, 1967. *Mojo* magazine's description of this first outing strikes me as being almost tongue in cheek: "Young British-blues master Green in excelsis: not much to do with the Californian edition of Fleetwood Mac."[28] That is putting it mildly.

Peter Lewry's book on the complete recording sessions is the ideal companion tome with which to listen to these early ventures. Try reading it with several glasses of the alcohol of your choice in hand, in order to simulate the sinuous realm in which it was recorded. With loving care he chronicles the details of each session and its emotional background. "Following a string of gigs at regular blues haunts, Fleetwood Mac finally went into the studios of CBS in New Bond Street, London to begin work on their first album. The resulting LP, *Peter Green's Fleetwood Mac,* is regarded as one of the classic British blues albums, and reaching number four and spending 37 weeks on the album charts. Several tracks were held over until 1971 and released on the compilation album, 'The Original Fleetwood Mac.'"[29]

In my opinion, it was The Classic British Blues album, bar none. The cut "Drifting," which was one of those held back in 1968 and released only later in compilation form, is the best gauge by which to measure the entire band's direction and spirit. "Drifting" has the ideal mix of blues bite and rock raunch. It is a mystery to me as to why this gorgeous and harrowing track was omitted, but its later inclusion does also draw attention to exactly how rapid was the rise and fall of Green's unit.

By 1971, at which point the surviving Fleetwood Mac was releasing the brilliant "Future Games" featuring both Christine McVie and Bob Welch, the world was already well prepared to memorialize and wax rhapsodic about the missing Green element, suggesting quite mistakenly that *this* was the real Fleetwood Mac. Actually (and as much as I loved, and still love, the original lineup), it was merely the *old* Fleetwood Mac which had been infused with a *new* and considerably less destructive spirit.

As fetishistic sound engineers the world over would like it to be a well-known fact, its important to note, as Mike Ross does on behalf of Vernon and the band, that this first album for Blue Horizon was recorded on a four-track machine, the complete live recording, including live vocals, without any overdubbing whatsoever. "The band wanted to create a club sound on these tracks, so we set up some speakers in the studio, placed microphones directly in front of the speakers and recorded the tracks."[30]

Songs such as "Cold Black Night" and "My Heart Beat Like a Hammer," two early Spencer tunes, show Green and the band at their finest and fittest, revealing the massive respect they had for the original black purveyors of the artform they were channeling in so spooky a fashion. Meanwhile, however, the original compositions by Green—"Looking for Somebody," "I Loved Another Woman," "Merry Go Round," "Long Grey Mare," and "The World Keep On Turning"—sent chills down the spines of blues lovers everywhere. It still does, almost 40 years later.

In "Looking for Somebody," when Green moans, "I got a feeling, the blues gonna be my only way," it does not help for us to know his eventual fate.... It is all the more heartbreaking that Green himself seemed to know instinctively that he was doomed from the start, except that he blames it on the woman, or on the other man, or on the world. *The way things are,* that is the most primal reason for having the blues. It also has in it the gentle wafting aroma of abstract regret, of a solipsistic sorrow, of the melancholy that accumulates around the way things could be, or might have been, or should be. Nonetheless, what he seems to have suffered from so severely was definitely some form of fulfilled-dream syndrome: the horrible sensation that everything you ever dreamed of has come true but somehow you just cannot stand it anymore.

Soon enough, almost immediately in fact, as revealed in the way his songs began to take the shape of his darker emotions, he was suddenly singing the blues in reverse. He was King Midas in reverse, crushed by an inexplicable guilt that prevented him from following through on the marvelous successes that were the direct result of his own gifts and hard work.

MR. WONDERFUL:
RELEASED 1968, BLUE HORIZON RECORDS

This quirky follow-up is difficult to call a sequel. In fact, it could almost have been a double-album debut, with the *Mr. Wonderful* material being a literal extension of what Mac had accomplished in their first outing. Once again, the music was pure, scintillating blues, rough in form and raw in content, this time with the addition of a horn four-piece section and an uncredited Christine Perfect on piano.

One has to remember the sheer speed and appetite that consumed the young Mac players. Since they had no inkling that their career would last very long, or that they even had a career at all to speak of, they were rushing full throttle forward into the next musical moment. Some people have expressed slight disappointment in this follow-up record, coming as it did so soon, too soon perhaps, after their initial launching. After all, the level of their playing, and the immediate diversity of their material, has already raised expectations to a high degree.

Producer Mike Vernon has observed that these days, it can sometimes be as long as 18 months or two years for a follow-up to a current release, especially if the initial release managed to chart well and create the usual expectations for the follow-up to be stellar.

But in the heady days of the 1960's, things were a lot different. As if to celebrate the release of Mac's debut album in February of 1968, the band headed back into the studio to cut two new titles. Within four weeks we were back in New Bond Street looking to record enough material for their second album. To a degree, the band's first album only partly emulated the energy surges of their stage performances. The plan was to aim for a dirtier, gutsier sound. We did our best to set up the band as if they were on stage.[31]

Only one month after the release of their first album, the band released the first of their incredible singles, and it was seemingly in the single format that this band achieved their most experimental forms of expression. This is an odd irony considering that singles are more generally considered commercial fodder to support long-playing records.

Steve Clarke has expressed the opinion that coming after two excellent singles, "Black Magic Woman" and "Need Your Love So Bad," *Mr. Wonderful* was some sort of abdication from their roots. It was not. It was an evolutionary leap forward and away from them. Once again, they were unconcerned at this stage with selling records, only with making them, and they produced cover art for the album (a nude and crazed-looking Mick Fleetwood clutching a child's doll near his private parts) which seemed to almost presage a proto-punk in your face attitude toward their own audience.

Mr. Wonderful is especially notable for the creative growth it displays in Green's writing and playing on this volatile mixture of reinterpreted blues standards and his own sizzling hot originals. "Rolling Man" and "Love That Burns" are clear indications of his prowess at its peak, but "If You Be My Baby" and especially "Trying So Hard To Forget" are even more obvious flags about his precarious state of mind—dramatic, emotional flags that none of his friends or bandmates seemed to notice.

Mr. Wonderful was released in September 1968 and did "good business." It was a grand introduction of Mac for the growing legion of blues lovers on both sides of the Atlantic. It was still, however, the straight goods in terms of gritty white blues within a traditional format, albeit with the drastically avant-garde approach of Green's playing. But it could never have prepared the audience for their third release, the genuinely experimental *Then Play On,* which would open wide many ears, eyes, and minds.

ENGLISH ROSE:
RELEASED 1969, EPIC RECORDS (U.S. ONLY)

Since *Mr. Wonderful* was not given a North American release, a mixture of old and new material was rapidly assembled and released under the title

English Rose in order to capitalize on the band's U.S. tour. The album featured nearly all of the band's prior singles, along with a few tracks lifted from *Mr. Wonderful* and a handful of new Danny Kirwan songs, originally intended for some future project. Again, their album cover art was created specifically for shock purposes, with Fleetwood, ever the game exhibitionist, featured in glaring drag and hyper makeup.

On a personal note, this is the first album by the group that my old friend Gerry acquired and played for me, thus introducing both of us to a 40-year love affair with their music. It was doubly unique in that the combination of songs, arbitrary at best and mixing old and new styles, could not help but convey the sense of a highly experimental approach to both blues itself and music making in general. The sequencing of singles not usually heard together, followed by new songs colliding in sentiment, made it a truly surprising and illuminating introduction to the group's style and sensibility.

PIOUS BIRD OF GOOD OMEN:
RELEASED 1969, BLUE HORIZON (UK ONLY)

This album was the exact reverse of *English Rose*—in this case, a package assembled for Britain only. The original vinyl format of this record was released in August 1969, in order to "preempt" the imminent release of the new Reprise label's *Then Play On*, the band's first foray on a big label. This record hit the charts in August and eventually climbed to #18, quite extraordinary for a huge raft of steaming blues at that time.

Essentially, *Pious Bird* (a rather obvious attempt by CBS to cash in on the wild success of the "Man of the World" and "Albatross" singles) contained four single releases, two album tracks, and two additional titles that featured Mac in a supporting role behind the Chicago blues pianist/vocalist Eddie Boyd. During this period, the 18-year-old guitarist Danny Kirwan, late of Boilerhouse, joined Mac and left a lasting musical mark: a profound stylistic influence that lasted long beyond his own sad breakdown.

According to Vernon, though considered by many not to have been a legitimate Fleetwood Mac "album," it nevertheless created quite a demand for the band's burgeoning output. Not surprisingly, it also drew a large amount of attention for its cover art, which featured a nun in complete formal habit carrying a large stuffed albatross—and clearly almost nine months pregnant!

BLUES JAM IN CHICAGO:
RELEASED 1969, BLUE HORIZON/CBS RECORDS

Blues Jam in Chicago is perhaps a labor of love more than anything remotely commercial: the exploration of their own music's roots by the gritty white cockneys playing and recording with their creative black elders. Vernon readily admits both the album's powerful emotional content and its lack of any market position, as well as the occasionally edgy feelings elicited by the encounter between the wealthy young white upstarts and the quite literally poor old black originators.

> There can be little doubt that of all the albums released on the CBS/Blue Horizon labels, the double "Blues Jam" was the least successful commercially and the most ignored by Mac fans. Recorded in one day, this project threw together the members of the band and a handful of the leading Chicago blues men: Buddy Guy, Otis Spann, Shakey Horton, Honey Boy Edwards, J.T. Brown and S.P. Leary, under the guidance of Willie Dixon.[32]

For those of us who did listen to and love this record, and there were quite a few despite the sales, it was an astonishing tour de force for the band, sweating in the shadows of the masters and desperately trying to impress them (and succeeding, by the way) in a way that far surpasses all the other attempts to get famous white rock stars and their black progenitors together on vinyl. Excursions such as the Rolling Stones in London with Howlin' Wolf, or Clapton's own forays into the darker origins of his music, pale by comparison to the sheer ego, rage, competition, nerve rattling, false starts, accidents, live commentary, and incredibly strong versions of pure, colorless blues found in this set.

Jeremy Spencer was completely awed because he was playing with J.T. Brown, the living legend who had played with Elmore James, the sole reason for Spencer's existence in the blues realm. And Green, keeping his own up-and-down egomania in check, was thrilled to be in the same spiritual space, Chess Records in Chicago, as one of his all-time heroes, Otis Spann. Within a week of this recording, they would also appear together in New York, working on Spann's "The Biggest Thing Since Colossus"—and it really was!

These sessions were also a landmark since it was the last time that Fleetwood Mac would play or record any "straight ahead" blues material. However, as I have tried to suggest elsewhere, this remarkable band, even subsequent to the departure of their fearful leader, continued to produce what I have described as a unique and revolutionary form of blues known as "pop blues." Indeed, it was so revolutionary that no one seems to have noticed that Fleetwood Mac merely camouflaged their blues, covered it in a shiny varnish, polished up the production values, increased the tempo until even a blues slug felt like dancing, and thus achieved astronomical pop success by wearing their new disguise. Beneath it all, however, beats the hammered blues heart of Fleetwood and McVie.

THEN PLAY ON:
RELEASED 1969, WARNER BROTHERS/REPRISE RECORDS

Then Play On is the unalloyed masterpiece of Mac's grand early period. A quintessentially experimental stew of ancient blues roots with psychedelic hippie-era sounds, this record also clearly defined a new territory for Fleetwood Mac. It is as fresh today as it was then, simply because it offered us a strange hybrid, the first of many from Mac—which, although it defined the group, could not itself be defined. It also shows the creative results of the band, most particular Peter Green, ingesting the drug that would both expand musical consciousness and shrink personal identity at the same time. It was the best of times and the worst of times.

Almost immediately following the Blues Jam at Chess in Chicago sessions, the band was in the studio again recording the beginnings of the strange single, "Man of the World": "Shall I tell you about my life....they say I'm a man of the world." It is perhaps the saddest non-blues song ever penned by a famous singer, apart from John Lennon. The sentiment encapsulates Peter Green's quickly melting mind at that time, containing a bluesy plea for the usual solution, "And I need a woman, to make me feel like a good man should....I don't say that I'm a good man, but I would be if I could." But Green quickly follows this plaintive call with the essence of his emerging challenge: "I have everything I need, I wouldn't want to be anyone else....but I just wish I'd never been born." Inexplicably, this too was still a hit record.

One of the many things that bothered Green in 1969 was his earlier label's release of the rough-and-ready *Blues Jam* in the same time period as his colossal new foray into the extended acid jams of *Then Play On*, correctly assuming they would confuse the public and interrupt sales of the new direction. This concern for sales serves as another irony, considering Green's infamous aversion to money, profit, and the well-earned rewards for all his labor. But then again, Green was an enigma. If nothing else, his insights about his music are often peculiar, leaving us better off if we listen to what he sang rather than to what he said. And what he sang and played on *Then Play On* was masterful, majestic, magical, dark, and doomed.

In the notes to the Warner Bros/Reprise second release of 1970, which included the suddenly popular and wildly weird "Oh Well, Parts One and Two" for commercial purposes, the band is described as "flexing the blues muscle that earned them a solid reputation among musical purists." True, but while flexing that muscle, they are also putting it to an entirely different heavy-lifting exercise. Whereas before they had engaged in a kind of emotional wrestling match with the blues and its lost-love content, here they are involved in a titanic boxing match with themselves, with the blues, with rock music, with drugs, and with the music industry in general.

It is the strange swan song of a group that does not quite know its about to meltdown and transform almost overnight, even though "Closing My Eyes" and "Show Biz Blues" are emergency wake-up calls from a rapidly descending "nowhere man" who would very soon wave goodbye, both to his mates and to his own sanity.

Danny Kirwan rises to the occasion and fulfills the early promise that his mentor Green saw in him with the opening track, "Coming Your Way."

Sinuous guitar lines weave in and around a fast-paced romp into the ether. Kirwan's other contributions—the beautiful "My Dream," "Although the Sun Is Shining," "When You Say," and "Like Crying"—all have a blues-based core but are covered in a mysteriously sweet icing that belies their darkness. His playing and voice are simply superb. He would last for three more records before having the nervous breakdown which to this day has rendered him a sad shadow of his former self. But here, one can hear the full force of his youthful brilliance.

Poor Jeremy Spencer is not featured on *Then Play On* because he had nothing to contribute to its forward-moving momentum. The new creative evolution had no space for his traditionally sliding and slashing guitar style, which pretty much limited him to channeling Elmore James or old-fashioned rhythm-and-blues rockers. He would last for only one more record, the truly transitional *Kiln House* in 1970, by which time he was fractured to a degree that made him perfect fodder for a street-based religious cult.

As per usual, it was Green's fiery intelligence and masterfully emotional playing that made and makes this record a permanent classic. *Then Play On* would reach the top five on British charts and was the group's first solid commercial success in America, largely because it appeared to be a drugged-out rock record rather than a booze-drenched blues record. It was both of course, because this kind of incredibly gifted music knows no boundaries. It is only we who draw the lines around music. The sound itself is always pressing and breaking through those lines, much to our good fortunes.

With its suitably lysergic cover painting by Maxwell Armfield of a god-like nude figure riding a magnificent white steed across a Lucy-in-the-Sky landscape, the album immediately declares its intention to take the listener on both a wild ride and an extended trip. And indeed, many listeners tripped for hours while studying that cover.

Recorded between April and July 1969, this breathtaking roller coaster of human feelings manages to maintain an uncanny stillness and calm at the center of its maniacally beating acidic heart. "I've got things to do, I move every day, I hope you don't mind 'cause I'm coming your way." And come they did, and come and come and come. *Mojo* magazine called it the last and greatest recording of the Mac's first phase.

In the most accurate sense, the band's early "blue horizon" was expanding drastically. Engineer Martin Birch describes the working method: "Peter would come in and show me the feel and structure, lay down the basic track, and when we were happy with the drums, the bass and the two guitars, and I would work on the song until it was fully recorded. Then I would do the same with one of Danny's songs, and it would alternate like that until the record was done."[33]

Mojo magazine also pointed out that this way of working, while it created and produced great recorded music, was indicative of a band in the throes of fragmentation. I would go further and compare it to the lamentably disintegrating Beatles' recording of *Let it Be* in that same fateful breakup year. There were also the classic kind of creative disputes over material, such as the "Oh Well" masterpiece. Fleetwood and McVie almost convinced Green not to release it at all, either as a single or on the album. However, one can never really convince a Peter Green of anything. "Oh Well" not only became a single, but a surprise hit. And it was eventually included on the album itself, which made for a better work of art in the long run. Once again, the addled Green, though imploding from within psychologically, was still brilliant enough to create and communicate forcefully beautiful and emotionally compelling music to his supposedly sane listeners.

And no one at all can ever explain the wistful elegance of Kirwan's instrumental "My Dream." It is simply his own "Albatross." The fact that this depth of soulful and sorrowful music can be conveyed through the sheer joy of their intertwining electric lava flows is a testament to something. But it is something so sad that we can only contemplate it from a distance, for fear of being consumed by the molten flow. We are only slightly soothed by Green's gorgeous piece that follows it, "Underway." But where are on earth are these men taking us?

Mojo magazine's editors have made some of the most astute observations about the morphing qualities of this band. First of all, they note that you can sense the immediate future of the band from the songs themselves. This, by the way, would also have been true if we had all listened more closely to The Beatles and *Let It Be*, if we all had not loved them so damn much!

Green has too often noted that "Show-Biz Blues" is about "why I left Fleetwood Mac" Gee thanks, Peter, but instead of explaining your most obvious song, how about instead try explaining something truly weird like "The Green Manalishi (with the two-prong crown)"? That song's elusive qualities are of the sort explored by writer Richard Brautigan in the same heady period, and trying to hold on to its meaning is definitely like picking up mercury with a pitchfork.

Mojo's album collection tome clearly identifies the special qualities of *Then Play On*:

> *Then Play On* delivered symphonic, elegiac rock, so far removed from the rough-hewn white-blooze of only 18 months previous, Green was rightly proud of the album upon completion and remains so: "I loved every minute of it. There is nothing I feel I could have done better. A Californian aesthetic was already looming—the wave-washed beaches and rolling highways suggested by Green and Kirwan's wistful guitar sounds and Fleetwood's tires-on-the-road thump. Americans loved it. One can only wonder what Fleetwood Mac might have achieved had Peter stayed and created a fourth album.[34]

For my money, Peter Green's astounding ode to the art of onanism, "Rattlesnake Shake," with its tongue-in-cheek mockery ("Well, I know this guy, his name is Mick, and he don't care if he got no chicks...just jerks away the blues.") is well worth the price of admission to his incredible musical carnival.

What other blues group could spark almost physical fights between young friends as drunk as the band was, as they passionately argued who the better blues performers were, America's Paul Butterfield Blues Band or England's Fleetwood Mac? But of course, that was long ago and far away, before they became LA's Fleetwood Mac, then America's, and finally the world's Fleetwood Mac. We will never see or hear the likes of their last early masterpiece, *Then Play On*, again.

Other significant record releases of the same period: Tommy by the Who; *Everybody Knows This Is Nowhere* by Neil Young; *Beckola* by Jeff Beck; *A Salty Dog* by Procol Harum; *Stand Up* by Jethro Tull; *Abbey Road* by The Beatles; *Astral Weeks* by Van Morrison; *In The Court of The Crimson King* by King Crimson; *Hot Rats* by Frank Zappa; *Live Dead* by the Grateful Dead; *Trout Mask Replica* by Captain Beefheart.

The Going of Green: Madness and Manalishi

3

Gifted and visionary musicians often feel compelled to advance beyond or leave musical structure behind. It is one of their inherent impulses to renovate all the musical history before them and to build a new structure out of their own musical visions. Such musicians often also feel that any musical structure at all is an impediment, that structure amounts to sandbags placed along the banks of a wild river designed to keep it obediently in place. And usually, if they are gifted enough, the creative collaborators surrounding them tend to allow them a wide latitude in the pursuit of that vision, often to the detriment of the visionary himself, who without realizing it has stepped off the edge of a precipice into empty space, suspended briefly in the air only by the antigravitational force of their own genius. But without those sandbags, sometimes provided by a gifted producer such as a George Martin for The Beatles, their musical river will overflow its banks, spread out across the entire soggy landscape and cause a kind of creative flooding that seldom reaches their intended audience. This is because without the river banks or sandbags that permit a musical structure, which the visionary always disdains, they are basically living and working in a messy artistic swamp. Inspiring and enlivening for you, perhaps, but confusing and alienating for the members of your "audience." Remember them?

In the case of Peter Green, so racked by guilt at his youthful success that he needed to sabotage it in an equally powerful way, the music he had begun to make by 1969 was no longer keeping within the banks of his gloriously talented blues river. It was too late for sandbags, it—the river was not just overflowing and flooding, it was boiling up and evaporating. I firmly believe that

Green chose "the blues" unconsciously, almost as a means of containing his growing dissatisfaction with life in general and his own culture in particular. He chose it the way a deeply depressed but manic person chooses a carefully considered costume with which to meet a hostile world. And I say that as one of his biggest fans! In other words, the blues provided Green with a kind of camouflage, a container for his grief that fit his sadness perfectly. Unfortunately, it could not conceal or contain his incipient madness. Further aggravated by his choice of incredibly dangerous chemicals, his personal darkness eventually overtook him entirely. Not only was the blues no longer capable of sustaining the balance it had once provided him, no music of any sort could ever do so again. He had lost his paddle, and the raging river that once nourished him now turned on him and utterly drowned him. To put it plainly: Peter Green could not take the heat so he had to get out of the kitchen. Alas, since he was a master chef who had personally turned up the heat way beyond its limit on all burners, there was no one else to blame or hold responsible.

Let us take an inside look at the personal and profession dysfunctions of the visionary early lineup of the group he had founded with a couple of gifted drunks who keep musical time better than anyone in the world. This chapter's title says it all—genius, paranoia, drugs, money, power, meltdown.

* * * * * * * * * *

There is nothing worse than the premature loss of a great artist, whether it be Robert Johnson, Bix Beiderbecke, Hank Williams, or Billie Holiday. It was even more sad in the case of Green, who did not die but merely hung around and slowly faded into the shadows. Early producer and true believer Mike Vernon certainly knows whereof he speaks: "In my own personal estimation, Peter Green was just the very best blues guitarist this country has ever produced, and if anybody wants any proof all they have to do is listen to the Otis Spann album I did with Mac, *The Biggest Thing Since Colossus.* Some of the guitar playing on that is absolutely stunning and its all from the heart." And Fleetwood, whose pain at losing his early musical mentor still twinges today, declaims: "Peter Green was responsible for forming Fleetwood Mac, which was very much a blues band, but 'Oh Well' demonstrates how strong a songwriter he was. We did the track around the time we did *Then Play On.*"[1]

"Oh Well" (discussed in more detail in the last chapter) was the furthest thing from a blues song imaginable, and yet it presaged a fresh direction which was then gestating and would have developed into a fully formed style had the darkness not overtaken Green. And in April 1970, with both the album *Then Play On* and the singular two-sided single "Oh Well" both burning up the charts, Green composed his swan song, literally. It was, however, not only his swan song from Mac, being the last piece he would compose and release with their name on it. It was also a swan song from all reason. And as we can all recall from that gifted artist of darkness, the Spanish painter Goya, the sleep of reason produces monsters.

This intensely disturbing last song has the texture of a howl out of hell, which is not something Green was simulating or trying to poetically evoke, since it actually was a howl from hell captured on a deceptively innocent little 45 r.p.m. record: "The Green Manalishi." The direct inheritor of Green's unhappiness at being a rock star, which he expressed so succinctly in "Oh Well," this anthem of angst is just the kind of song you want to avoid singing if you happen to be perched precariously on the edge of what used to be yourself. But even that song, in all its phenomenal weirdness, was still a hit. Martin Birch, who engineered the song, said, "The weirdest session I've ever taken part in. Peter wasn't communicating very much and Jeremy was well into his Children of God thing [the cult that would capture his interest, and his mind, the following year]. The whole atmosphere was very, very strange." Green's own take was suitably off-kilter: "Making 'Green Manalishi' was one of the best memories. Mixing it down in the studio and listening back to it, I thought it would make number one: lots of drums, bass guitars, six string basses, tracking on it, double-up on bass guitars, all kinds of things, Danny Kirwan and me playing those shrieking guitars together."[2] All kinds of things? Was he at the same session as the others?

McVie observed Green's departure sadly but stoically, perhaps realizing that at least he and Fleetwood still might have a future together, but not knowing what it could possibly be without the "Green God."

> In Spring 1970, Peter Green, who'd been thinking about leaving for some time, suddenly said enough is enough. It was right in the middle of a European tour, but he worked out all of the contracted gigs, and left six weeks later. He just didn't want to be a guitar star anymore...all the pressures, possibly coupled with a degree of acid loss, seemed to put him off the rock scene. At the time he left, he was getting into free form playing, spacing out—and I think his solo album [*End of the Game*] was probably a reflection of the state of his mind that summer.[3]

Early bassist Brunning was equally concerned, "I was very worried about Peter around that time. He and I had worked together on Dave Kelly's solo album on Mercury, and I invited him round to my house to listen to it. But he refused to listen to the record, saying he had no interest in music. This was certainly not the Peter I knew."[4] And the soon-to-be-scintillating Christine McVie was experiencing it all in quite a personal way, "John and the band were working up a new album and a stage act following Peter Green's departure that May. They were down to a four-piece, and just before the start of a tour, they suddenly decided they needed another instrument to fill out the sound....[A]nd there I was, sitting around doing next to nothing and knowing all the songs back to front because I'd been watching them rehearsing for the past three months."[5] This is typical modesty from the quiet and taciturn former Miss Perfect. Far from doing nothing, she was just voted top female vocalist and was releasing a solo record, or planning to, but her entry to Mac's lineup would definitely keep her quite busy for the next 36 years.

Very briefly, the chain had been interrupted but not broken. Sooner or later, the members of Mac, and their global audience, would come to realize that they would never, ever loosen the ties that bind.

* * * * * * * * * *

In February 1971, while in the middle of yet another successful tour, Jeremy Spencer suddenly dropped out of sight, and out of mind. Eventually he was traced to a "religious" colony known as the Children of God, one of the more unfortunate side effects of the searching sixties. The weak links were beginning to unravel and threatened to sink the whole enterprise. Almost as if self-doubt was contagious, Spencer too had begun to wonder darkly about his fame and fortune, just as Green had started to a few months before. Fleetwood tried to communicate with him, but had to give up and grudgingly accept his strange decision.

"Jeremy, my small friend, took flight one day, never to return," was how he sadly recalled the vanishing. Why was it so difficult to keep the individual parts of the whole together? Better for them not to wonder at the way their magic worked, since their challenges were, once again, only just beginning. The departure of Green was to be the first of several interregnums for the band.

* * * * * * * * * *

In order to understand the extremely utopian states of mind that caused such turmoil when apparent comfort and happiness were so close at hand, it helps to remember just how disorienting the sixties really were, whether or not you were involved in the same pursuits as the figures being discussed in this book. It was disorienting for all of us; they just happened to produce the emblems of that sensation, with which the rest of us identified so personally.

One of the clearest critical glimpses into that momentous historic period was carried out by the late Ian Macdonald in his masterful study of both The Beatles and the history they catalyzed, in which he probes the slackening of control and behavioral standards that arrived with this tumultuous decade. Most importantly, he isolates the "anti-elitism" of the sixties as one of its primary distinguishing characteristics; but he also points out that this sensation, far from restricted to the counterculture, was intrinsic to the general democratic spirit of the age:

> As such, the popular rebellion against authority was well underway before the arrival, in 1966, of its would be hippie/anarchist leaders. Persisting in the background while the flower children and Maoists enjoyed their Warholian fifteen minutes of fame, the Sixties' anti-authoritarian mood of cheeky undeceivability

continued to make way for the quiet inner revolution of attitude and assumption with whose consequences, propitious and otherwise, we live today.[6]

Anyone interested in a deeply probing analysis of this still confusing decade and its after effects is advised to read Macdonald's clear-headed and entertaining take on the whole spectacle:

> Most of the work of this Revolution was inspired and facilitated by the productions of science. A culture of convenience is inevitably a culture of laziness. Pop music too has played a role in reinforcing the manifest relaxation of goals and standards since the Sixties.
>
> While the instantaneous/simultaneous mentality introduced by the Sixties suited new idioms like pop and television, it had a less benign effect on older forms. The crucial thing that died as a result of the instantaneous/simultaneous outlook was *development:* development of theme and idea, of feeling and thought, of story and character. The ultimate root of this degenerative trait lies in the psychological change introduced Western life during 1963–73: the Revolution in the Head which The Beatles played a large part in advancing and whose manifesto runs willy-nilly through their work, rendering it not only an outstanding repository of popular art but a cultural document of permanent significance.[7]

This is, in shorthand, the notion that, "we want the world and we want it *now,*" and it inspired many other people, fellow musicians and otherwise, to seek out an apparently immediate answer to all existential questions. And to seek instant but notorious results in the miniaturized and speeded up enlightenment process afforded by certain psychic drugs. Peter Green is an example of the worst effects of these procedures to increase the velocity of evolution itself, along with Syd Barrett of Pink Floyd and Brian Wilson of the Beach Boys, among others. Macdonald wrote that:

> The Sixties seem like a Golden Age to us because, relative to now, they were. Our former way of life...far away from us on the other side of the sun-flooded chasm of the Sixties, where courtesy of scientific technology, The Beatles can still be heard singing their poignant, hopeful, love advocating songs. The true revolution of the Sixties, more powerful and decisive for Western society than any of its external by-products, was an inner one of feeling and assumption: a revolution in the head.[8]

It is my contention that while The Beatles propagated a "revolution in the head," Fleetwood Mac promoted a "revolution in the heart," allowing the emotional content of everyday relationships, especially the demanding and difficult sort, to be explored through their music. The revolution in the head lasted only a very short time, though its effects are long term; while the revolution in the heart has lasted far longer, and its effects are even more impactful; since, unlike the head, the heart remains utterly connected to the real world of feelings, needs, loyalty, and betrayal. These are the key elements that Mac has both celebrated and been burdened by over 40 years, and they are the elements that an ever-expanding audience began to relate to as the band left the blues behind, then took a road less traveled in the mid-1970s, and finally evoked with searing commercial success from that point onward.

Neither revolution was kind to Peter Green, or to his fellow meltdown cases, Jeremy Spencer and Danny Kirwan. Green was ready, he thought, to get with the program, but in his case a deep melancholy only experienced by certain kinds of singer-songwriters would not allow him to come to the party. But the party would go on without him. The same decadelong party, with its decadelong hangover of the 1970s, would almost eat up all the members of Mac with its relentless appetite for fresh minds. Almost but not quite, since the two mainstays of the band, Fleetwood and McVie, were historically and hysterically notorious party hounds whose survival to be the reflective old geezers they are today is nothing short of a miracle.

Fleetwood remembers the party more than most people with his history even have a right to:

> Fleetwood Mac arrived in America during the first week of May 1968, after several months of frothing anticipation on our part. We came straight to Los Angeles and played Shrine Auditorium with the Who and Arthur Brown. From there we went to San Francisco, where we were met at the airport by Judy Wong and two local musician friends of hers, Jerry Garcia and Phil Lesh of the Grateful Dead. Our first album hadn't yet been released in the States (it would be in June), but the Dead had heard about Peter's playing via the transatlantic rock grapevine, and they wanted to meet the Green God in the flesh.
>
> San Francisco was everything we had heard—hippie capital of the Aquarian Age, and more. We loved San Francisco in those days. We became friendly with the Grateful Dead, playing with them on the triple bills that Bill Graham promoted, and even letting their rambling, jamming acidic style rub off on us. The Dead took good care of Fleetwood Mac, keeping us high, occasionally putting us up at their Haight-Ashbury house, and getting us gigs. We were good friends with their sound man, the legendary Augustus Stanley Owsley III, who was always urging us to try some of the superior LSD-25 he was alchemizing. Fleetwood Mac's second tour of America began the first week of December 1968. The first gig was opening for our friends the Grateful Dead at the Filmore East. It was there, after the show, that we reconnected with Owsley. We figured he made the best, most pure LSD available. We all wanted to try it, and if not his, whose?[9]

LSD was first synthesized from the ergot fungus of rye, after 25 attempts, by the Swiss chemist Albert Hoffman in 1938 at the Sandoz Laboratory, whiles searching for a cure for migraine. He found it in spades, albeit accidentally, since melting away the identity portion of the mind itself, as well as the many illusory boundaries between oneself and others, will most certainly eliminate headaches of all kinds. However, LSD-25's unusual and unfathomable properties were not fully realized until 1943, when he casually absorbed some through his fingers and experienced, "an intense stimulation of the imagination and an altered state of awareness of the world." That is putting it mildly!

In his 1956 book *Heaven and Hell,* a follow-up to the 1954 document of his experiments, Aldous Huxley would lend intellectual and philosophical credence to the use of these radical mind-altering substances, referring to them as "aids to visionary experience" that provide access to a place, or a zone, suffused with what he termed "preternatural significance." Towards the end of his masterful study of personal psychic exploration, *The Doors of Perception* (of which rocker Jim Morrison became an obvious early big fan when he named his group), Huxley summed it up: "But the man who comes back through the Door in the Wall, will never be quite the same as the man who went out. He will be wiser but less cocksure, happier but less self-assured, humbler in acknowledging his ignorance yet better equipped to understand the relationship of words to things, of systematic reasoning to the unfathomable mystery which it tries, forever vainly, to comprehend."[10]

We do not know to what the Mac group considered this an aid, apart perhaps from making more compelling music, but they plunged into the maelstrom big time. Poor Peter Green however, for reasons not solely attributable to the drug, went out the door but never quite came back. Its effect on him, just as on Lennon, would be a subtle combination of astonishing insights and a general lightening up of his hard-edged self-esteem problems, while at the same time creating new and unexpected esteem issues quite beyond measure. For Green too, the new compassion was merged with a severe and abrupt schism in his self-image, revealing to him in brutal terms what was real and what was not. Or so he thought.

In his *Revolution in the Head,* Macdonald aptly describes it as "a powerful hallucinogen whose function is to temporarily dismiss the brain's neural *concierge,* leaving the mind to cope as best it can with sensory information which meanwhile enters without prior arrangement—an uncensored experience of reality which profoundly alters one's outlook on it." Delivered by Dr. Timothy Leary to the existing underground pharmacy of marijuana, mescaline, and magic mushrooms, LSD came to the attention of the media in early 1966 as state legislators moved to ban it. Allen Ginsberg (freshly dosed with enough LSD to receive a nocturnal visit from his idol, the dead British poet William Blake) urged that all healthy Americans over the age of 14 should take at least one trip in order to perceive what he saw as the true machine nature of America.

Sadly, many people who were far less prepared than Huxley was to have their worlds transformed for 12 hours or longer, followed his advice and discovered, to their dismay, a paradox at the center of the experience. This was the fact that universal empathy often does not translate into actual love for individuals, especially since the "individual" always appears to vanish completely through a harrowing tunnel of self-negation through the acid experience. In the case of Peter Green, he suspended his usual dark melancholy blue streak long enough to take a dive into the cosmic swimming pool, but he got tangled up and became terribly frightened of the deep end. Just as it had for John Lennon, the drug changed everything, providing a direct and unmediated pipeline to the collective unconscious and an open door to breathtaking and brilliant creativity—at first. Until the solipsism sets in, like the rust that corrodes a singer-songwriter's armor, exposing us all to the terror behind the mask. Hardly a face at all, really; more a symbol of a face than an actual face.

Also like Lennon, Green was poised to take his band mates to the "top-ermost of the pop-er-most"; unfortunately, he himself would not be coming along for the ride. Money was "evil," he had discovered; he did not want it. He could not have dreamed just how high his little blues group would ascend into the world of pop royalty after his departure. Meanwhile, Lennon's other half and balancing act, Paul McCartney, once remarked in the mid-1990s that he felt like the sixties is just about to happen, that it felt like a period in the future to him, rather than a period in the past. That's because the sixties *are* a future time, and they always will be.

* * * * * * * * * *

The singer-songwriter who started out with plaintive moans about classic blues scenarios would somehow, in only one short but frenetic year, end up singing about the impossibility of his lot in life. He would go from growling about being a "rambling pony, rambling from town to town" and lamenting that "Last night I dreamed about my baby, I woke up and the tears were runnin' all down my face, you know I was dreamin', that some other man was takin' my place," on the early record; to groaning that, "I've got to find a place to sing my words, is there nobody listening to my song?" and pleading "Tell me anybody, now do you really give a damn for me?" on the last record. How was such a tragic trajectory possible: to go from singing the blues and thus transcending them, to really having the blues and being unable to open your mouth anymore?

How did the blues go from being a symbol of an existential condition to being an actuality that consumes the victim instead of helping him rise above it all? The last single produced by Peter Green for his quickly evaporating band was "The Green Manalishi," a song released in April 1970 and so strange that it has become a cult favorite. The year 1970, of course, was also a terribly down period filled with artistic losses. The Beatles finally broke up after years of rancor; Diana Ross and the Supremes split up; Simon and Garfunkel parted company, old friends no longer; Brian Wilson withdrew from public life into a room in his mind; John Lennon all but vanished into the Dakota in New York, in a self-imposed exile from the rest of humanity; and several trailblazers died—Janis Joplin, Jimi Hendrix, and soon to follow, Jim Morrison. Unfortunately, the main part of Peter Green also died; yet he remained amongst us as a pale ghost, mumbling about the shadows of Satan. Maybe it was the devil's music after all? The only certainty is the common links shared by passionate poets. Green had the same immense vulnerability as Lennon and Wilson, and like them, he too would walk away from the rest of us, lost in the dark night of himself.

Manager Clifford Davis sums things up this way:

> I've read many stories about why Peter left the band. None of them accurate. There were several reasons. First, he no longer wanted to be tied down to a particular musical format. He wanted to be free to play with whoever he wanted to and not to be constrained by the rhythm section of Fleetwood Mac. He also had other differences with members of the band. They were quite strong differences musically and personally. Although he and Mick had been together in a variety of different bands over the years, he constantly complained that Mick was slowing up rhythmically all the time. His main complaint about John McVie, like Mayall before him, was John's drinking.[11]

Personality clashes also ensued with wunderkind Danny Kirwan. "Peter had a problem with Danny, who was going through this whole thing about 'I'm the glamour boy of the band, and I'm really as good as you but you're getting all the attention.' That really made Peter fed up.... The only person he had no problems with was Jeremy Spencer, he liked him very much."[12]

Of course, that may also have been because Spencer, a closet religious fanatic with secret bibles sown into his jackets, was clearly almost as disturbed as the esteemed "Green God."

Davis remembers the moment of the final split, "We were sitting in a bus in Sweden. He came up to the back of the bus to sit with me and said, 'I'm leaving the band. Apart from anything else I've had enough of these shits, Clifford. But it's actually a bit deeper than that.'"[13] In fact, it was so deep that Green would never get to the bottom of it, even after sporadic stays in mental hospitals and ill-advised shock treatments, followed by medicinal cocktails probably more harmful than his original drug of choice. Even working as a graveyard attendant would not cure his ills, not surprisingly.

Fleetwood remembers with a philosophical attitude: "It was not an irrational move, it was a very deliberate move on his part. He had obviously come to the end of the line as to what he could do creatively with the band. If there were other things involved, I was not aware of it. We were always the best of friends, as he was with John McVie." For McVie's part, there was considerable anguish involved, and he was often described as devasted. "Ahh, it was, I'm not kidding you, it was trauma city! We were in the middle of a European tour. We just didn't know what to do. The whole period was beyond belief! It was very hard to find yourself out on a limb without Peter, who had become the band's writer, guitar hero, lead singer and the main focal point of the band. And for that to go, I mean it was very traumatic."[14]

Brunning has commented that as Green's illness took over, his creative fire began to sputter out. He was becoming both aggressive and dismissive about music altogether, giving away all his guitars, vowing never to play again, and growing his fingernails to a weird length to ensure that no one ever expected him to. Paranoia about money overtook him. He threatened the band's accountant, David Simmons, with a shotgun. Simmons's crime? Performing his role as an accountant by forwarding large sums of money owed to Green as a result of his own brilliance. Menial jobs, such as a hospital orderly, doomed him to a peripheral existence, even though the band made sure the royalty checks kept coming, whether he liked it or not. He did not. Quickly, Green entered the wretched realm of living legends: the gloomy circle of vegetating geniuses whose loss seemed so irredeemable to us because they were so irreplaceable.

Some magical things happen only once. For Fleetwood Mac, that one thing was its founding member, Peter Green. It is not surprising that they all believed their career was over just as it was getting started. They were wrong. But losing a genius can take the wind out of your sails. Luckily, there was a veritable storm of winds just waiting to happen a few years down the road. All they had to do to reap the whirlwind was to stay alive. But staying alive proved a difficult task in the late 1960s and early 1970s, both professionally and personally. The road of excess was always there, beckoning in its soft creative voice.

I have written elsewhere about the urge to transcend and the appetite for the edge that seem to accompany the singer-songwriter's unique lifestyle, and I have suggested that this quest for an "artificial paradise" designed to sustain creativity far precedes the notoriously self-indulgent decades being covering here. In fact, it was the nineteenth-century French poet Charles Baudelaire, author of *The Flowers of Evil* and *Paris Spleen*, two delightful odes to altered consciousness, who wrote in his 1860 study called "Le Paradis Artificiels" of his allegiance to the Le Club des Haschichins, and who dramatically stated the case for artistic consumption:

> The man gratified by this sense of loveliness, unfortunately so rare and so transitory, feels himself more than ever the Artist, more than ever more Noble, more than ever more Just. The eyes have a vision of eternity, sounds take on colours and colours contain music. Suppose you look at a tree gracefully waving in the wind: you attribute to the tree your passion, your desire or your melancholy, its murmurs and its writhing become yours, and before long you are the tree. In the same way, a soaring bird first represents the immortal desire to fly above things human, but already, you yourself are the bird.[15]

Peter Green had "the immortal desire to fly above things human" in spades. Icarus could have been his middle name. And this search was something he inherited as an oblique kind of legacy from generations of whacked-out poets before him. In the highly entertaining study *The Pursuit of Oblivion,* Richard Davenport-Hines takes the reader on a wild trip designed to show how prevalent and inherent this urge has always been in the human animal.

In her review of the book, Christine Kenneally draws attention to the central and ancient ritual being played out across history's stage.

> In a sunless room in Bengal in the 1670s, a group of English sailors enacted a scene that would in spirit, be repeated in basements, bedrooms, and alleys of the Western world for centuries. First, they each swallowed a pint of bhang, a local drink. One of the sailors then sat and sobbed all afternoon, another began a fistful with a wooden pillar, yet another inserted his head into a large jar. The rest sat about or lolled upon the floor. They were completely stoned. Psychotic, depressed, or mirthful, the sailors' behavior was induced by bhang's crucial ingredient—cannabis, also known as ganja, charas, grifs, hasish, hemp, or marijuana. Their drug-addled afternoon, reported firsthand by the merchant Thomas Bowery, who sat sweating throughout it, is the earliest account by an Englishman of recreational cannabis use.[16]

This scene opened *The Pursuit of Oblivion,* which is most accurately described as "a history of emotional extremes", and it is a good indication of the antiquity of the urge to travel inward. This may have been the first report. Reports about the life of Peter Green, and others of his ilk (sensitive and creative souls with a tormented sense of self) are merely the most recent. The basic message of the book is best applied to the uniquely intense areas of artistic enterprise, in which the practitioner is always on the search for an edge that is further away than the last one he or she explored in their work. Intoxication is not unnatural or deviant. But it does come in different flavors, and some of them are more acceptable to society than others, and indeed, some of them demolish the user more rapidly and finally than others. And, as Christine Kenneally asked in the *New York Times,* "After all, who hasn't longed for oblivion or dreamed of ecstasy. Who hasn't wished for something, anything, to take the edge off daily life?"[17]

Green, of course, was partially doomed by this inner desire, both to increase the edge and to take it off at the same time, only one of his many conflicts with himself and the world. But far be it for me to psychoanalyze Peter Green; I respect his talent too much for that. My only intention is to place his shining talent in the context of others who shared his curse. After all, it is not as if he was the only one taking in the raw sunshine of these chemicals and herbs; his entire band worshipped at the church of alcohol, smoke, and pharmaceuticals. It is just that he was the one who succumbed most severely to the occupational hazards of a professional dreamer.

With Green gone, the band started to reexamine its lifestyle. Not enough to change it, of course, but just enough to marshal their forces and continue forward, wherever that was. Twenty years after this period, the band still seems to subscribe to their philosophy of never trying to replace historic figures, but always trying to go on. And go on they did. Timothy White had an accurately gritty take on their early charms in his comprehensive chronicle of creative mayhem, *Rock Lives:*

> What has always rescued the band from artistic dissolution, as well as a tatty backstage sordidness, is its candor about individual sins and shared illusions. Rock and Roll was once synonymous with scathing honesty, but in an era when the music is rife with hypocrisy and specious accommodation, the family tree of Fleetwood Mac continues to bare its fairest foliage as well as its gnarls. You may elect to go your own way, but its how you travel the twisted route that makes the destination worthwhile.

White's description of this early phase of the band's long history is also suitably grimy:

> In the beginning there was hot-wire limey blues, and the brisk hoisting of lager that blurred the band's rainiest days. Peter Green invited Mick Fleetwood— who had been dropped from Mayall's Bluesbreakers for chronic drunkenness— to join his own fledgling outfit. To flesh out the sound, Green chose guitarist/ prankster/Elmore James impersonator Jeremy Spencer. Sensing a good time was brewing, veteran Bluesbreakers bassist—also temporarily ousted by Mayall for excessive intoxication—came swiftly on board. McVie: I was a full-on blues bigot, and I felt the Bluesbreakers were getting too jazzy.[18]

Here, White captures some of the essence, "The Mac's prowess as a live act— further augmented with the addition of third guitarist Danny Kirwan— became the stuff of legend."[19]

The fact that they never stopped connecting to newer, younger, and bigger live audiences, and that they simply loved playing live music, was indeed the ongoing power source they needed to survive, thrive, and evolve. Perhaps, White defers, but "the best question for any crystal-gazer might be: but is the future really *worth* the past?"[20]

It is if you are Fleetwood Mac. This is a key example of the phenomenon I would most associate with the group in all its phases and permutations: their ongoing commitment to conducting that "revolution in the heart.". It is the touchstone that enables them, year after year, to transmute the personal anguish of human relationships into an art form that both celebrates and liberates them at the same time. It is what makes them, even today, blues musicians par excellence, even if their later music is not recognizable as the blues. It is in fact, the pure indigo of the heart's longing that they manage to capture and transmit to us. That is indeed Mac's lot in life, as well as their role in our cultural life.

By undertaking what I call their "revolution in the heart," by allowing their convoluted private lives to become the raw material for their public personas as musical artists and performers, both the band and its music became emblems for the enigma of romance. They remain emblems for that same perpetual enigma to this day. The enigma never goes away, and neither will they.

* * * * * * * * * *

During the heady period that drew the sixties to a close, Mac was about to launch itself into the stratosphere of a change they could never have even imagined, let alone planned or prepared for. Given the status of Peter Green as the symbol for all the band stood for, his departure may have affected more mortal bands in a profound way. For Mac, it was still a profound change, but for quite different reasons, since their new mantra became survival at all costs. It simply never seemed to occur to Fleetwood and McVie, even given all the trials and tribulations they were facing, that their creative partnership might be coming to an end. Far from it, in fact, and although not guided by conscious decision making (this band was never guilty of doing anything consciously), their next direction would insure a tangible link with their future.

That link was blonde, female, talented, and incredibly bluesy: the link's name was Christine. For years, the steady rocking pianist had been lurking in the shadows—in the nicest possible way, of course—and now her time was near. She was a well-known figure in blues and music circles in general, a talented professional with a quirky voice and serious writing skills. This was not a case of Sir Paul McCartney putting wife Linda into his post-Beatle band Wings, or even of John Lennon (who should be a Sir) forcing his avant-garde girlfriend on an unsuspecting world. Unlike her famously infamous female peers, she actually belonged exactly where she was. She was the real thing.

Christine Perfect had been a stone's throw away from the very beginning of Mac's collective career in 1967, as the headliner of Chicken Shack. In August 1968, she married bassist McVie and took his name (kind of a shame, really, when you have a name as "perfect" as hers already) but she still played only a behind the scenes private role with the band, given that the "Green God" was still ascending. The general public was largely unaware of her quiet presence, even though she provided piano input on their second recording, *Mr. Wonderful,* and later more major input on their first post-Green recording, *Kiln House,* produced the year of Green's meltdown and departure. That general public certainly knows who she is now, though I still do not believe the giant audience that eventually enveloped both her and her new band ever really adequately appreciated the true stature and depth of her musical gift. She not only *saved* Fleetwood Mac after its guitar avatar left the rational world, but she is largely responsible for their new musical consciousness in its entirety.

In order to fully grasp how daring and experimental Fleetwood and McVie really were at heart, one has only to think of how rare a blues chick was in the macho, testosterone-driven domain of white blues punks on drink and dope. That, plus the fact that she was ostensibly "replacing" Peter Green, a daunting task almost as nerve-racking as Green replacing Clapton. But Christine McVie's nerves were considerably stronger than Green's, as evidenced by the fact that not only did she survive the transition, and not only did Mac itself survive and thrive after the transition, but that she contributed in a major way to the second phase of the band's historic career, and that she played a crucial role in the gargantuan third and final phase of the band's rise to rock royalty. She was not just a good replacement for an ailing mate; she was and is a great complement to the band's whole musical philosophy and its ongoing commitment to a revolution in the heart. This is largely because she provided much of that heart.

Christine McVie is one of the greatest white blues singer-songwriters in history. She is also one of the greatest artists, black, white, or otherwise, that the pop music field has ever produced. And though many of us lamented the sad going of Green and the madness of his Manalishi, some of us were patient enough to realize that his replacement was in it for the long haul. She was hot, in every sense of the word.

Here is how Miss Perfect described the transition:

> Fleetwood Mac were my favourite band at the time. They were like a drug. They were *so* good—Jeremy Spencer, Danny Kirwan, Peter Green, Mick Fleetwood and John McVie. They were an enigma. They had a real magic about them that was infectious. They did their first American tour, gone for six weeks and I didn't hear from John once. When he came back, he proposed to me. Ten days later, we were married and I left Chicken Shack. Then Fleetwood Mac went to Europe and the bombshell hit. Peter went off with the German jet-set and did way too much acid for his own good. He came back and said, I don't want to be in Fleetwood Mac anymore, I don't want to do anything.[21]

And for a long time, he did not. Then Spencer disappeared one day while he went out for a magazine, ending up two days later in the Children of God cult. Christine explains it this way:

> So we called Peter Green and begged him to come over and help us complete the tour rather than being sued. Peter cam over, and the remainder of the tour was done without singing, a totally instrumental tour. We did a version of "Black Magic Woman that lasted 45 minutes. Peter refused to sing, and that's when I really learned to jam.[22]

And she could jam with the best of them, and always could. Chicken Shack had been my favorite blues band after Mac. Their guitarist Stan Webb was gifted, in an equal but different way from Green. And Christine McVie had always been a star waiting to explode. She did just that. It was perfectly clear that if Christine McVie had not been close at hand, and with the musical ability and authentic blues chops to step into the long shadow cast by the burned-out shell of Green, Fleetwood Mac would undoubtedly have folded its cards early and left the game. It was probably even more abundantly obvious to the band's rhythmic leaders that they had a daunting challenge ahead of them to carry on the blues torch dropped by the perplexed Green. If they could carry on at all, which was doubtful back then, they would have to rework the engine of their band. Fortunately, Christine had been trained in the school of hard blues knocks known mysteriously as Chicken Shack.

* * * * * * * * * *

In some ways, Chicken Shack struck me as being as good as or occasionally better than Fleetwood Mac, as guilty as it makes me feel to say so. This was largely because they were unburdened by the angst-ridden guilt of the bipolar Peter Green, thriving instead on the erratically unique guitar and vocal stylings of Stan Webb, a truly manic performer without the depressive downside. Webb, and the profoundly gifted pianist, writer and husky-voiced chanteuse Christine Perfect, were capable of some of the finest white blues the world hardly heard, overshadowed as they were by the towering stature and legend of Green's Mac. But it would soon be Christine's Mac, a whole new Mac game that suddenly seemed worth playing all over again the second time around.

If there was a secret underground link between the two bands, apart from blues and instrumental excellence, it would have to be Mike Vernon as a producer of both. Vernon recalls, "I saw how they got their name: they used to rehearse in a chicken shack on the smallholding belonging to Andy Sylvester's parents. What I found interesting about the band was that they had a girl pianist who also sang. That was unusual because apart from Joanne Kelly, there weren't any girls in Britain singing the blues."[23] Sylvester was also a bass player with a shuffling style almost as uniquely smooth as the incomparable John McVie. But though Vernon immediately loved Christine's "plaintive, appealing interpretation of the blues," he was also captivated by the flaming guitar work of Webb. "Stan immediately struck me as being a complete extrovert, a complete and utter lunatic with a very exciting visual appeal on stage."[24]

Chicken Shack played on the same bill as Fleetwood Mac during their historic first outing in 1967 at the Windsor Jazz and Blues Festival, a concert at which Mac would debut along with the ironic mixture of John Mayall's Bluesbreakers (featuring young Mick Taylor as Green's replacement) as well as the headlining act, the newly formed Cream featuring Eric Clapton, the guitar giant that Green had himself replaced. The concert was a veritable summit meeting of mammoth musical egos, all perfectly poised to soon launch themselves together into the waiting arms of America's summer of love.

Chicken Shack's debut recordings were crisp and perfect renditions of pure white British blues: *40 Blue Fingers* and *O.K. Ken?* are vintage 1968 masterpieces of the genre; soon to be followed by *100 Ton Chicken* in 1969 and *Accept,* a heavier rock-oriented direction, in 1970. By that time, Christine Perfect would already be off on her own, settling into life as Mrs. McVie, and closely watching the insanity and creative chaos of Fleetwood Mac unfold and unravel, from the inside out.

* * * * * * * * * *

Meanwhile, back at the Mac ranch, things incredibly were going from bad to worse. It is paradoxical, especially considering that in 1969, as they were in the process of melting down—or at least as Green was descending further down into his own pit—the band itself was commercially on top of the world. But that, of course, was precisely what frightened and dismayed the gifted guitarist so much in the first place, unable as he was to reconcile his own Jewish working-class roots with the lofty heights of rock royalty he had scaled. As Diane Cardwell once remarked, it is the universal irony of icons: they freeze in the very image they themselves created. And, of course, the lofty heights of his experiments with psychic drugs did not help. He seems to have been doubly doomed from the start: destined to succeed triumphantly, but doomed to crash and burn abysmally.

Now, of course, Green was not the first or the last rock star to suffer the slings and arrows of outrageous fortune. But he did it with a certain all-out aplomb that few others can match, though many have unintentionally tried. It is now a universal truism that rock stars have become the romantic poets of our age, devoting themselves with special energy to fast lives, early deaths, or worse, taking the vegetation route. Just as in the classical age of melancholy poets, there are many occupational hazards associated with complete self-absorption. One need only consider the poet Shelley drowning in the Spezia Bay, or Byron succumbing to a deadly fever in Greece, or John Keats dispatched by consumption in Rome, or Novalis expiring of the same affliction.

The list of doomed musical performers is equally dramatic and maybe more extensive: Buddy Holly, Otis Redding, Ricky Nelson, Stevie Ray Vaughn and the majority of Lynard Skynyrd all victims of plane crashes; Duane Allman and Berry Oakley in motorcycle collisions; John Lennon and Sam Cooke shot to death; and Brian Jones drowned (some say murdered) in his swimming pool. Then there are the illnesses, the suicides, and, of course, the ever-popular substance abuse: Jim Morrison, Jimi Hendrix, Janis Joplin, Mama Cass Elliot, Gram Parsons, and a list of specific acid meltdowns that is simply too long to accurately compile. But few made their departures in so dramatically silly a manner as Green. Much as I sympathize with his battle against inner demons, which was exaggerated fatally by his chemical diet, his outrageously simplistic and guilt-ridden anti-money crusade was merely a mania that went too far and paralyzed him, as did his submerged anger, rage, resentment, and insecurities of monolithic proportions.

One observer has commented that sure, happy people can create great art too, but the old Romantic myth of misery as a muse tends to die hard in our culture. This is especially so because we, the adoring audience, are often guilty of enabling these gloomy outlooks through the ultimate rewards of our attention to their celebrity and our contribution of money to their cause, which is usually one of downfall. In Green's case, he seems to provide ample evidence of something that scientists have recently begun to suspect, namely that the human brain appears to be hardwired for anger and rage. In fact, a student of anger, Dr. Richard Friedman, has suggested that strong evidence from neuroscience suggests that people share this ancient emotional neural circuitry with all our animal cousins.

The deep-seated rage in Green, which early on provided the foundation for his exquisite rendering of a unique brand of almost spiritual blues, also seems to have been at the base of his essentially narcissistic personality. Anticipating an assault from a world in turmoil, he swiftly began to crumple under the weight of his already shaky and low self-esteem. It is always amazing to the public that figures who appear so self-assured and aggressively confident are often riddled with much more doubt and fear than the average and supposedly untalented person. As doctors have pointed out, just because our brains may be hardwired for basic emotions such as anger, fear, and the urge to hide from ourselves and others does not necessarily mean that we have little or no control over the impulsive kind of behaviors associated with the significantly lower levels of brain serotonin, associated with ailments such as deep depression or personality disorders.

It now seems clear to everyone, as it was certainly obvious to those close to him who loved Green and his prodigious talents, that his story started to unravel in the earliest days of the superb band he created. Unfortunately, no one back then was able to step in and declare that Green didn't just have a deficit of serotonin, he may just have been missing any at all, so severe was his over-reaction to stardom. Never before had so much adulation been offered to someone who responded with such alarming paranoia to people saying he was the greatest thing since sliced bread. A cursory glimpse and listen to even just the singles released by the band under Green's tenure reveals him to be ambivalent at best, even from the beginning—"Black Magic Woman" and "Need Your Love So Bad," both from 1968; "Albatross" and "Man of the World," both from 1969; and "Oh Well I and II" and "The Green Manalishi," both from 1970.

In "Need Your Love," with original lyrics penned by Little Willie John, Green amplifies the primal urge at the bottom of most if not all blues music: "Now when the night begins, I'm at an end because I need your love so bad. Why don't you give it up and bring it home to me, or write it on a piece of paper, so it can be read to me. Need a soft voice, just to talk to me at night." Green was already somewhat paralyzed in the headlights of love even then, not even reading the love letter himself but having it "read to him." The night was not a good time for Green. It always returned to haunt him with ever greater demons, eventually too strong to be defended against.

In "Black Magic Woman," Green is already revealing a strange relationship with The Devil and his dark army, which rivals even his relationship with the woman he appears to be singing about, making of her a mere cipher for his immortal fears of being dominated by the dark forces at work around him. This "woman" has him so blind he cannot see; she is black magic and is trying to make a devil out if him, although he never says exactly how. He pleads for her not to turn her back on him, since she just might break up his magic stick, whatever that is. Either way, she has a spell on him that is turning his heart to stone, and suddenly, Green has merged his own song with the older Willie John song, declaring that he can't leave her alone, and once again that he needs her love so bad, so bad, so bad.

"Albatross" is so gorgeous that no words could ever be necessary, yet the looping and overlapping guitar lines in this exquisite and very strange instrumental still seem to be saying, "I'm lost; please help me." It is unclear just to what the "albatross" refers, apart from its nautical lore as a good luck symbol —an image that somehow collides with its more common meaning, that of having a weight that burdens you and pulls you down. In this case, Peter Green would soon turn out to be the albatross hanging around the group's neck himself, quite nearly sinking the band he had so passionately and joyously formed only three years earlier.

"Man of the World" is a bizarre song that competes with John Lennon's "Nowhere Man" for the most self-flaying declaration of doubt and disillusionment—and to my mind, Green wins that contest hands down. Green's audience must have mistakenly thought he was still purring the blues when he admitted there was no one he would rather be but that he wished he had never been born. This was not the blues, however; this was a blue life disintegrating in public. He wants to feel like a good man should, a slight nod to the old blues motif of a good woman's redemptive powers. But he then slips in a bit of pained confession: "I don't say I'm a good man, oh but I would be if I could."

But clearly the most shocking of all, especially since just like all the other singles even this would become a hit despite himself, is "The Green Manalishi," a tour de force of suffering seldom seen or heard in the entertainment industry. His final statement within the format of Fleetwood Mac, it still sends chills down the spine to hear it 37 years after it floated onto the charts as one of the oddest songs ever to ascend the pop charts. Along with the equally angry anthem of "Oh Well," another inexplicable hit even with is weird division into a rock movement and a classical movement, Green seems to have single-handedly invented a kind of protoheavy metal music, without realizing it, just by baring his scarred soul. "Oh Well" also has a dangerous personal identification with God, which could not have boded well for either his bandmates or his still loyal audience. He first declares that the audience should not ask what he thinks of them, since he might not give them the answer they want to hear. Then he announces that when he talked to God, that same response is what he himself received from the creator of the universe. God "told" him to stick by His side, and He would be Green's guiding hand—as long as Green did not ask God what He thinks of him. Heady stuff, to say the least.

"Manalishi" goes even further, yet even here he is still standing on ground tilled by the bluesmen before him, for he echoes Little Willie John's feeling that "when the night begins he's at an end" by gasping almost breathlessly over a wall of nerve wracking guitar waves, "Now when the day goes to sleep and the full moon looks. And the night is so black that the darkness cooks ..." It is then, in what the ancients called the hour of the wolf, that "You"—presumably the Devil himself, disguised as the evil of money incarnate—come around making him do things he does not want to do (such as successfully entertain millions of people) and busting in all his dreams, making him see things he does not want to see, such as reality. He announces that this Devil is the Green Manalishi (thought to be a money clip) with the two-pronged crown, which all through the night is either "dragging us up or bringing us down." Most importantly, he declares, that Devil leaves him here, trying to keep from following him.

Poor Peter Green, pursued by invisible enemies in a musical world that quite nearly worshipped him, joined the ranks of the great acid burnouts such as Syd Barrett, Rokey Erickson, and Brian Wilson; but also like them, his own prior psychological makeup contributed equally to his fall. And poor Peter Greenbaum, the outsider child he buried so young and so deep inside. For him, only a special condition will suffice to ever adequately explain how he came and went so quickly. A German word—perhaps appropriately, given his own oppression and his own culture's background of social distance from the power brokers—so perfectly encapsulates Green's destiny. The word is "Weltschmertz," and its meaning is: a kind of sentimental pessimism, an existential malaise, leading to the deep depression caused by the ongoing comparison of an idealized potential world with the real world of actuality. In Green's case, the combination of drugs, depression, insecurity, and his own mixed-up mysticism, made it simply impossible for him to occupy the actual world of challenging but everyday paradoxes instead of the pure world he imagined in his LSD-soaked mind. The good world he wanted so badly would not let him exist comfortably in the bad world in which he had to live with the rest of us.

In terms of making his art in a form which would resonate with his fellow human beings, Green would also have done well to pay attention to that lovely adage by another English poet, Francis Bacon, back in 1625. Bacon declared that, "Fame is like a river, that bears up things light and swollen, and drowns things weighty and solid."[25] Bacon's observation, however, also helped the band Green founded achieve a level of success and market worship that he could not have begun to imagine—without Mac knowing it of course, since they were too busy being sudden rock stars. But Bacon's insight could have also have helped Green adapt the content of his message and slightly contour the form in which he delivered it. The same sentiment, archaic sounding at first until one appreciates what he was really saying, certainly helped Fleetwood Mac soldier onward and upward after his departure.

In many ways, Peter Green can be favorably compared to many other extremely gifted but fragile young artists who burned too brightly to last very long. In discussing another young and radical firebrand, the nineteenth-century French poet Stephane Mallarme, editor Angel Flores raised a glittering issue in the form of one of my favorite phrases. This phrase applies perfectly to Green, as it does to many of the gifted who departed too soon, so soon that a legend starts to develop around their disappearance. And it applies to Green now simply because he deserves it, and especially because of the way a dizzy history has formed around his departure and its effects on the music world: he converts absence into diamonds!

In fact, one of Mallarme's experimental poems from the dawn of the twentieth century, "Windows," provides a veritable epitaph for the going of Green: "Is there a way for Me, who knows bitterness, to shatter the crystal insulted by the monster, and to escape with my two featherless wings—even at the risk of falling into eternity?"

FLEETWOOD MAC, *KILN HOUSE:* RELEASED 1970, WARNER BROTHERS/REPRISE RECORDS

Kiln House is, admittedly, an odd little record. Some people consider it more consistent than *Then Play On,* and perhaps that is true. This is the band trying to regain its balance and foothold after the abdication of its fearful leader, and wondering if it had a future. With a withering Jeremy Spencer facing the full force of Peter Green's absence, a staggering void that he could never fill, it feels as odd as it sounds. The album also reveals the brief flowering of Danny Kirwan, who would weave extraordinarily beautiful music for several more albums before himself cracking up in the worst psychological sense of the word.

Mostly however, the album reveals the band asking itself, "Where the hell do we go from here?" and allowing us to listen in on the vague and slightly shaky answer that results. Back to some sort of manicured rock and roll roots, a temporary way-station before the arrival of the rebirth, although it does feature an uncredited Christine on piano, as well as the trippy cover art design.

From the opening track, the fun but soft-centered "This is the Rock," the record announces a seemingly new direction, though in fact most of the Jeremy Spencer–driven songs are a fallback position, assuming a new stance by retreading some of his favorite rhythm and blues and early rock and roll roots. Listening to it in the same session as Peter Green's first solo record, released in the same year, is a shock to the system: Green, as whacked out as he was, still appears to be making light-year leaps into the future of heavy metal music that had not yet even been invented, while Mac sounds like it is pausing to ponder its own future.

Among the peculiar mix however, are several small diamonds studding the otherwise lame tributes to Buddy Holly. These gems are by the gifted Danny Kirwan: "Station Man," "Jewel-Eyed Judy," "Earl Gray," and "Tell Me All the Things You Do" are superbly crafted rock songs.

PETER GREEN, *THE END OF THE GAME:* RELEASED 1970, WARNER BROTHERS/ REPRISE RECORDS

Do not listen to what they say about this record. Listen to the record. This is the kind of music that cannot be listened to and written about at the same time. It says something very strong and powerful, but in a peculiarly fragile and tentative voice. Spaced-out noodling? Don't you believe it! The decay of genius? Most probably. However, Green always had far more genius to end up with than most people start out with, so I would caution the listener from jumping to conclusions just because of the composer's mental state while making the record.

The sounds in this superb little declaration of independence are no more addled than the other brilliant experimental directions taken by Charlie Parker, John Coltrane, and Ornette Coleman in the jazz idiom. Certainly as blasted on acid as "Bird" Parker was on heroin, Green still manages to pull together some masterful playing and several moments of blistering brilliance, despite the apparent aimlessless of the six instrumental jams on this record. "Hidden Depth" and "The End of the Game" in particular, while no longer capable of being called "songs" in any traditional sense of the word, are nonetheless charged with a fiery intelligence, even if it is one that is largely melting away before our ears.

Meant to be taken quite literally by Green, the title track sums up his entire enterprise as an electric guitarist extraordinaire, churning and grooving at a furious pace until it begins to slowly trail off as if exhausted. And then, in one of the most painful moments in recording music history, the track suddenly ends abruptly with the actual sound of an actual plug being pulled out of an amplifier and frying everything into a deep dark silence. End of the game, indeed!

Green would not resurface in the music business, apart from occasional anonymous guest spots, until nine years later, with his strangely mystical album *In the Skies.*

THE ORIGINAL FLEETWOOD MAC:
RELEASED 1971, CBS RECORDS

One can only imagine the chagrin caused by the late release of these initially rejected tracks from the early Blue Horizon days. They are, of course, scintillating as usual, especially the portions that include actual impatient exchanges between Green and the engineers. Weirdly, the year this compilation was released, the "new" Fleetwood Mac would be releasing one of the best records ever, the underappreciated *Future Games;* this is covered in the next chapter devoted to the Bob Welch years.

The title is an indication of how far the group had both risen and fallen in the short space of those three accelerated years between their founding in 1967 and their implosive mutation by 1970. It shows how rapidly a legend can form itself around a gifted but self-destructive creative performer. For those of us who sorely missed Green, and we were legion, this was a beloved chance to get one more hit of that magical time. "First Train Home," "Watch Out," and "Leaving Town Blues" are inimitable examples of what the "original" band did best—hardcore, unvarnished, electric white blues, dripping with scorn, sarcasm, and exquisite instrumentation.

One terrific bonus was the inclusion of a track itself called "Fleetwood Mac," first recorded on April 19, 1967, before FM even existed. It is a blistering instrumental jam-romp featuring just the rhythm section and Green, while they were all still deployed within the Mayall school of blues. Listening to its rumbling momentum, recorded as it was during a session while the boss was away, gives us all the obvious reasons why the trio simply had to leave and form their own band of the same name. Chemistry like this does not grow on trees!

Other significant record releases of 1970: Bridge Over Troubled Water by Simon and Garfunkel; *Bitches Brew* by Miles Davis; *Black Sabbath* by Black Sabbath; *Live At Leeds* by the Who; *A Question Of Balance* by the Moody Blues; *Abraxas* by Santana (featuring Peter Green's song "Black Magic Woman"); *The Twelve Dreams of Dr. Sardonicus* by Spirit; *Tapestry* by Carole King; *Sweet Baby James* by James Taylor; *Plastic Ono Band* by John Lennon; *All Things Must Pass* by George Harrison.

Rebirth: The Coming of Christine Perfect and Bob Welch

4

Without the lyrical complexity and ethereal Californian production spirit of Bob Welch, Fleetwood Mac would never have survived, let alone evolved, after its early rise and fall. Welch is definitely one of the most gifted, easy-going and underrated musicians in pop history. His poetic contributions to their catalogue, *Future Games* (1971), *Bare Trees* (1972), *Mystery To Me* (1973), *Penguin* (1973) and *Heroes Are Hard To Find* (1974), are among their best recordings, though not their most popular or bestselling. And then, after Welch "Los Angelesized" the group, along came Stevie Nicks and the mercurial genius Lindsey Buckingham. It was off to the races by then.

From the beginning, Mick Fleetwood and John McVie have always had the greatest good fortune in their choice of collaborators. First and foremost, they had each other, a strong creative and personal bond that continues to this day. From their own early collaboration as a superb rhythm section, to their later selection of collaborators for their band as it slowly evolved and became more and more famous, their good fortune has appeared to be an unending series of unbelievable good-luck moments. But observed from the aerial view of a 40-year history, each of those moments has also been saturated with a sense of inevitability, of fate or destiny playing a hand. An old adage sums up their own personal responses to these pivotal moments: Chance is the fool's name for fate!

One of their most revealing songs, from the 2003 record *Say You Will*, summed it up nicely and offered a title that at least partly explains both their longevity and the twisting detours of their long and winding road from gritty blues group to polished pop group: Destiny rules. Considering the brilliant trajectory that enabled them to move from Peter Green to Bob Welch and finally to Lindsey Buckingham and Stevie Nicks, this may as well be the slogan for Fleetwood Mac. In it, Nicks put forward the sentiment in a way which truly encapsulates how the band has felt its fate to be in the hands of a greater power—a positive and fateful power that helped them succeed almost in spite of themselves. The sentiment is basically this: we may have been together in another life, perhaps we were together in a parallel universe, perhaps our paths are not supposed to cross twice; but when we see each other again, as we always do, it appears that destiny rules, and the spirits are ruthless with the paths they choose. It is not being together, it is just following the rules of destiny. And that is exactly what two ideal collaborators such as Fleetwood and McVie must have felt in their choices for the musicians to help them express their band's vision. With incredible "luck," they managed to work with a truly great sequence of players, each of which added one more piece to a strange and chaotic puzzle.

* * * * * * * * * *

By now, you will have noticed the fact that I believe Christine McVie is probably one of the most gifted, most underrated, most underappreciated, and most important female figures in rock music history. Hers is much more than the story of a band spouse who somehow joins the stage show, à la Linda McCartney or Yoko Ono. She is single-handedly responsible for the rebirth of Fleetwood Mac, and she along with new singer songwriter Bob Welch, a talented Californian with a tantalizingly soft mystical side, would together lay the groundwork for everything the band would accomplish in the future. In fact, she and Welch *were* the future.

Of this period, as he usually is, Fleetwood is the most forthright in his recollections:

> The very phrase, Musical Chairs conjures up an atmosphere like the game suggests—you're in you're out, you're up you're down. In other words, compared to those beginning days, Fleetwood Mac would become less focused and set out on a musical roller coaster. Peter Green's influence, now gone, left Jeremy, Danny, John and myself feeling a vacuum, to say the least. It was sink or swim, yet we found, slowly, ways to remain buoyant. Into that vacuum first came Christine McVie, who from the moment of becoming part of the band injected new creative energy, which grew over the years to become a unique musical style that still to this day is a major part of Fleetwood Mac.[1]

That is putting it mildly; to put it in the vernacular, she saved his hide. But Fleetwood, ever the pragmatist, has always had a knack for expressing what he believed to be a sense of inevitability for his band.

> So Greenie left us, and we thought, oh shit! There were mutterings in the ranks about breaking up the band, but I never understood why. It never occurred to me to quit. I simply thought we were too stupid to do anything else. McVie

and I were a bass player and a drummer and we needed a band. You simply keep going if you're a musician. The whole philosophy McVie and I had, and still have regarding Fleetwood Mac is, if someone pulls out, we're still here.[2]

But, as the erstwhile drummer confides, all that determination was cold comfort to Jeremy Spencer and Danny Kirwan during the summer of 1970. With Green gone, he explains, Jerry and Danny were deeply affected (another understatement, since Green's absence literally pushed them over the edge of their own fragile selves) since they themselves were now fronting the band and their morale was low to nonexistent. In Fleetwood's mind, they were all terribly depressed and nervous because they had lost their "supreme leader."

In a brave attempt to muddle through, Fleetwood took over leadership of the band from Green, and in Christine Perfect McVie, he also acquired some frontline assistance. She was the "best blueswoman and the prettiest musician in England," as well as being John's wife. At the time, Christine firmly believed that she had not only quit her band Chicken Shack, but also resigned from the music business altogether, in order to happily assume the role of homemaker. She always was, and still is, a quiet homebody. Her retirement lasted all of two months. Her last gig has lasted 36 years.

* * * * * * * * * *

Christine Perfect was born on July 12, 1943, in Lancashire, England. Another alumna of the British Art College system after a musically encouraging upbringing, she too found herself immersed in the blues at an incredibly young age. After acquiring a degree in teaching and sculpture, she joined forces with Andy Sylvester and Stan Webb to send their new band Chicken Shack into the stratosphere.Most notably for her, she played keyboards with Chicken Shack on the same historic playbill at the Windsor Blues Festival as Mayall's Bluesbreakers (with future husband McVie still playing bass for them at that point), and Peter Green's Fleetwood Mac in their first 1967 appearance (with temporary bass player Bob Brunning). At this stage, she was personally also a hardcore Fleetwood Mac fan, likening them to a drug with a kind of mysterious magic that was clearly infectious.

Under the illusion that she was retiring from the music business, an industry never quite suited to her temperament, in 1969 she left Chicken Shack, even though her wonderful blues song, "I'd Rather Go Blind" gave them their only really big hit. She was also honored as Best Female vocalist in Melody Maker's readership poll. Her retirement seemingly lasted about ten minutes: a solo album, Christine Perfect, was released, but almost immediately she joined John McVie as both life and musical partner, and in 1970 she was featured on their remarkable first post-Green album, *Kiln House*.

Earlier in 1970, just as Green was losing his bearings, the entire band had collectively moved in together, assembling their now familial army in the country domicile that would provide the title for their next album, the truly transitional *Kiln House*. This was an ancient, eccentric coasthouse near Hampshire and Surrey, where they repaired to live in two adjoining kiln houses that were used for drying hops and converted for domestic use. Fleetwood, exhibiting some of the communal and antiurban spirit of the times, felt it was a "wonderful ménage" of bandmates, wives, children, and roadies. His little commune included himself and his pregnant wife Jenny (sister of his brother-in-law George Harrison's wife Patty); Jeremy Spencer, his wife Fiona, and their son Dicken; Danny Kirwan and his girlfriend Claire; and their road crew, Dennis Kean and Dinky Dawson, up in the attic. They stayed in the country for six months, finding the break from former band madness and city frenzy truly inspiring, trying to work as a four-piece band (something they would never actually accomplish, since somehow five was the magic Mac number). Fleetwood recalled:

> We were smoking lots of hashish in chillums. Great blocks of the stuff lay about. While our summertime at Kiln House was nice, we were feeling enormous pressure as a band. Pete was gone, we had to prove that we could stand as one of England's more progressive bands. This gave us terrible cases of nerves, and long evenings were spent quelling mutinies and threats of disintegration.
>
> The pressure was on to record the successor to *Then Play On* and it made us sick. I felt a kind of soldierly duty to somehow carry on in the face of hippie lassitude and hash torpor. It took me four hours one night, but I talked everybody back into the band.[3]

As his wife Jenny confirms, "They'd had it but Mick talked them back in. He would not let go. He will *never* let go of Fleetwood Mac!"[4] Prophetic words indeed from Mrs. Fleetwood, since he is *still* holding on three decades later.

It simply cannot be overestimated how radical and experimental it was back in 1970 for Fleetwood and McVie to replace their reigning guitar god with a blueswoman, no matter how accomplished she was. Imagine the reaction in English blues purist circles—"blues cultists" may be more a more accurate term. Either way, the band was letting go of the drunken macho lechery of their early days—and apparently, of all that made them a blues band. The purists in England, a crank bunch when it came to their blues heritage, stridently rebelled, accusing the newly reformed progressive rock unit of turning their wealthy backs on tradition. They remain angry to this day.

I was 16 when I first discovered the blues version of Mac, and 20 when they made their shift into new and uncharted territory. Somehow, it just seemed logical that they would evolve along these somewhat mystical and possibly psychedelic lines. Besides, the new music they were making, especially what came after *Kiln House* was truly remarkable in every way, at least for those with open ears. But the patriarchal politics of the rock music world has deep roots and deeper emotions.

One feminist music critic, Ellen Willis, has long observed the inherent stresses in this industry. She responded to her own bewilderment about the role of women by asking the culture around her the basic question: can a feminist still love rock and roll? And she explained her position by clarifying that love does not preclude tension and conflict, indicating that her primary subject matter has always been the "bloody crossroads where rock and feminism meet."[5] Willis and others continue to appreciate that paradox, and so should we, to discover the place at which women's liberation and musical liberation at least seem to intersect, what she calls the function of rock and roll as a catalyst for the moment of utopian inspiration. This is the "out of time" moment when we not only imagine, but live the self that you would be in the world that could be. Willis continues:

> Whenever I listened to music during the sixties and seventies, I was listening for the voice of that utopian moment, through the filters of pop conventions and clichés, the performer's defenses and cover ups: it was the spiritual equivalent of listening for the "pure music" through an old scratchy recording. But feminism made me lust for the voice without the filters, and so I longed for a female rock and roller who would be my mirror.
>
> This is an old story in pop music: the flip side of listening for that pure utopian moment through those obscuring filters was embracing the poignancy of the filters themselves, representing as they do the condensed stories of human joy, tragedy and resignation inadequately but insistently expressed.
>
> And it occurred to me that one of the measures of the advance of women's liberation in rock and roll is the increasing variety of filters available to female performers, from new variations on the old staples of sex and romance to ironic deconstructions of same to sheer brattiness, to the pop feminist clichés that are now an integral part of our culture's canned fantasy life. Women—performer, fans, critics—have now achieved more power to construct their own filters out of the cultural detritus, and fool around with them, as men have always done.[6]

One of those "filters" is the blues idiom. Another is even more universal, namely the male-female polarity itself, which has always formed the bedrock of the blues in the first place—women cause the blues, but only women can cure the blues. And although today there are a multitude of respected women rock artists, as well as female musicians in all the other idioms as well, it was rather rare back when ex-Chicken Shack chick Christine McVie joined her husband's "blues band." There were quite a few soul singers, and the occasional anomaly of a Janis Joplin or a Tina Turner, but for a blonde blues crooner to join forces with the besotted boys and contribute to their musical mayhem was an oddity indeed.

The editor of the *Rolling Stone* study "Women in Rock," Barbara O'Dair, is still puzzled by it all, however:

Given the evidence, it seems odd that there would be such a dispute about women's contributions to rock and roll over the years. But Madonna's struggle for legitimacy despite her accomplishments is but one example of the deep and pervasive hegemony of the men in the rock establishment. Their ambivalence for power-sharing with their female colleagues manifests itself in a kind of willful ignorance, aggressive indifference, and sometimes, even outright sabotage.

Power-sharing of course, has been an issue from the early days. Rock was born black and taken by enterprising whites to a mainstream audience. Women have been engaged in making this history all along, ever since a woman laid down the tracks of the very first blues recording (Mamie Smith, "Crazy Blues," 1920).[7]

There are literally acres of incredibly talented blueswomen laboring in the tall shadow of Bessie Smith and Memphis Minnie—some well known, some less, some totally unknown, but all integrally involved in the suddenly accelerated evolution from blues to rock. Throughout the 1950s, blues music was a means of bringing together the polarities of rural and urban life. In addition, radio stations began to pop up like mushrooms in the postwar period, and, as the feminist critic Ariel Swartley has pointed out, both bluesmen and blueswomen found themselves "haunting another sort of crossroads": their songs were the place through which white America discovered black music. Swartley argues, "Blues may have been the coal that stoked rock's runaway train in the fifties and sixties, but traditional players were left at the crossing, playing to dwindling audiences, slipping into retirement, or dedicating their musical talents to the church. At about the same time though, a younger generation of mostly white guitarists had begun tracing rock's roots back to the old records."[8]

As we now know from the histories complied by dedicated critics who insisted on giving credit where credit is due, the blues revival was propelled by a variety of fuels: left-wing populism, the civil rights movement, and the empowerment of black culture in general, and the mostly white, restless, suburban generation's search for what Swartley accurately calls an "ecstatic authentic connection." "Whatever the source though, in the United States, female blues artists were given the cold shoulder. Europe was a different story."[9] Indeed, it was, so much so that a talented young woman in London would become the pianist/singer/songwriter frontline performer for the greatest white blues band in history, Fleetwood Mac.

There is indeed a blues "matriarchal line," with a uniquely long and rich history, even if we don't always recognize it. But astoundingly, a rumpled pair of white Englishmen did recognize it, and they staked the future of their already famous group on that line. By doing so they would accidentally (because almost everything they did was accidental, as they themselves would be the first to admit) create a seminal new form of music altogether. There was no name for it yet back then, but it was inevitable that they would later expand the premise even further. The term that most closely defines what that new form of music felt like is "pop blues"—an unrelated concept, devised by the gifted but troubled producer Phil Spector in order to differentiate his own sound from that of rock and roll. Pop blues describes perfectly the new shape of things to come within Fleetwood Mac. Indeed, it is the only phrase that can describe what they began to write and perform during the transitional period of 1970–71, and that can capture its creative and commercial paradoxes.

And when Mac succeeded in enlisting the services of the of the soft-spoken Californian, Bob Welch in 1971, a unique moment in their history had been reached. Their second phase allowed them not only to emerge from the blues shadows of Peter Green, but to literally catapult themselves into the progressive rock arena of the seventies and beyond. Supported commercially by the advent of FM radio (which may as well have been called "Fleetwood Mac radio"), their new hybrid sound would lay the foundation for everything else that followed.

* * * * * * * * * *

Two wonderful lines from Ariel Swartley help describe this momentous collaboration in process. First, history is the straight yarn of time knit on a circular needle. This will be born out again and again during the circuitous growth of the band the world now knows so well. Second, combustion, however spontaneous, comes from a mixture of elements. This is never more clear than when outlining the serendipity, even the shocking synchronicity, that controls the destiny-drenched evolution of this same band. These facts of creative life would eventually make Mac a household word, even if that word was to be synonymous with the ultimately dysfunctional impact of their long and winding road through creative chaos.

That chaos needs to be understood and appreciated in the context of the way Mac always made their music, and the way their personnel changes made their career first grow and then explode. Christine McVie simply waded into the torrential rapids and started immediately making her presence felt. She brought some desperately needed balance and warmth to the mercurial mix, and her feminine energy, with a husky smoky voice that smoothed some rough edges, proved to be a kind of saving grace. When she joined the band for its fourth American tour in the second half of 1970, her husband has commented that "she's more mellow than Mick and I put together. She has a great ability to accept situations and put them in their proper order. That's her strength." Although it is not difficult to be more mellow than that maniacal rhythm section, it is true that a certain stoicism does come through all her work, as well as her serious professionalism.

Steve Clarke believes that this stoic side of McVie allowed her to withstand the slings and arrows of the many arduous years to follow. That stoicism, or the ability to accept whatever fate dealt out, was tested royally the following

February, when Jeremy Spencer went missing in Los Angeles. "His on the spot decision to throw in his career with Fleetwood Mac in exchange for eternal salvation with the Children of God has become as legendary as Green's own disappearing act."[10] The band's post-blues, California-influenced sound, typified by Kirwan's breezy rockers and Christine's effortless vocals, was more suitable for American audiences than the grim relentlessness of Fleetwood Mac's blues period. But Spencer seemed to find it difficult to commit to the band's new music."[11]

Los Angeles had long been a stomping ground for all kinds of eccentrics and religious fanatics. Since the Sixties, its streets, boulevards and airport lounges have been ideal hunting ground for fringe sects. Spencer was perfect material for the Children of God, with his little-boy-lost air and hippie appearance. Clearly Spencer was psychologically unsuited to playing a pivotal role in the band. Arguably, he had never been cut out for the leading role he occupied post-Green.[12] Equally unsuitable to the task of following the intense musical path of the brilliant Green, Danny Kirwan would hold on for only part of another year. Drugs, alcohol, mental instability, and the incapacity for fame, all took their toll on each of the three guitarists from the founding family of the band.

Green not only remains to this day a legendary guitar genius, but also serves as a cautionary tale about the dangers of both indulgence and insecurity. When the band returned to England to prepare for their 1970 tour, Fleetwood observed, "We were sad and mystified to hear Peter's solo album, *End of the Game,* which had just been released. Free-form acid-rock jams wove in and out of each other, meandering this way and that. It made me wonder what had gone wrong with my dear old friend."[13] While many of us listeners knew exactly what went wrong, we still considered Green's post-Mac opus to be a masterpiece of experimental rock. It still holds up today as a pure expression of electronic madness. But of course, just as Green had intended, it plunged in the opposite direction from where the money was. You could always count on Green to do something exceptionally uncommercial.

Meanwhile, the newly reformed Mac was slowly inching its way towards new heights in wealth and popularity. And some of their newest guitarist/ singer/songwriter's charm, grace, and elegance would go a long way to positioning them on a more accessible global stage. Back then, in early 1971, Bob Welch was just what the psychiatrist ordered for this band.

* * * * * * * * * *

Bob Welch was born on July 31, 1946, and raised in Hollywood, the son of a movie producer and an actress. As strongly influenced by the West Coast mentality and spirit of Brian Wilson's Beach Boys as his own eventual replacement would also be, he passed through the ranks of several bands before being approached in 1971 to take Fleetwood Mac in a new direction after their recent implosions. Joining without an audition, as per usual with Mac, the first American member of the band instantly put his melodic and mystical stamp on their output. Welch got along especially well with Christine McVie, and together they shared a certain laid-back vibe and casual but creative writing style that went a long way to erasing some of Mac's former madness.

On several occasions, Fleetwood himself has commented that Welch "saved" the band, and this is completely true. His five albums with Fleetwood Mac (*Future Games, Bare Trees, Penguin, Mystery to Me,* and *Heroes Are Hard To Find*) are all superbly accomplished masterpieces without which the band would never have been in a position even to contemplate the next stage in their strange evolution, let alone actually make the move. But when he first joined in 1971 and began collaborating creatively with the band—especially with its new female member, with whom he shared a certain simpatico style and sensibility—everyone was hopeful of a more healthy and balanced future.

Future Games, the first recording released with Welch on board, and the first to officially have a public declaration of Christine McVie's new important role, was a radical departure for the band. It remains one of the best produced, most beautifully written and artistically holistic of all their efforts. To this day, it still has the fresh appeal, untainted by time, of a great work of art that has no clear territorial designation. It could have been made yesterday, simply because its hybrid qualities cannot be compared to anything else in the music industry. Unbeknownst to them at the time, Welch and McVie's entrance into the hallowed ranks had brought about the invention of a completely new form of expression. While that form still cannot be categorized, its lush gentle tone makes it clear that Mac was expanding its reach far beyond the blues of founder Peter Green.

* * * * * * * * * *

For a time in mid-1970 and early 1971, it appeared that this was not just some romanticized "band on the run," but a full-fledged band on the rocks. The blues boom, which lifted Fleetwood Mac to international prominence almost from the instant they struck their first chords in 1967, and which reached a peak in 1969 and 1970, was suddenly exhausted and enervated by 1971. The ride appeared to be over almost as quickly as it had begun. By this time, the British father of the blues, John Mayall, had more or less abandoned straight blues for a much more jazzy, free form, Californian hybrid style of his own. Eric Clapton's long-awaited solo record after the implosion of Cream, *Clapton* (1970), was disappointing to hardcore fans of the British blues, of which he was the principal young exponent. His tour de force, *Layla and Other Assorted Love Songs,* only seemed to provide evidence that many of the most gifted blues purveyors were jumping ship and embracing hard rock music.

Steve Clarke confirms that, from a British point of view,

Fleetwood Mac had more or less ceased to exist after Peter Green had left the band. Now that Spencer had followed suit, Fleetwood Mac had achieved a dubious notoriety as the band who hatched weirdo guitarists. In the new musical setting of the early Seventies, they found themselves in a musical no-man's land with their espousal of good, honest musical values that sounded increasingly like a cry from the distant past. Financially, their best chance for survival was to court the American audience. This is perhaps why Fleetwood Mac took an instant liking to Bob Welch, a young well heeled Californian hippie who, over the next three years would become an integral, if ultimately frustrated member of Fleetwood Mac.[14]

Apparently, it was largely Welch's personality that appealed so much to the struggling band that they embraced him, and his lyrical, mystic, melodic style, with open arms. This is par for the course for Mac, operating as they do from some deep intuitive source that has little resemblance to logic or reason, yet they were never, ever wrong. They did not seem to require a traditional audition from the new musician. Christine McVie has stated that during their initial encounter "Bob never actually played a note. All we did was sit around and talk until dawn, and we just thought he was an incredible person."[15] And from the very outset, this incredible person was stunned to discover that the ongoing operating method of his new band, in keeping with their origins and early history, was one of creative chaos. Their modus operandi remained unchanged: reaching for the finest sound available without any rhyme or reason beyond achieving the perfection of that sound.

It has been widely reported that the "audition" itself was a shock to Welch, who was more used to and more comfortable with a highly professional approach to the making of music. For instance, quite understandably, Welch expected the leaders of the new band he had just joined to provide him with direction, telling or at least showing him what to play. He assumed that *they* would provide the material for *him* to play. Not Fleetwood Mac. From the band's wobbly perspective, newcomer Welch *was* the new leader, and he was expected to create and provide new material for *them*. But he discovered that "[t]hey didn't talk about direction, except to make it clear that they didn't want to do blues." Basically he was colliding head on with a creative tradition dating back to the first introduction of Kirwan and Spencer. In addition, given that the band's state of mind and morale was at such a low ebb, he was also expected to rejuvenate both their creativity and their confidence—no simple task.

But as Christine put it at the time, "Bob is like a breath of fresh air because everyone was on the verge of cracking up when Jeremy left." And indeed, he was the fresh air they desperately needed. He was the first actual American in a band that was beginning to feel and to be almost American in spirit and musical sensibility. Welch was crucial not just to survival but to growth, which is why it is all the more shameful that his phase of Mac, from 1971–

74, with its five intriguingly different recordings, is often overlooked and underappreciated, mistaken for a mere hiatus before the blockbusters. On the contrary, it was their most inventive period, bar none.

According to Welch, their first encounters were rather intimidating, since he was clearly entering into a group lifestyle that had all the makings of a communal experience. He slowly began to fit in though, since there seemed to be a generally simpatico feeling among all concerned.

> We spent a lot of time socializing, which really meant a lot of time sitting around smoking and drinking a lot of brandy. The band let it be known that they were *not* looking for a Peter Green clone, which suited me, because I was basically more influenced by Steve Cropper than Peter's hero B.B. King. I didn't think *anybody* could be as good as Peter Green anyway. He had the body of a twenty three year old cockney but the soul of a fifty year old black bluesman.[16]

Welch has often described the convivial, if odd, initiation ceremony conducted by the band for its new frontline man as a kind of dreamlike scenario. He hung out with them for about a week, mostly sitting around Christine's kitchen table, where all important Fleetwood Mac business was executed. They drank a great deal of coffee and wine, smoked a lot of "good hash," and talked, and talked, and talked. Mostly they discussed Jeremy Spencer and Peter Green, and how they had been crushed by LSD. Welch could clearly see that they were traumatized, having gone from being one of the most successful bands around to having two of their front men leave within months of each other. He also noticed that they were similarly traumatized by the Los Angeles vibe, New York, and the United States in general. "I did have some songs that I'd put on tape over the years. Mac said, so let's hear them. Danny and Chris seemed to like my songs, so I kind of got the message that they were looking to change their style. They hadn't specifically thought *how* their style was going to change. They had done no conscious planning. They were simply looking for something they hadn't done before."[17] The band would certainly get that in spades.

And Welch would rapidly learn that his new bandmates never appeared to do any conscious planning. From the beginning, until Welch's period, and later into the blockbuster glory days in 1975, they relied utterly, totally, and magically on their own special brand of creative chaos. It never failed to cause immense personal and professional angst, and yet it never failed to launch them into ever higher commercial successes.

They never quite translated into a comparable success at the cash register. Creatively, however, with the mysterious five-album phase of hard-to-define and ever-evolving Mac music over which Welch presided, they were musically very advanced. What Bob Brunning has called the "cracks in the Fleetwood Mac organization" were clearly beginning to show. But the band still pressed on, returning to the UK to prepare the next album. There was *always* the next album. And after all, soon enough, without knowing it, that next album would be the one to catapult them over the top. That would, of course, be after Welch, but it would also largely be *because* of Welch.

Like *Future Games* (1971), the first Welch-led record with Christine officially on board, *Bare Trees* (1972) was a vastly underrated and yet singularly rewarding listening experience. It also yielded the first fresh hit single penned by Welch. The shockingly soft and melodic "Sentimental Lady" was both a clarion call towards the future and a rapid shift away from the band's gritty, albeit far from meager, origins. But while the tour, the single, and the album itself started to suggest a vital rebirth that was already underway, one of the major "cracks" was just now reaching the stage of disrepair. Welch was immediately sensitive to the recklessly unstable attitudes and behavior of Danny Kirwan, the last survivor from the Green days. "I thought he was a nice kid, but a little paranoid, a little bit disturbed."[18] Apparently, and not surprisingly, the most important thing to Fleetwood and McVie (and therefore to the band they created) was loyalty. Kirwan had been Green's protégé, and Green had been their blues god, so they were hanging on to him out of the most misguided kind of communal support—that is, until even they saw the overly sensitive young guitarist go too far.

It was during the 1972 tour to support *Bare Trees* that Kirwan simply burned his one bridge too many. As Welch remembers it,

> We had a university gig somewhere. Danny started to throw this major fit in the dressing room. He had a beautiful Les Paul Gibson guitar. First he starts banging the walls with his fists, then he threw his guitar at the mirror, which shattered, raining glass everywhere. He was pissed out of his brain, which he was for much of the time. We couldn't reason with him. Next thing, he goes out to the mixing desks out in the audience and would not come on stage to play![19]

A musical nightmare quickly ensued. Kirwan flatly refused to play, but instead decided to heckle and advise them loudly from the mixing consoles. After the "concert," he was swiftly, and finally, fired.

Once again, it appeared that the invisible burden and angst of Peter Green's "retirement" had weighed down and sunken another brilliant young blues performer. For Brunning, and for our musical history, the departure of Kirwan was clearly the closing of a major chapter in the band's early growth. "He was the last link with the blues and r'n'b phase of the band. He had been a talented and soulful protégé of his mentor Peter, and had contributed much fine work to the band's repertoire."[20] The band would now enter a new phase of their checkered career. But it would be, as Fleetwood himself has said in a masterpiece of understatement, "somewhat fraught."

* * * * * * * * * *

Others have described this middle phase as the band's fifth "incarnation," but that is not entirely accurate. I prefer to call their very fertile second phase a rebirth. A rebirth is a new or second birth—a renewed existence, activity, or growth, a renaissance or revival. That is what occurred by expanding the post-meltdown band to include Christine McVie and Bob Welch. There was still considerable continuity at work creatively, even if it was in the midst of their signature chaos.

There was also a kind of evolutionary extension of the group's musical message and its recorded product that rarely happens once in the industry, let alone twice. But as for actual reincarnation, the audience would still have to wait until 1975 for that, and it would surprise everyone, including the band itself. The rebirth brought about by the coming of Christine McVie and Bob Welch (and to a slightly lesser extent through the temporary addition of Bob Weston and Dave Walker) would lay the groundwork for the ultimate reincarnation brought about by the arrival of Lindsey Buckingham and Stevie Nicks. That reincarnation of the band's soul, so to speak, in which upon the death of the body it returns back to earth in a different, completely new body or form, would later become crystal clear with the mercurial and manic presence of Buckingham and Nicks, whose Californian sensibility would forever stamp itself upon Mac's identity.

However, only in retrospect, and with the benefit of historical hindsight, does it appear that the unbreakable chain of the Mac continuum would manage to triumph, let alone survive at all. From the inner perspective of the members, this band was simply perpetually breaking up, over and over again, in slow motion. And since the raw material for their new music would be the personal relationship nightmares of the members, they would also give a new and ironic meaning to the phrase, "breaking up is hard to do."

Mick Fleetwood, always the best spokesman for his band's almost simultaneous rise and fall and rise again, put it this way:

> Things went downhill from there. At this point, 1972, Fleetwood Mac had spent the past five years either on the road or making records, with varying degrees of success. We had stood both at the top of the charts and looking over the precipice of failure. For the next two and a half years, we went through hell. In the wake of Danny's departure, we expanded to six pieces, then deflated to five, and finally pared down to a quartet. We made records that were both good and indifferent, and at one point we almost lost the band entirely. It was that close. It was a crazy and confused time, a period in our collective history. That underlines the fact that nothing ordinary ever happens to Fleetwood Mac.[21]

Bob Welch was equally philosophical about what it meant to be a member of Mac. "When I met them they were going through a sort of a weird phase, and it continued in that phase until after I left. I consider the whole period to be a foundering stage. They had begun as Green's band, a hot blues band, hit singles in Europe. Then when he left, Spencer and Kirwan didn't exactly know what they were doing, and when I left they really had no idea."[22]

Welch may have felt they were floundering, and perhaps they were, given their disastrous choice of Savoy Brown rocker Dave Walker to briefly front the band; nonetheless, this period gave birth to incredibly inspired songs that rapidly moved them into new and uncharted territory. Each of the five Welch-driven albums pushed the band closer and closer to the reckoning place: that special creative destination where the explosive talents of Buckingham-Nicks would lift the band higher than they ever imagined possible.

Most crucial of all perhaps, Welch somehow convinced Mick Fleetwood that it would be a good creative decision to move the band to Los Angeles, establish themselves in the Californian musical environment, and all but transform into an American pop group. Who could have guessed then that his recommendation would be the end of his own involvement, but also the beginning of the latter-day Mac that an army of invisible fans had been waiting for? But until then, some rebalancing and realignment still was required for the Mac machine. One of the reasons for their relocation to California was a bit of a survival mechanism. The band let Dave Walker go almost as quickly as he was hired, and Bob Weston was asked to leave after Fleetwood discovered he had embarked on an affair with his wife, Jenny. Then suddenly, their management team attempted to hijack both their name and their growing brand.

After the obscure album *Penguin* (called by Christine a "really weird out in the ozone kind of album"), they released one of their best post-blues records, *Mystery to Me*, an album that mostly featured and focused upon the strengths of their newest melodic member. The band went back to America in 1973, the year of *Mystery*'s release, in order to "earn its bread and butter." "Hypnotized" was the gentle but compelling Welch hit from this record, and at first their concerts were ideal supports for the record, with audiences in America being far more open to their stylistic changes than the blues-roots fanatics back home in England.

As Samuel Graham pointed out in his early study of the band, after canceling their 1973 "make or break tour,"

> Mick was fried, he couldn't go on. Their manager was adamant. He warned them that he *owned* Fleetwood Mac. He also warned them that he refused to lose his reputation and business because of the whims of a bunch of irresponsible musicians. He warned them that their careers would be over if they didn't do what he told them. Welch said, this guy thinks we're his slaves! So, Fleetwood Mac scattered to the winds, with plans to regroup as soon as possible. They were ill-prepared for what was about to happen to them.[23]

Another incredible understatement, since they were always ill prepared for everything that happened to them, whether it was success, failure, or in between. That, after all, proves once again their chief modus operandi: caution thrown to the winds of pure creative chaos.

Fleetwood characterizes the managerial escapade as the hijacking of his band, perhaps the ultimate artistic nightmare any band ever had to endure. Davis describes it in almost noble terms, "The story of the fake Fleetwood

Mac stands as one of the most sordid and depraved episodes in the history of popular music. That the group managed to hang on, fight back and eventually prevail is also one of the most inspiring sagas in the music business, still preserved in the oral tradition of rock musicians."[24]

Following the collapse of the *Mystery to Me* tour, as well as the collapse of Fleetwood's already strained marriage, the besieged musicians went off on their own to recuperate. John McVie went to Hawaii to pursue his love of solitary sailing, Christine retreated home to England, Welch went along with the band's gear to Los Angeles, and Fleetwood flew off to the game preserves of Africa, until he and his wife Jenny decided to get back together again. Meanwhile, the faux Mac, assembled by their grasping business advisor, lasted only ten days on a tour that confused audiences and enraged the musicians. The band learned that their management had them in an apparent contractual headlock.

Unable to record as Fleetwood Mac, unable to tour as anybody else, court injunctions had been placed against them, and their concert fees and royalties were frozen. The lawyers that Fleetwood hired indicated that the band had signed contracts years ago, as "drunken teenagers." It appeared they did not even own their own name. The tiny shreds of band credibility remaining were strained utterly. Once again, it certainly seemed like not only the end of the game but also the end of the road. Once again, it was not. Bob Welch convinced Fleetwood to make a fresh start in Los Angeles. They all settled into rented quarters in Laurel Canyon and Malibu, with Fleetwood himself assuming the role of their new manager—perhaps a good idea at the time but one that would later prove equally disastrous.

The band's label, Warner Brothers, based on their long history and loyal fan base, decided to give Mac another chance to prove themselves stateside. In June 1974, the weary musicians started work on the new album, *Heroes Are Hard to Find*, the first of their records to be recorded entirely in America. After some 43 shows, however, it was Bob Welch's turn to become the latest weak link in the Mac chain. The strain of reconstruction had been too much for him. He also felt that he had reached the end of what he could contribute creatively to the band. So he gracefully withdrew after the tour, on good terms with his bandmates—a rare occurrence for a group so used to the sturm-and-drang storms of ego inflation and mental collapse usually associated with their clockwork like personnel changes. Welch was slowly being worn down by the perpetual angst that always accompanied the creative working methods of Mac. He was also amazed that the band's management was almost as out to lunch as his fellow members appeared to so often be.

The manager in question, Clifford Davis, still to this day defends his purpose in attempting to recoup his losses and capitalize on the group's impending demise. He claimed the ownership of the name of the band, its creative content and its future, if any. His "New Fleetwood Mac" was comprised of various members of various other groups in his management stable, with absolutely no members of the real Mac ever being connected to this bogus American tour. This, despite a false claim in an article in *Let it Rock* magazine that Fleetwood and Christine came to him and agreed to front a band put together around them, something the band has always categorically denied. It was clearly a perfect example of the fact that the band had evolved into a "brand" and that someone was trying to sell that brand, whether it contained an actual product or not.

Welch recalls that the "New Fleetwood Mac" tour was a complete and utter disaster, with both promoters and audiences alike being irked and offended by the obvious masquerade. A lawyer representing Mac stated that what really happened was not an altruistic move to save face and retain the group's good name by putting together a new band as an act of goodwill. Instead, it was a case of a business man profiteering from an asset, which in this case consisted of a name. According to Welch, this sordid scenario high-lighted the distressing fact that they were not receiving all that they should from various royalties, for which the manager was responsible.

The event not only disturbed the element of trust that had for years tacitly, and contractually, existed between Clifford Davis and Fleetwood Mac, but the real band's credibility became highly suspect, especially among promoters and record labels. Fortunately, Warner Brothers sided with the band and negotiated a new contract with them directly—although the label may have done so more out of potential profits than out of loyalty. For the band itself, Welch has commented, "It was a depressing situation. Positive, in that we survived, but very paranoid." By then, he should perhaps have known that the evolution of this incredibly tenacious blues-rock-pop group was always completely dependent on paranoia as the principal reason for its existence. And that, seemingly, nothing on earth could kill the engine that drove it for-ever forward.

But alas, Welch's own engine had run out of steam. He was a consummate pop craftsman and perfectly gifted pop stylist, although the mysterious music he produced with Mac was difficult for their audience to fully comprehend or appreciate. Tired and frustrated with how hard he had worked to keep the band afloat during the Clifford Davis scam and after the disappointing response to his *Heroes,* he can be forgiven for seeing the end in sight. He was looking for bigger indications that the difficulties had been worth it. But Fleetwood Mac just turned another page. Just like Peter Green before him—and Jeremy Spencer and Danny Kirwan, for that matter, although for very different reasons—Welch doubted the balance between crap and creativ-ity. Apparently only the ultimate stalwarts, the original founding roadhounds who played drums and bass for the band, would ever be able to withstand the full force of that tornado and still manage to go on.

For Fleetwood himself, at the center of the vortex swirling around him, Welch had been more than just an integral part of Fleetwood Mac. In charac-terizing the Welch years, Fleetwood comments,

Bob always used to wish that he had the same kind of background as us in a lot of ways, because it leads you more to an emotional content than a technical one, and that to me, is the most important thing—in anything really, when you get down to it. He'd be practicing for hours, doing all these jazz licks, then suddenly it didn't really mean anything. I think while Bob was in the band, he got to understand that side of it and appreciate a sort of angle that he never got involved in before, which is just a simple, honest approach to music. It's a way of having sympathy for other players, for not over-extending yourself. It's taste, really.[25]

Putting aside for the moment the founder's astounding definition of a "simple honest approach to music" that leaves in its wake a totally wrecked crew of drug burnouts, cult crazies, psychotic breakdowns, ego inflation, mercenary machinations, and personal relationship hell, one has to admire his gentlemanly good manners when it comes to how he feels about every single member of his group. He even produced and promoted Welch as a solo artist, such was his respect for the talent that had somehow helped him and McVie emerge from the loss of Peter Green to the impending arrival of the platinum personalities yet to materialize on his horizon.

Subsequent to his departure from Mac, and prior to their own pop explosion on the global stage, Welch worked with the trio he called Paris, a venture he called a cross between what he wanted to do and what he thought would sell. His own creative philosophy has often appeared to be similar to that of Mac itself, but without the manic panic and chaos. He seemed most comfortable when exuding a highly passive hold on just how to chart a course toward his own future. As if having learned something uniquely central to the Mac creed, he once commented that it seemed to him the less you make plans, the more things begin to take shape. He often wanted to be able to plan things carefully, but admitted that it did not usually work out that way, frequently observing that things seemed more vital when plans were not made.

Eventually, a good solo pop album by Welch would materialize in the magic year 1977, the same year *Rumours* was released, with Fleetwood, McVie, and Buckingham (Welch's Mac successor) contributing to an excellent remake of the Welch song "Sentimental Lady" (originally on Mac's *Bare Trees* from five years earlier). With McVie and Fleetwood producing, and with Buckingham's gifted arranging, it became a well-earned hit for the likeable Welch.

Given the strange public amnesia about Fleetwood Mac's post-blues, post-Green, post-England days, and the lack of both critical and public appreciation for the crucial role he played in moving closer to the *Rumours*-era style and sensibility, the most important line in Samuel Graham's early study of the band is, "Someone of his talents and intelligence deserves not to be inconsequential."[26] Fortunately, the music magazine *Uncut* has remedied some of the missing attention so richly deserved by Welch. In their piece on the band's history, "Five Go Mad," they at least had the grace to produce a special sidebar devoted to this highly creative, quirky, oddly mystical, and romantic musician. Calling it "Fleetwood Mac's Forgotten Man," the magazine captured at least some of his major importance to the band's future, although still identifying the period between the departure of Peter Green and the arrival of Buckingham-Nicks as something of a "nadir" in Mac's history. I believe they are only partially correct in that respect. Once again, too much worship is paid to the massive sound of the blockbuster cash register that began ringing in 1975, and not enough attention is paid to the five records that Welch helped manifest.

In the 2003 issue of *Uncut* magazine, covering the band's eventual reunion to release *Say You Will*, Nigel Williamson characterized the transition period well enough:

> Although Mick Fleetwood and John McVie remained as a bridge between the two eras, the band would probably not have survived the early 70's without the considerable input of American guitarist Bob Welch. When he got the call to "audition" for Fleetwood Mac, he was stranded in Europe, unable to afford a plane ticket back to his native Los Angeles. He's sold his electric guitar and arrived at the band's communal home in Acton Hampshire with little more to his name but the clothes he was wearing.[27]

This feeling is seconded by Mark Trauernicht:

> Strongly influenced by Welch's more melodic style, it was the first Fleetwood Mac music to make a complete break with the blues-rock sound of the Peter Green era. He had become the dominant musical force in the band. Welch was to make one other lasting contribution to the Fleetwood Mac story. Shortly before he quit towards the end of 1974, he persuaded Fleetwood Mac to relocate from Britain to L.A.[28]

A lasting contribution, indeed. Musically, Welch made it possible for Mac to even remotely consider the vaguely new-age mystic romance that would become their later trademark, by introducing it intravenously and in slow motion over his four-year stint. Materially, he made it physically possible for the eventual encounter between the rock-warrior Fleetwood, on the hunt for a new front muse, and the producer-wizard Buckingham, on the hunt for creative survival.

Bob Welch's records are among the finest ever produced by the band, and they deserve to be listened to for what they are: sophisticated and charmingly hybrid pop-rock ventures which pushed the group ever closer to the self-defining pop-blues of their "zenith." His melodic machine was single-handedly responsible for the continuation of Mac until their next evolutionary leap. But like all good things, he didn't last long—just long enough. Welch, master of the spooky transition, expressed it best in his own song's words, "Fate Decides": "Funny how fate plays another trick again. The hand of fate decides. The hand of fate revolves, and you're caught in the middle. Part of the whole design. Fate decides."

The addition of this Californian resulted in a profound contribution to the new sound, with fresh-spirited records that are a vertigo-inducing stew of styles and impossible-to-classify formats. Welch was the bridge leading to the other shore of musical alchemy at work in the heads of the collaborative and combative bassist and drummer. This bridge would also provide access to a maturity and clarity of sound and sensibility which would prove remarkably satisfying to the appetites of the 1970s musical audience: jaded and bored, alarmed and offended by the bloated places post-1960s rock music had visited. But that audience could never have anticipated the true scale and monumental bloating that would result in the late-1970s Fleetwood Mac. Only a pop music industry expanding beyond all familiar proportions, one consumed by the corporate over the creative, would have made such excess not only possible but wildly celebrated.

So, once again reduced to the bare bones of their rhythm section and a husky voiced female lead singer, Fleetwood Mac began to look around for any hopeful glimpses that they had a future at all. According to Stephen Davis, Fleetwood told the McVies not to worry, he was sure somebody good would *turn up*. These sentiments would prove hauntingly prophetic, considering the tidal wave of success that would greet the next phase of their long history.

FUTURE GAMES: RELEASED 1971, WARNER BROTHERS

This is one of Fleetwood Mac's finest records, either from the old or new period, and whether featuring the original or the morphed lineups. Whereas *Kiln House,* as intriguing as it was, felt like a transitional and tentative pause that fell back on the 1950s-rock-and-roll obsessions of Spencer, this is the first new and fully fledged work created by a rejuvenated band with a fresh vision. The second phase of Mac's creative life was now firmly in place.

Released in September, in time for their latest American tour, it was for Fleetwood the "new look Mac, devoid of past trademarks." He was especially fond of Welch's new guitar addition, relishing yet another gifted instrumentalist in their ranks, and their shift toward "country rock." For the first time, this record was presented without their customary provocative cover art and design. Instead of Fleetwood in drag, or doing something menacing, the cover was shot by his sister Sally and showed her two children playing near a river in Salisbury with an inner tube—a strangely innocent image, yet somehow befitting the softer and more melodic sounds contained within. Fleetwood has stated that the image depicted the band's own hope for their future and the new optimism the record represented for all of them.

One element of inescapable bad-boy behavior still remained, of course, with a shy and petulant John McVie refusing to have his photograph on the back cover and using instead one of his beloved penguins instead of himself. "Then he got very drunk," Fleetwood commented in his autobiography, "and got a penguin tattooed on his arm. That's where all the Fleetwood Mac iconography started, after that we always had penguins plastered on album covers and every other available surface." Thus armed, he declared, "we prepared to attempt the re-conquest of America."[29]

The conquest, supported by the sheer brilliance of Bob Welch's oddly breathy voice, jagged swirling guitar, and mysteriously obscure lyrics, would launch them into the arms of an ever-widening audience that was just now waking up to Mac's new charms. The word ethereal is the only one to adequately capture the essence of what they were up to here. To this day, about 36 years later, I still do not know the meaning behind many of the songs, especially Kirwan's gorgeous ballads, such as the album's opener "Woman of A Thousand Years." But the music is so powerfully beautiful that meaning is often happily left behind. "Woman of a thousand years, how are your sons of a time ago? Do they still admire your silvered ways? As you go down to the sea and golden sand. Flying down from on high, she is gone, and then appears, from the water's edge . . ." Whatever this song means, once you hear the musical vessel that contains them, you too will forget the part of your brain that always craves understanding. Words fail to convey how reassuring this strange and sad song is, and like the whole album itself , its words are carried on the back of a pop instrumental prowess which was just then in its nascent stage.

Mark Trauernicht's assessment on the Mac Web site, One Together, is a very sound one: "*Future Games* shows just how capable Welch was in fulfilling his part of the bargain. Considerably different from any of its predecessors, *Future Games* indicated a change of direction for the band, eschewing blues in favour of a mellower sound. Welch's west coast influences are prominent, as is his interest in the supernatural, particularly in the title song."[30] Indeed, the song "Future Games," a deceptively soft piece with a hard heart that is one of my favorite cuts from one of my favorite albums, is a peculiar little anthem to both forging and curing our own "karma": "All of the wild things, tomorrow will tame, talking of journeys that happen in vain. And I know that I'm not the only one, to ever spend my life sitting playing future games . . ."

The whole record seems to be about the future—not surprisingly, perhaps, given the trauma the band had just experienced, but the first of many to come. Christine McVie's lovely piece "Morning Rain" is suffused with the hopeful energies of starting over again: "Clear as the morning rain, seeing it very plain, we've got to start again. Everything's going around in my head, the future's new and the past is dead. Pull out the stops, turn on the light, cause away from the darkness everything seems bright." Kirwan, however, while trying to start again, seems in several of his finest songs to be bound up inextricably with the past. In "Sands of Time," a hauntingly lovely piece, he depicts "the falling sands of time, blow my mind and drifted by, to and fro the trees still bend, wondering what the host will send. We will go down to the sea, bathing in light we will be free to wander. The magic of a blackened night can go so far, but not seem right." While in his song "Sometimes," he seems to be mourning the recent loss of a certain friend or mentor: "Sometimes I get to thinking about the times we used to have...but now you've gone away and left me so alone. Taking the sun from the sky, lifting our hearts to the day, thinking of new revelations, talking with nothing to say ..." Perhaps he needed to heed the calming advice of the new guitarist-leader of the group, Bob Welch, who sang in one of his more raucous romps: "Lay down your burden of sorrow, lay down your burden of hurt, lay it all down, for paradise here on earth..."

Other significant record releases of 1971: If I Could Only Remember My Name by David Crosby; *Ram* by Paul McCartney; *Sticky Fingers* by the Rolling Stones; *Surf's Up* by the Beach Boys; *Blue* by Joni Mitchell; *Imagine* by John Lennon; *Wildlife* by Wings; *Hunky Dory* by David Bowie.

Bare Trees:
Released 1972, Warner Brothers

With an even more sedate and calming cover design than the last one, containing a desolate but tranquil landscape shot photographed by John McVie, Mac quickly tried to both capitalize on and consolidate their new lineup and fresh creative direction. It is hard to say whether their public image was beginning to reflect their new soulful music, or whether the music itself was an unconscious reflection of their new public image. Either way, it was a hidden masterpiece, recorded in their usual whirlwind fashion during a brief week's break in their touring schedule of Europe and North America. Apparently upon returning to America, the tapes were damaged by the x-ray machines at the airport, and yet more labor had to be devoted to their repair at a studio in New York.

It was during this tour that Danny Kirwan's long-simmering psychological problems began to manifest themselves in earnest and he was fired by Mick Fleetwood. The album yielded a couple of impressive singles that were hits of the sort that emerge from the "progressive rock" and "underground music" scenes. Since the music that Mac was making at this time was a curiously unique hybrid, no one knew what else to call it but progressive. Yet that is exactly what it was and still is: not exactly blues, not exactly straight rock, not yet pop, but a mesmerizing mixture of them all.

Kirwan managed to write some of his most tender and poignant lyrics just before his breakdown. It is also ironic to note that this second phase of the band's history was to be much more heavily focused on songwriting, on lyrics as poetry, as songs with a discernible, if obscure, message, than anything prior. Kirwan himself called the music something no one had ever heard of before, in his raucous rocker "Child of Mine": "Heavy country blues keep a rockin', k-k-k-keep that soulbeat a sockin'." This was a new and exotic form of music making that had yet to find a niche, though it soon would on the burgeoning alternative radio networks just then forming on the horizon. Kirwan still let a little of his blues roots leak out, however, when in the same song he intones: "I miss you again, I let the sunlight through my eyes, I won't cry..."

Two singles, with an A-side of Christine's plaintive plea in the gorgeous ballad "Spare Me a Little of Your Love" and a B-side of Kirwan's sweetly gentle and albatross-like "Sunny Side of Heaven," started to climb the charts. But the best of their new softer and highly commercial direction was conveyed by Bob Welch's almost too gentle "Sentimental Lady," a perfectly crafted love song that was both a hit for Mac and an even bigger hit for Welch when he re-released it as a solo record several years later.

Welch had the unique ability to encapsulate in a single song the travails of personal intimacy as well as the larger social picture in which we all lived. "Cause we live in a time, when meaning falls in splinters from our lives, and that's why I've traveled far, cause I come so together where you are..." His warm voice, like crushed velvet, was both reassuring and threatening at the same time—especially when he focused, as he often did in his writing, on the reasons why life in the real world conspires against our contentment: "You are here and warm, but I could look away and you'd be gone...sentimental gentle wind, blowing through my life again, sentimental lady, gentle one..." This gentleness was always creatively balanced with the darker and more alarmingly isolated tones of Kirwan's own writing, making for a perfect contest between hope and despair, as in the title track by Kirwan: "I was alone in the cold of a winter's day, you were alone and so snug in your bed... bare trees, grey light, oh yeah, it was a cold night." And Kirwan's desolation found perhaps its ultimate expression in his almost indescribably beautiful musical rendering of a Rupert Brooke poem from the first World War, "Dust": "When the white flame in us is gone and we that lost the world's delight stiffen in darkness. Left alone to crumble in our separate light. When we are dust, when we are dust..." Unfortunately and most sadly, by this time the white flame in Kirwan had clearly gone the way of Green.

But it was Welch and Christine McVie whose writing was beginning to mature drastically and start to build the emotional structure that would become the band's trademark in the coming boom years. Her "Spare Me a Little" and "Homeward Bound" both serve as veritable announcements that she was tired of all the rock business merry-go-rounds: "I want to sit in my rocking chair, I don't want to travel the world, as far as I'm concerned I've had my share. Well it all seems the same when you've done it before, there is no end in sight, or my own front door. Buy me a ticket, homeward bound." And by this time, Welch's inherent interest in the supernatural and all things mystical was playing itself out in the theater of his songs, to great effect, as in "The Ghost": "Hold on until the ghost appears, that day is gonna last for years...just a blue star hanging out in space, earth town is such a lovely place, strange winds coming from the sky, lovers gotta say goodbye..."

The new Mac had arrived. They were hip, they were cool, they were obscure, and they were pure California, inside and out.

Other significant record releases of 1972: Nilsson Schmilsson by Harry Nilsson; *American Pie* by Don Maclean; *Manassas* by Manassas; *Exile On Main Street* by the Rolling Stones; *Music of My Mind* by Stevie Wonder; *School's Out* by Alice Cooper; *Sail Away* by Randy Newman; *Close to The Edge* by Yes; *Foxtrot* by Genesis; *Transformer* by Lou Reed; *African Herbsman* by Bob Marley.

MYSTERY TO ME:
RELEASED 1973, WARNER BROTHERS
PENGUIN:
RELEASED 1973, WARNER BROTHERS

These two releases should probably have just been one single album, much in the same way that *The Beatles* (The White Album) and Mac's own *Tusk* a few years later should have been individual and drastically edited recordings. Neither Dave Walker or Bob Weston (who would later be fired for having an affair with Fleetwood's wife) added much substance to the proceedings. Both albums were recorded within the space of three strenuous months.

On *Penguin,* the addition of strange rockers like "Road Runner" weakens the mix, and Walker's "The Derelict" has no place at all here. Inclusion of the rock chestnut "For Your Love" and the cowritten Weston track "Forever" is simply too sappy, even for the later Mac. Luckily for all of us, when a group is as supremely talented and creatively gifted as Fleetwood Mac, a couple of weak songs, such as Weston's instrumental "Caught in the Rain" on *Penguin,* cannot have a lasting effect on the album in its entirety. That is what the "skip" button is for, after all.

Both *Penguin* and *Mystery to Me* still yielded great music and a few strong hits, with one by Christine, as usual, being among them. Her "Remember Me" captures the essence of a blues lament within the churning pace of a fast rocker. Meanwhile, Welch plunges further into the poetic shadows that most suited his style and sensibility. "Bright Fire" admonishes us, or someone: "Don't let the waters of caution remove you, don't let the fire of saints compel you...I've seen the future burn blue before me eyes, and all through the dust and the green magnesium fire, don't let the violence blind you, you're gonna come through alive. Don't dam the river that's running through you, stop saving up for a time that may never come..."

Welch, when he sang to us that he had his share of blue revelations and that now he knew that time was a region to be passed, seemed to sum up the melancholy dimension that followed on the heels of the sixties. He said something on our behalf, as all great songs do, even if we did not quite always understand his meaning. That could be because as time went on, it became clear that Welch was not necessarily singing about our earth at all. A strong metaphysical quality, verging on an esoteric religious feeling, coursed through all his work. "Night Watch," on *Penguin* (on which an uncredited guitar is played by the "living ghost" of Peter Green), is a good example of this tendency: "Take this shadow from my eyes and tell me everything, take the desert from my soul and lift me up from down below. Well I have wondered why I live, now I know you must forgive. Let me stand inside your magic shadow."

Mystery to Me yielded a fine hit for them in Welch's "Hypnotized," but it was the twin messages of powerful love and powerful distaste in his songs "Emerald Eyes" and "Miles Away" that seemed to capture the core of dissatisfaction covered by the armor of amour. In the first track, Welch shares a fondness that makes his life bearable, "She's still a mystery to me, the way she sails away slow, makes your day to day life easy. Emerald eyes is a mystery, she's my place of serenity..." Whereas, in "Miles Away," he chooses to provide a commentary on what might be the shallowness of the very culture that supported his own best interests: "The swamp is getting deeper all the time, and the faces that I see don't seem to shine. Now there's too much Warhol hanging off the wall, and the mystery that there used to be is gone. Let me go, miles away, let me ride, just miles away. Now I know that I can't say what's black and white, but if I could fly I think I'd try tonight..." There just might be a contagious quality to the stresses of playing in the big time, and if so, it seems that Welch somehow caught it—perhaps from Kirwan, who caught it from Spencer, who caught it from Green. One way or the other, Welch would soon fly away; but before doing so, he would help create one more very strange and mysterious Mac album.

Other significant record releases of 1973: Can't Buy a Thrill by Steely Dan; *Pink Moon* by Nick Drake; *Dark Side of the Moon* by Pink Floyd; *Birds Of Fire* by Mahavishnu John McLaughlin; *For Your Pleasure* by Roxy Music; *Raw Power* by Iggy Pop and the Stooges; *Fresh* by Sly and the Family Stone; *Goodbye Yellow Brick Road* by Elton John; *Quadrophenia* by the Who; *Here Come The Warm Jets* by Brian Eno.

HEROES ARE HARD TO FIND:
RELEASED 1974, WARNER BROTHERS

Heroes certainly are hard to find, and it is so difficult being one yourself. Some of our heroes are those talented songwriters who manage to articulate something we all already feel. That is precisely what Welch, even at his most obscure, always did so well, although this art of articulating what others all feel would rise to truly astronomical heights when the upcoming *Rumours* lineup began to tell their personal stories of marriage mayhem. But the roots of relationship hell were all present here, long before the arrival of the Buckingham-Nicks wrecking crew. Before then, however, the band had to survive in order to arrive at that destination. The year 1974 was wicked for Mac in general, and for Welch in particular. He was simply running out of steam.

Though almost universally panned as a confusing romp, *Heroes Are Hard To Find* is actually quite a visionary album. In some ways, it approximates and anticipates Mac's experimental *Tusk*, five years beforehand. In many ways, I firmly believe that if Welch had not departed at the end of 1974, the next album he created with the band would have had the same dank, murky, muddy, swirling weirdness that *Tusk* had. In other words, if Buckingham-Nicks had not joined the group and produced their market masterpieces *Fleetwood Mac* (1975) and *Rumours* (1977), Welch would have plowed right on through to that rugged and strange *Tusk* territory. But naturally enough, the audience would not have been any more prepared for *his* next Mac record than they were for *Tusk*, as evidenced by the solemn but inescapable fact that they were not even ready for *Heroes*.

Yes, 1974 was hell on earth for Fleetwood Mac. One wag referred to part of the problem as the "Clifford Davis Blooze," touching on the pathetic management attempt to coopt and preempt their own talent and its product. The rest of the problem was a simple case of burning out, something Mac seemed to do every few years or so. In fact, they tended to burn out more than most bands even succeed at all.

Heroes was their first recording made entirely in the United States, under the producing reins of Bob Hughes. Cath Carroll's excellent book on the band during this period, primarily concerned with the behemoth *Rumours,* had some interesting insights:

> A blues thread still runs through *Heroes Are Hard to Find,* and the live approach is still there, the club din of ride and crash cymbals, swampy blues guitars, and unfussy vocals always sitting back in the mix. With this album however, the band's style expanded, with perhaps a little too much over-considered variety.

> Bob Welch, like Lindsey Buckingham, his successor in the band, admired Brian Wilson and the Beach Boys. This is apparent when both Welch and Buckingham produce vocal harmonies. However, on this album, Welch's Beach Boys tribute, "She's Changing Me" is just that, a reproduction, rather than an integration of Wilson's influence which Buckingham incorporated into *Rumours* All of this expanded the boundaries of the band and set a precedent for its future arrangements on both *Rumours* and *Tusk.*[31]

While much of what Carroll says in her fine study is true, I cannot quite agree with her assessment of the contest between Welch and Buckingham as creative producers. *Heroes* was produced by the Mac committee method under the tutelage of Hughes, whereas Buckingham is a technical wizard and producer genius whose personal production values are stamped all over every Mac record he ever touched. But Carroll also comments astutely on what I have already suggested is one of the great travesties in record industry history: "In 1998 Fleetwood Mac was inducted into the Rock and Roll Hall of Fame, but the board's decision to induct "only the two classic-Mac lineups of 1968 and 1975 generated a great deal of unhappiness from some former members. Bob Welch noted that the Eagles had supposedly overridden a similar board decision to include only some former band members, and he wondered why Fleetwood Mac could not do the same."[32] I also wonder, and lament; it is still a mystery to me.

Other significant record releases of 1974: Grievous Angel by Gram Parsons; *Valentine* by Roy Harper; *Crime of the Century* by Supertramp; *The Lamb Lies Down On Broadway* by Genesis; *Sheer Heart Attack* by Queen; *I Want to See the Bright Lights Tonight* by Richard and Linda Thompson; *Down by the Jetty* by Dr. Feelgood; *Sheet Music* by 10cc; *Average White Band* by Average White Band.

A youthful Mick Fleetwood, circa 1966. (Courtesy of Photofest Inc.)

Fleetwood Mac, the early days, 1969. *Left to right:* Danny Kirwan, Mick Fleetwood, Jeremy Spencer, John McVie, Peter Green. (Courtesy of Photofest Inc.)

The middle Welch years, 1974. *Left to right:* Bob Welch, Mick Fleetwood, John McVie, Christine McVie. (Courtesy of Photofest Inc.)

John McVie in action, 1975, the year of *Fleetwood Mac,* the album. (Courtesy of Photofest Inc.)

The classic *Rumours* lineup, 1977. *Left to right:* John McVie, Christine McVie, Stevie Nicks, Mick Fleetwood, Lindsey Buckingham. (Courtesy of Photofest Inc.)

The *Tusk* period, 1979. *Left to right:* John McVie, Christine McVie, Lindsey Buckingham, Mick Fleetwood, Stevie Nicks. (Courtesy of Photofest Inc.)

The *Tango in the Night* period, 1987. *Left to right:* Lindsey Buckingham, Stevie Nicks, Mick Fleetwood, Christine McVie, John McVie. (Courtesy of Photofest Inc.)

The *Say You Will* period, 2003. *Left to right:* Mick Fleetwood, Lindsey Buckingham, Stevie Nicks, Christine McVie, John McVie. (Courtesy of Photofest Inc.)

Reincarnation: The Coming of Buckingham and Nicks

5

"Ah, that feeling again...magic. The undeniable sensation of rightness that came from moment one when Stevie and Lindsey became part of Fleetwood Mac. It was as if Merlin himself could not have concocted a spell more perfect."

—Mick Fleetwood

Bob Welch, master of the spooky transition, transformed Fleetwood Mac into a Californian pop band with his mystic charm and melodic beauty. He also made them more than ready for duty when Lindsey Buckingham and Stevie Nicks arrived on the scene some four years later. This was synchronicity in action. Once Welch was gone, Fleetwood recalled hearing the haunting harmonies of another Californian folk-rock duo and took a bold move into an utterly radical rock territory: he increased the female content of the band and merged it with a guitarist-producer genius who could complete the jigsaw puzzle with his wistfully bopping melancholy. All the while, Fleetwood and McVie continued toiling in the background, providing the spine and soul of a new, improved, and genuinely prescient pop group poised for world domination. Anyone who wanted to know what the next phase of the plummeting phoenix known as Fleetwood Mac would be in 1975 only had to listen to the record made by Lindsey Buckingham and Stevie Nicks two years earlier. Entitled *Buckingham Nicks,* it contained all the nascent elements of a brand new wave for Mac to surf.

By now it is quite clear that Fleetwood and McVie were and are masters of surfing a crashing wave in the best way possible. To gain the best effect, they always managed to rise to the top of a wave, and capitalize on its full strength, by standing at the point where the wave is just about to break. Before breaking, a wave is approaching chaos but is not yet there; the wave still exists. Fleetwood and McVie had somehow learned the art of being on the verge of chaos, especially creative chaos, but never actually arriving there, which would mean their total dissolution. They were geniuses at managing insanity, of having people and things dissolve all around them, but without ever being in danger of actually dissolving themselves—the zen of chaos.

Once again they were surfing on the crest of a breaking wave known as Fleetwood Mac, which by now had taken on a life of its own and only had to be slightly prodded with a stick in order to reach the big time that always seemed just around the corner. But this time, the big time really was just around the corner; and the big stick they were given, like a gift of manna from heaven (or hell, in the case of all the suffering involved with their newest partners) came to them in the form of two more Californian dreamers.

It was to be a case of spontaneous combustion, right from the start. But, as Ariel Swartley once pointed out, combustion, however spontaneous, comes from a mixture of certain elements. Before those elements are in place, no amount of hoping can just start the flame. Another characterization of a performer, originally made by Terry Sutton about Janis Joplin, also comes closest to capturing the essence of an ensemble of performers such as Fleetwood Mac: These were its parts. Its whole is less the sum of its parts than the movement between them. The emotional movement between Buckingham and Nicks, charged with dark hubris at the best of times, would soon be perilously but creatively merged with the intense and abstract emotional movement between the historical and hysterical parts of Mac, charged with a mania for making music even in the worst of times. The result would be spontaneous indeed, even though it took a full ten years for it to "suddenly" explode on an unsuspecting musical world.

This manifestation of the platinum personality phase of their history clearly places them, in terms of the roller coaster ride of pop-mania, with its ultimate benchmark being set by The Beatles, at the top of the circus tent of commercially successful and wildly popular music. They could, ironically enough, be placed next to the Fab Four (not too close, of course, but nearby), and finally be appreciated as what they obviously became: the "Famous Five." But before that transformation could take place, Mac had to absorb the tumultuous two.

* * * * * * * * * *

Lindsey Buckingham and Stevie Nicks are so intertwined, personally, professionally, and creatively, that their lives can be viewed in tandem, since that indeed is the way the art of their songs is mutually crafted and delivered. Buckingham was born in Atherton, California, on October 3, 1949, and Nicks was born in Phoenix, Arizona, on May 26, 1948. They both attended Atherton High School, Buckingham one year behind Nicks, and their merger into one of the top-selling songwriting teams in history seems inevitably destined to occur.

They met each other at a party where a casual sing-along was in progress, apparently a Beach Boys song according to accounts, and from the moment they began to harmonize together, they instantly realized the creative charge that existed between them. They later explored this charge, or tried as best they could, in a youthful band called Fritz, which played locally; they opened for Jimi Hendrix and Janis Joplin, and even performed at their own 1967 graduation party. Ironically, in that year's summer of hope, as Peter Green was forming Fleetwood Mac in London, England, Buckingham and Nicks were forming a romantic and musical bond of their own that would come into full fruition seven years later, when they were utterly stunned to be invited to join the revolving-door band on the strength of their first and last solo record together.

Their peculiar love affair, so fraught with the ups and downs of highly emotionally and self-centered artists and their egos, would form the crux and crucible of the dynamic energy that came to be synonymous with the soon-to-be globally famous pop group, Fleetwood Mac. Their quite beautiful harmonies, when merged with the voice and feeling of Christine McVie, would create that unique and signature melodic style that would soon make Mac into a corporate brand of astonishing scale, scope, and influence.

Nicks added her own touch of mysticism in her song "Rhiannon," which scaled the charts in 1975. It was one of several very clever and intimate pop songs that Buckingham and Nicks brought along with them into the fervent mix that was Mac. Due to their readiness—indeed, their almost prefabricated "Mac-ness"—the first album with them featured, *Fleetwood Mac,* the eponymously titled record sometimes called "the white album," was able to be created in an astonishing 10 days! The working environment was charged with the crystalline knowledge of future cash. And it was almost as creatively cohesive as the old Peter Green days, maybe even more so.

* * * * * * * * * *

"The Beach Boys showed the way. It was Brian Wilson showing how far you have to go in order to make your own musical dream come true. Later, I would relate to Brian's struggle as an artist against a machine that tended toward serving the bottom line."
—Lindsey Buckingham

As I mentioned previously, if anyone *had* listened carefully to the self-titled *Buckingham Nicks* album of 1973, their only recording under that name, they would have clearly heard the future of Fleetwood Mac. That record, especially the track "Frozen Love," not only told the whole story, but it also seemed to be a prophecy of the whole whirlwind ride that was awaiting them. Unfortunately, few people bought or listened to the record. It would be rereleased to much acclaim in 1977, after *Rumours* made blissfully obvious to everyone the chemical and emotional magic of the newest combination of sounds and souls.

But Mick Fleetwood listened in 1974, and he listened hard. He admits to being floored by the technical prowess of Buckingham's guitar style and the gorgeous harmonies he produced with his young girlfriend Nicks. Fleetwood at that moment heard the future of Fleetwood Mac as clearly as if as time machine had opened its jaws and spit the sultry couple out onto his lap.Just as he had twice before, he felt that same spine-tingling sensation: he heard the future when he first bumped into Peter Green, and he heard the future again when he was first introduced to Bob Welch. But this time, he heard a future in the harmonic convergence of these two Californian folk-rockers and his old friends the McVies, a future that the rest of the world would also hear, very loud and very clear. In each of these three cases, it was the powerful electric charisma of the three distinctly different but somehow simpatico lead guitarists that would lead the way. It is actually not as far a leap—from Peter Green (or "The Blue Bomb," as I used to call him, in honor of his ethnic origins), to Bob Welch, a gifted practitioner of sustained restraint in his playing, to Lindsey Buckingham, frenzied and neurotic in his perfectionist stance—as one might imagine.

In 1975, as the myth goes, everything changed. Many observers have pointed out that in the previous eight years, with the ever-imploding and mutating band going through nine different personnel changes, their artistic and creative standards were evolving apace, but the one thing they lacked was enough stability to capitalize on their own talent. With this current lineup, they would have not only a rare stability lasting more than a dozen years (and now, historically, even longer), but also a firm grip on the magic of making hugely successful hit records. This, of course, is both ironic and paradoxical, considering that stability itself was still always the furthest thing away from the actual personal and professional interactions between these *final* band members. In fact, as we now all know from following the rock soap opera they quickly became, it was their unstable vulnerability as people that somehow clicked with a public ready to engage in the seriously schizoid flip side to the sixties.

The seventies, the decade of a dream deferred, and the eighties, the decade of a dream cashed in, would be the perfect social and political fodder for the new Mac's strategy for world domination: turn the basic blues into a slickly produced pop package that celebrates the transcendence of suffering through a compulsive immersion into its very core. It would become the soundtrack for a society intent on living as if there was no tomorrow. By diving so deeply into their own personal lives, sustaining their professional relationship for the sake of the music while their emotions and psyches melted down in public, they succeeded in capturing the tenor of the times as few before them had done. Who were these people? And how did they come to express the private feelings of so many listeners?

* * * * * * * * * *

In 1974, Mick Fleetwood was starting over once again. During the search for new studios in which to record the follow-up to *Heroes Are Hard To Find,* a much misunderstood album that met with a less than lukewarm response, an accident brought him into contact with the couple who would not only impact the career of his band, they would make that career a utopian reality. Buckingham recalls that,

> Mick Fleetwood was shopping in a supermarket somewhere and bumped into Thomas Christian. They got to discussing studios—because the group was getting ready to think about another album—so Thomas suggested Studio City in Van Nuys. So Mick went there and to demonstrate the qualities of the studio, the engineer Keith Olsen played him tracks from our Buckingham Nicks album, which was made there. As it happened, Stevie and I were in the next room working on some demos and I went in to see Mick stomping his feet to our music. A few weeks later, Bob Welch left and we were invited to join.[2]

In the middle of 1974, at the same time as Mac was doing its regular dissolving trick, Buckingham and Nicks were busy working on material for their follow-up record to their fine debut record. But there would be no follow-up, at least not the way they expected.

Buckingham and Nicks brought over a raft of demo tapes of the songs they had been developing for their second release and bestowed them on a stunned Fleetwood. The collection included the prototype versions of songs such as "Landslide," "Monday Morning," "I'm So Afraid," and the song that would become a performance signature of the future Mac, "Rhiannon." These songs were all absorbed into the Mac soup, and the band convened in February 1975 for studio sessions. In a remarkable 10 days, they had the debut album of the newly rejuvenated Fleetwood Mac, called by the name that would make so many listeners imagine that it was their first record. It was actually their 10th record, but who was counting? They were ready now, finally, to become an overnight success, a full decade since first forming in England. Wilfred Sheed once sarcastically remarked that Englishmen who go to California never recover. It seems true in the case of two drunken lads from London who had suddenly started to scale the heights of a pop world that was largely being orchestrated by a new Los Angeles sensibility.

Fleetwood and McVie had now become old hands at following the fickle finger of fate. Was it by chance that they agreed to move to Los Angeles? Was it by accident that they encountered their new collaborators there? They would not think so at all, having long ago learned that chance is the fool's name for fate. Welch had said that "fate decides," and Nicks would eventually say that "destiny rules." One cannot argue with their strong sense of events following a course of their own design. Fleetwood sums it up quite nicely:

> I've always felt a sense of depth and destiny about Fleetwood Mac. We always did everything on instinct. Nobody ever auditioned for Fleetwood Mac, and that's one of the reasons nothing ordinary ever happened to this band. Somewhere up there, I've always felt, was a little magic star, looking out for us. People were *meant* to be in this group![3]

It is not surprising that Fleetwood feels so maneuvered by fate. He has noted the goose bump feeling that arises when you just know something is so right.

> Several things were obvious from the start. Fleetwood Mac once again had a front line of three singers and songwriters, but more powerful than ever. Those early rehearsals reminded me so much of the energy that exploded when Peter Green brought us together with Jeremy Spencer. Right from the gitgo, we could tell that this was going to *play*. Lindsey was a brilliant player, and Chris and Stevie sounded as lovely as falling water. Plus, the vibes and energy were shimmering.
>
> I also found Stevie to be the most endearing combination of beatnik poet and cowgirl. From [t]he beginning she was determined to bring a mystical quality into this version of the band.[4]

Christine McVie, who instantly bonded with the new and additional feminine energy in the group, almost as an antidote to the bluesy and raucous masculinity that had pumped it forward for so long, also felt what she called "gooseflesh." She could not believe how great the three-part harmony sounded and wondered how long it could last, as if perpetually prepared for the Mac curse to descend on them again. But, naturally, no one could have imagined, even as secure as they were in the magic of this new compound they had created, just how big their "first" record would become, or indeed, that anything as remotely enormous as *Rumours* lay ahead of them. Even more impossible to imagine would have been that they would still be at it a decade later with a new record in 1987, then again with a 20-year reunion record in 1997, and then again with a special documentary called *The Dance* in 1998 that would clear the path for yet another late reunion in the early twenty-first century. Years later, Stevie Nicks confided her amazement that any of this had happened at all: "We fell into the American Dream, out of nowhere. We were just nowhere."[5]

So, with almost half the new record being provided by their new and exhilarating cohorts, John and Chrstine McVie moved into action in their Malibu beach sanctuary, and the former Chicken Shack "chick" moved into the well-seasoned second and most mature phase of her writing career. There she penned "Over My Head," a huge hit single for the group; "Say You Love Me"; "Warm Ways"; and "Sugar Daddy." Buckingham continued working on his opus "I'm So Afraid," and Nicks convinced her new mates to rerecord one of her songs from their duet record, "Crystal." After that, there was, and still is, no looking back.

* * * * * * * * * *

Once these players were in place, all of the ingredients had been prepared for a tasty pop dish that would set new standards, both in production values and in personal content, that only they would be able to reach again and exceed with their follow-up—if they all survived together. Either way, all of the essential elements were now synchronized and the listening audience was poised to hear the sound of spontaneous combustion. But there was also, quite literally, a considerable degree of combustion among the players themselves, in the form of the sort of personal fireworks we have come to expect from the institution of Fleetwood Mac. This would be both the beginning of the "platinum personalities" of the band and an ongoing development of their remarkable continuum, a pattern formed from the instability and off-kilter challenges of their creative way of working confidently through sheer pandemonium.

Of Buckingham and Nicks joining the band, Christine McVie recalls that Fleetwood came back and announced that he had found a fantastic guitar player. They did not know "who the girl was," since it was really only the guitar player they were interested in at the time—a new replacement for the long electric shadows of both Green and Welch, not to mention Spencer and Kirwan. In other words, the new heart and soul of the band, instrumentally speaking. But since, as Fleetwood has often explained, the band always functioned from a "go with the flow" attitude, making room for two new players seemed as easily done as said. He also explained to his main collaborative partner, bassist John McVie, the sole condition for Buckingham's joining the group was that hiring him meant including Stevie Nicks. He was especially cautious and sensitive to Christine's role and her potential reaction to another female presence in the group. Luckily for all concerned, especially the listening audience, Mrs. McVie's big-hearted response was an open invitation to more fresh talent in the band, especially since as a quiet introvert she seldom sought out the limelight anyway. She was quite content to let the newcomers jump into the bright lights while she remained, like her husband, content to contribute her gentle greatness from the shadows of the sidelines.

Fleetwood has often expressed his faith or strong belief in his own intuition, and having listened carefully to "Frozen Love," and having heard the future hiding there, he was utterly convinced of the newcomers complete rightness for their sudden role as Fleetwood Mac's new "stars." He firmly believed that Lindsey and Stevie were exactly what the doctor ordered for his ailing band. "Even though we were looking for a guitarist at first, we found that Stevie and Lindsey came as a duo. Their loyalty to one another was apparent, they were very much a couple, and a powerful package."[6]

What was not immediately apparent, however, since it had been withheld by the duo upon the invitation to join, was that their bond was not quite as secure as it first appeared. They were actually in the process of breaking up in slow motion, just as the group itself had been from the time of their inception. What would become even more apparent, especially in the near future of their upcoming massive stardom, was that their loyalty to the music was almost indestructible. Even when Nicks and Buckingham proceeded to fall apart as a couple, they remained creatively committed. And even when Fleetwood split from his wife, and the McVies, after years and years of troubled togetherness aggravated by his alcoholism, finally divorced each other, they too remained wedded to the musical group. This deep tenacity and hunger for ultimate success would hold them all in good stead during the making of their blockbuster and even beyond, keeping them as together as a scarily dysfunctional family.

The link of the shared desire of this group as a whole, bonding them all through a force hard to define for mere mortals like the listening audience, would form the emotional glue that no amount of excess, drug addiction, or interpersonal mayhem could unstick. Fleetwood Mac would eventually evolve into something like a cult in its own right. There was just no leaving.

* * * * * * * * * *

There were fireworks aplenty, and they emerged in an ongoing public display of personal hubris and animosity that eventually become the band's trademark. But mixed in generously with the personality and relationship clashes, there was always a staggering amount of talent waiting to be effectively harnessed. And if there was one thing Fleetwood himself was incredibly good at, it was harnessing the strengths of his collaborators while downplaying and defusing their weaknesses. According to the band's nominal leader, they worked on the new music together for several weeks, getting more and more excited all the time. They were hot and he knew it. He has described Lindsey Buckingham as the most creative guitar player since the bygone days of the "Green God," as he likes to call Peter Green; and as he watched Nicks dancing around the rehearsal room, he had the definite feeling that audiences were going to devour her. As usual, he was right on all counts.

But the insidious side of the business started encroaching immediately. Given his personal experiences with watching his close friends and band mates meltdown from the weight of the drugs in which they indulged, it is a little surprising just how easy it was for the new group, and for Fleetwood himself, to become entangled in ever more precarious lifestyle choices. As Fleetwood recalled, "There was a lot of cocaine around the studio, and we recorded our album in a somewhat Peruvian atmosphere. Until then, Fleetwood Mac hadn't had much experience with this Andean rocket fuel. Now we discovered that a toot now and then relieved the boredom of long hours in the studio with little nourishment. The devil's dandruff, in those days, was still the musician's friend."[7]

Almost immediately however, the famous inter-band competitions and jockeying for creative dominance took center stage, or at the center of backstage. Fleetwood reports that Buckingham was full of ideas about how the new band should sound, and that being a record producer at heart (almost as gifted as his own great mentor, Brian Wilson, in that respect) he felt strongly about how the music should come across. Buckingham especially butted heads right away with the main rogue alpha male of the outfit, John McVie,by trying to make suggestions to him about playing or tuning, when the taciturn and often supremely cranky bassist was simply above and beyond such input. For Fleetwood, however, ever the crazed optimist, all this proved very healthy in the long run, noticing that after the initial collision, there was a balancing act between their personalities. Indeed, it was an act that would continue, with great difficulty but still successfully, right up to the present day. Fleetwood noted that, "Lindsey was confronted by the fact that although he had been dominant in Buckingham-Nicks, now he was in a band, one which did things by consensus. Fleetwood Mac has always been a democracy"[8] True, a democracy of lunatics, but still a democracy nonetheless.

Leah Furham hit the myth right on the head when she referred to this period of the initial encounter, and the music that resulted, as a "harmonic convergence," a phrase that both describes the synchronicity of Mac meeting Buckingham-Nicks as well as the new-age overtones of what this would mean to the music's bottom line. In both senses of that term, creatively and profitably, the bottom line would become forever transformed, as would the motley crew of former Brits who had managed to morph into California pop-hipsters with an awesomely magic platinum touch. When the band convened to examine the result of this new collaboration, they were all quite stunned by the sense of predestined coherence to their new identity. Having finished the recording in June 1975, and titling it *Fleetwood Mac* for the purposes of "continuity," the freshly minted organization listened to the playback of their latest incarnation.

This really was reincarnation at its most obvious, even more sizzling in some ways than the vital rebirth that occurred with Welch. Fleetwood remembers thinking: *this record could be a monster*. As usual, he was absolutely correct. But all they had to do was persuade their record company of that same premonition. Up to that point, Fleetwood and the McVies had been producing records for the same company, Warner Brothers, for years, ever since the last Peter Green album, *Then Play On*. Their running family inside joke was that the band's usual average of 400,000 record sales per album would just about cover the cost of Warner Brothers' light bill! A bit of an exaggeration, but not much.

They—meaning mostly Fleetwood, the titular manager, agent, and resident den father—explained to the company that this was not just another Fleetwood Mac album. But the executive attitude was what he once called "ho-hum," and he readily admits that he could not really blame them. They felt the band's sales were somewhat static, which they were, and that they were a solid opening act but suffered from constant breakups, disintegration, and changing personnel with each album and tour. "The thought of selling millions of Fleetwood Mac records occurred to no one but the band, and record executives were used to the inflated fantasies of musicians. They heard them all the time. Another conflict with the label was over touring. I was determined that we had to take our music to our audience, even before our album was out on the streets. And so, against all conventional wisdom, Fleetwood Mac began its career as a touring band on May 15, 1975, in El Paso Texas."[9]

The fact that they always toured so relentlessly before, during, and after whatever latest album they were featuring, is one of the primary reasons for their longevity. We simply have to connect their tenacity at touring and performing, a hunger for live performance and for delivering music to their audience personally and up close to an intimately embraced fan base, with their ultimate long-term survival. Mick Fleetwood in particular has always believed in seeing the whites of their eyes as he delivers his music to his listeners. He is joined in this forever unsatisfied appetite for live music by his collaborator of so many years, the generally irascible and antisocial John McVie. And this shared commitment to never losing touch with their live audience has ensured their survival against all odds.

Unlike The Beatles—who became distantly detached from the howling of their own mass audience and almost instantly saw a downturn in their music's ability to communicate with them, as well as a drying up of their own creative well—Mac has managed to prove the crucial value of never stopping the two-way exchange that can happen only in live concerts. The Rolling Stones, today themselves a corporate behemoth, are almost the only similar musical giants of magnitude who learned this inviolable secret early on, and that is what has kept them on center stage: the combination of sweating performer and squirming audience that can never be replaced, no matter how brilliantly produced a group's studio sessions may be.

And ironically enough, this same Mac trade secret is also the way for us to understand the pivotal role of Buckingham-Nicks in their creative direction. The 1973 self-titled album by this duo of Californian folk rockers really was an excellent record, and it really did contain nearly all of the raw ingredients for making them members of Mac. But the audience never heard the record to the extent required to properly reward its fine songs with sales. Buckingham-Nicks had to have the touring and performing band to take the record out on the road and sell it to America.

As evidence of their perfectly positioned creative direction, one need only remember that half of the hoped for Buckingham-Nicks follow-up record literally became more than half of the next new Fleetwood Mac record. All Buckingham and Nicks would have needed to make it on their own back then was a fantastic backup band to present the record to its public. Then suddenly, on the verge of going under, they were invited to join Mac, and just as suddenly, they had the greatest backup band in the world. Their three-way harmonies with Christine McVie, and the alternating current moving from a Buckingham song, to a Nicks song, to a McVie song, gave them everything they needed and more. Of course, also ironically, their *new* backup band was actually 10 years old. And, as mentioned previously, the *new* Fleetwood Mac album that emerged in 1975 was actually their 15th record release. Nonetheless, it was indeed a harmonic convergence, with the writing, the harmonies, and the success to prove it.

But any central harmony among the group members themselves, as always within the Mac enterprise, was incredibly lacking. They would all soon embark on a roller coaster ride of immensely rewarding but intensely self-destructive proportions. It was the kind of ride made possible only if shared between intimate partners who also worked together professionally, and whose shared intimacy became the very core of their work as singer-songwriters. Such a ride has the kind of venom that is only possible between either siblings or ex-lovers. Ironically, it was probably the members of Fleetwood Mac sharing a lifestyle together as partners, collaborators, lovers, bandmates, ex-partners, and ex-lovers that enabled them to sustain the hunger to carry on. It was a surrogate family that produced a unique psychic armor for itself through living communally, both at Kiln House and earlier at Benifolds.

In this quintessentially Californian live work scenario, they put into practice a model their roots in the counterculture of the sixties had given them, a Grateful Dead–influenced, hippie-tinged arrangement, somewhat anarchistic but still somewhat utopian. It was dreamlike mirage that would collide head on with the mid-seventies arrival of monolithic stadium rock music. And they collided inevitably, with each other, together, and apart. They lived, fought, and played together as only an utterly dysfunctional family could have done. They just happened to be able to spin mesmerizingly mellow sounds out of the suffering they all shared.

Yes, the new band's coming together under the reincarnated leadership of two new frontline performers was certainly a harmonic convergence, at least in terms of the remarkably beautiful three-way harmonies of Christine McVie's smoked and stoked husky tones merging with the lovely shininess of Buckingham and Nicks's combination of sweet and sour emotional sauces. But there was very little harmony otherwise, as per usual. Fleetwood has observed that almost from the beginning, the demands of touring and remaining connected to their audience were exacting a toll on the freshly minted group:

One of the first things to break was John and Chris's marriage. John had been drinking heavily to cope with the pressures of launching the new band, and his moods began to blacken. He could be combative and quite frightening. And at that point, Chris decided she'd had enough. In San Francisco, the word went out that John and Chris were no longer occupying the same hotel room. This was all handled very low-key and there was no talk of breaking up the band.

They both knew it was too late for anyone to back out of Fleetwood Mac now, since too much was at stake, especially our pride. I know that Chris felt very bad about it, because she hadn't stopped loving McVie. So despite the heartbreak, especially John's under the circumstances, we all soldiered on.[10]

It was a harmonic collision, all right—soon Buckingham and Nicks would publicly break up, but still stay in the group; then Fleetwood's long-strained marriage would finally fall apart, and Fleetwood himself, ever addicted to fresh chaos, would eventually embark on a two-year affair with Nicks, while Christine would seek solace in the arms of the man who fixed her spotlight. And all the while, the personal entries and letters they would each pen in their diaries, containing everything from confessions to declarations, would slowly surface like ripples on the pop culture pond. Their love-hate letters to each other, and their diary entries to themselves, would be transformed into strangely haunting and universal anthems of a special sort of shared angst everyone could get into.

Everyone except, of course, the gifted but recalcitrant John McVie. Not being a songwriter or singer, he had to content himself with instilling raw rage into his brilliant bass lines. These razor-sharp ripples felt a lot like rumors, and they were. That's what John McVie said was going on, so why not call their first reincarnated Fleetwood Mac album what it really was—a slightly bent collection of rumors.

In a very real and ironic sense, that could be the generally inarticulate McVie's one lyric, a one-word song: "Rumours," spelled the English way. And they were all true. But they did not start in 1977 with the release of the album of the same name. They started the way everything always started with Fleetwood Mac—first, they lived the content of the songs, then they wrote the songs themselves. And in 1975, with the release of their first album *Fleetwood Mac,* to have that magical mixture of elements certain to cause apparently spontaneous combustion, they launched themselves onto the perilous voyage of self-discovery and mutual annihilation that we all listen to with such contentment.

* * * * * * * * * *

The first of several blockbuster singles was released while the group was still touring. In its newly remixed version, "Over My Head" sold more than 400,000 copies during its first month and found a spot in the American top ten in November 1975. This amazing accomplishment has to be appreciated in the context of Mac normally being content to sell that many copies of their whole album. With the approach of Christmas, Mac was somewhat collectively stunned by the fact that they had a gold record, a very successful tour supporting it, and four hit singles drawing from its content. Times were changing for the formerly British blues band, and they were not looking back—although sometimes looking forward was equally difficult, for the usual reasons.

Buckingham, ever the perfectionist and production control fetishist, had immediate adjustment problems. "I had mixed feelings during the first album," he once told the music press, "There were things important to me I'd given up for the sake of playing team ball."[11] But despite this personal and professional limitation, he also saw the writing on the wall, emphasized by giant dollar signs, which perhaps made his attempted adaptation more palatable. "There was never any conscious effort to fit into their styles other than say, doing their songs onstage. Maybe one of the reasons Fleetwood Mac has been able to survive for so long is that they've been able to change."[12] Yes, it was definitely one of the reasons. Christine modestly felt the presence of *something special.*

Of course, one thing that did not change was Mac's allegiance to the pursuit of both musical excellence and personal oblivion through the extensive use of drugs. Only the drugs changed. They moved from the expansion mode of the sixties, with mountains of hashish and acres of LSD blotters, to the party mode of the seventies and beyond, with mountains of cocaine and gallons of equally pricey champagne.

Other critics have noted the early effects of crossing this shaky borderline. "The chiffon-draped look with which Nicks would emerge was not the only enduring Fleetwood Mac staple to come out of the first heady months of the Buckingham-Nicks/Fleetwood Mac collaboration. It was during the recording of the *Fleetwood Mac* album that cocaine also surfaced in the group. The mid-seventies took a light view of the drug; if everyone was doing it, it could not be addictive, much less dangerous. Musicians with no time to spare and money to burn thought of the white fairy dust as a gift from the gods and used it accordingly. Fleetwood Mac was no different. "The subculture of drugs was really considered to be the norm in the circles we traveled in," remarked Buckingham.[13]

So quietly and with the subtlety of all truly destructive urges, the band embraced their new drug, which naturally assisted them in completing 90-city performance tours with all the fervor for which they were already famous. Touring always was, and still remained, one of the key features of their astronomical success. No matter how big they became, they never stopped delivering the goods to stadiums of writhing bodies. "And I loved it," declared Fleetwood himself, "For me, this was it. A band live is what a band is. Making records—twelve songs in eighteen months—is not what a band is. We were brought up to believe in playing live, and if you sell a few records, you're lucky."[14] I would say they were very lucky. Fleetwood continued:

> But it was the sound of this band that killed me. Chris and John were at the top of their form despite Chris giving John the elbow, as he so succinctly phrased it. And it was totally fascinating to watch our new members blossom into their own. Lindsey was incredibly fluid as a live guitarist, and I was immediately impressed with the amount of obsessive thought that went into his art. Being with us now, he was really forced to change his personality in some ways. Before he had been in control, now he was in an established band and had to tread a bit more lightly than he might have wanted to. After we made that first record, Stevie began to come out of her shell and talk as a person in her own right.[15]

Fleetwood has also remarked on the constant theorizing about why this particular version of Fleetwood Mac, the 10th line up in eight years, became so successful. According to him, the truth was, as usual, an accident. It was a matter, he said, of keeping one's ears open. He just heard them in the studio and he *knew*. That kind of knowing is what makes him one of the best musicians and best band leaders in the pop music world, bar none.

And yet, also as usual, destiny rules and fate decides. As Fleetwood put it,

> Ahh, cruel fate, bitter destiny! As Fleetwood Mac crawled and clawed our way back to the top, the gods were laughing at us and having sport. As *Fleetwood Mac* inched its way to the summit of the charts, our lives were snarled by disharmony and pain. In the year it took us to make our second album with the new lineup, the record that would change our lives forever (*Rumours*), we all got divorced. The whole band.
>
> In the past, events like these would have killed Fleetwood Mac. But not now. We all knew it was too late to stop. So we kept the band together, continued to work, and proceeded to make the best music of our career, in the form of a record that would become one of the biggest selling albums in the history of commercial recording.[16]

Original bassist Bob Brunning has a clear grasp of how this almost decade-long overnight success occurred. "Fleetwood Mac caught on as a performing band as it never had before, playing in huge stadiums all summer long. This was partly due to the success of the album, but also because of the important role played by the exotically costumed, foxy-looking Stevie Nicks. Fleetwood Mac had at last found itself a strong visual image to go with the fine rock music it had always been able to provide."[17]

At this stage, they truly appeared to have everything they ever wanted in terms of both creative and commercial success. Yet it was at this same stage that the glue holding them all together started to dry up and crack in the most dramatic and "Mac-like" fashion. In the midst of their little triad of relationships coming apart at the seams just when the brass ring was within their grasp, it has been observed that perhaps Fleetwood was the lucky one in the crew. He did not have to work closely in a professional format with his private partner, the way the McVies and Buckingham and Nicks did, so perhaps he escaped at least a little of that particular angst. But there were other forms of angst at which he himself specialized. Not working with Jenny Boyd, sister-in-law of rock god George Harrison, meant also not necessarily living with her, either. If too much togetherness doomed John and Christine, not enough togetherness doomed Mick and Jenny, while personal growth and independence issues seems to be the specialty of Stevie and Lindsey.

Given the dangerous drugs and relaxation techniques they were all employing to continue at their frenetic pace, it is hardly surprising that Fleetwood did not really even seem to notice that his own marriage was as destroyed as those of his long-time collaborator and his new found bandmates. "I was basically having a ball being crazy and being socially how I wanted to be," was his own take. Meanwhile, fellow rhythm master McVie often observed that they were living in a bubble called *us and them*. All of the band members were slowly being sucked down a drain of dazzling success and withering personal failure. Fleetwood, almost as if he had no control over the circumstances in which he found himself, comments wistfully about the real family crisis caused largely by his musical family and its demands: "I was stoned half the time. I watched them walk down the garden path , just in slow motion, going, 'Well, there's my wife and there's my two children, walking out of my life.' It was all like a dream."[18]

But the tours went on, and Mac went onward and upward. By December 1975 their six-month marathon of grueling service to a dream was winding down. The period has been called "emotionally disemboweling," and while that is slightly melodramatic, nothing else comes quite as close to describing the harrowing reality they lived through. But still, it had only been a dress rehearsal for their next and biggest ride of all.

It was a year since the almost utterly unknown newcomers had joined a famous but imploding rock band, and probably the most important year in their still young lives. Nicks notes the sudden shock of it all: "We were not famous. The record had just come out. We hit the road. Then within three months, we were all famous and on our way with the hits."[19] She was coming into her own, just as the band was coming into its own. She was a huge part of it, and she knew it. And as usual, she expressed it best in one of her classic Nicks dirges, "Landslide": "Well, I've been afraid of changing, cause I've built my life around you. But time makes you bolder, even children get older. And I'm getting older too. If you see my reflection in the snow-covered hills, well the landslide will bring it down." But first, a landslide would bring them all up, so high that the snow-addled view became distorted beyond recognition.

BUCKINGHAM NICKS:
RELEASED 1973, ANTHEM RECORDS/POLYDOR

All the secret ingredients were here, hiding in plain view two years before the fact. On my original vinyl edition of their first self-titled solo record—stamped "Collector's Edition" since it contains the original version of "Crystal," a big hit when rerecorded with the Mac-treatment on their new band's new record—I can clearly hear the oddly nascent stirrings of the sound that would make them both famous and infamous. With its sexually suggestive cover, a nude from the chest-up portrait of a classic hippie girl and her Svengali-like partner, it proved the perfect fodder for a 1975 cash-in by the label based on the surprising fact that the duo had just become household names as the newest comets to streak through the Mac solar system.

For once, the delirious hype on a record cover was actually quite true. Lindsey Buckingham and Stephanie Nicks first got together in 1968 in a San Francisco band called Fritz, opening on the same bills as big names such as Santana, Chicago, and Jimi Hendrix. Following the band's demise in 1971, the two remained together and released this album in 1973.

Even though he had heard the tape of this record only once, it was at the request of Mick Fleetwood that early in 1975 Buckingham and Nicks not only became part of Fleetwood Mac, but they actually *became* Fleetwood Mac. "Once you hear this album," the liner notes declare, "you'll know why." Now we all know why. It seems inevitable in retrospect, like most of the incredibly important events in all our own lives.

From the very beginning of this record, as he would throughout his Mac career right up to their latest recording in 2003, Buckingham is already bemoaning what appears to be his disintegrating relationship with Nicks. This ironic self-analysis would serve as the raw material for practically every song the duo ever wrote, whether together or apart. In the opener, "Don't Let Me Down Again," a song the band would resurrect and perform live from the lofty but cold summits of 1980, he is basically pleading with his lover not to treat him "this way." Wakeful ears will recognize immediately the basic thread of every blues song ever written: "don't treat me so bad, I'm the best you've ever had, you wanna leave now and find a new start, its gonna kill me if you break my heart. Once you let me down again, you're just bound to see the end." It could have been a Leadbelly song, for all intents and purposes.

But one of their most important and prophetic song follows it. "Long Distance Winner"—the title I almost wanted to give this 40-year appreciation of Fleetwood Mac—seems to contain many prescient moments that appear to encapsulate the dynamics of both their relationship and their future fame. This time, it is Nicks making a statement to her lover with a song that also serves as a cautionary tale for a band to which she did not yet even belong. "You love only the tallest trees. I come running down the hill but you're fast, you're the winner, the long distance winner. But not unlike the blue white fire, you burn brightly in spite of yourself, I bring the water down to you, but you're too hot, too hot to touch." Nicks then reprises her feelings in "Races Are Won": "Tell me I'm wrong, I can't believe you. We've tried a thousand times before. Rained on reasons kept us believing that there might still be more. Races are won. Some people win, some people always have to lose."

The two most important songs on their solo record are, of course, "Crystal," to be reproduced to great effect by Mac's eponymous white album in 1975; and "Frozen Love," the classic from the record that made Mick Fleetwood stand up and take notice. As mentioned, what he noticed was his own future. When Nicks intones the mournful celebration of her lover in "Crystal," she creates a magical kind of adulation: "Do you always trust your first initial feeling. Special knowledge, holds truth, bears believing. I turned around and the water was closing all around. Like a glove, like the love that had finally found me. Then I knew, in the crystalline knowledge of you." Amazingly, the Mac version of this song would only increase its weirdly worshipful tone, while at the same time injecting it with the necessary punch and unique harmonies to make it one of their first big hits together.

But few songs capture the essence of a love affair run aground like the harrowing "Frozen Love," the song that rewarded Fleetwood for always trusting his initial instincts. Again Nicks declares, with a considerable confidence that belied her own insecurities, "You may not be as strong as me, and I may not wish to teach you. It may be hard to keep up with me but I'll always be able to reach you. And if you go forward, I'll meet you there. And if you climb up through the cold freezing air, look down below you, search out above. And cry out to life for a frozen love." Comparisons of this quite beautiful but disturbing love song with either the title song of the latest Mac album, *Say You Will* from 2003, or with their shared closing epistles on the same record, "Say Goodbye" and "Goodbye Baby," will send chills up and down your spine.

This sensational love-hate dialogue is something like what Robert and Elizabeth Barrett Browning may have penned back and forth if they had been rock stars, if they had been even more dysfunctional than they were, and if their lives had been consumed by celebrity and numbed by cocaine. But for Mick Fleetwood, when he heard the dazzling guitar of Buckingham and the dulcid tones of Nicks, it was as if heaven had opened its gates and tossed him two new angels to add to his expanding playground. His genius is in large part the ability to recognize genius in its raw form, in the shape of Peter Green, in the shape of Bob Welch, and in the shape-shifting personas of Buckingham and Nicks.

FLEETWOOD MAC:
RELEASED 1975, WARNER BROTHERS

From the moment the needle hit the record groove in those lamented lost days of vinyl, we knew we were in for a strange ride. "This is a strange trip," one of my friends, who was inclined to talk that way, said in preparation. Those of us who had begun hearing about the otherworldly mythology of the original Fleetwood Mac in 1967 and who began listening in earnest in 1968 to their stellar "dog and dustbin" debut album, were understandably surprised when we first heard the reborn Mac under Bob Welch's writing and playing aura in 1970. Although the glorious presence of Christine McVie's voice and delicate songs ameliorated most of our young men's feelings of loss over Green's departure, it was the mysteriously lyrical second phase of Mac that kept our allegiance firmly in place.

Records like *Future Games* and *Bare Trees,* and most of *Mystery To Me,* are undeniable classics of bluesy and mystical pop-rock hybrids of the highest order. But of course, nothing could have prepared us for the arrival of Buckingham and Nicks. Some of my friends bolted at this point, abandoning Mac as sellouts, has-beens, or worse, and followed the flow leading to the hot loads of Led Zeppelin and sparkling heights of Genesis and Yes, great bands all. But the person who first introduced me to Peter Green's Fleetwood Mac, the one who played me those first three astonishing blues and experimental acid-rock records, also forced me to sit and listen carefully to everything from *Kiln House* in 1970 to *Heroes are Hard to Find* , in 1974. And he also forced me to listen and realize how, much to our amazement, Fleetwood Mac had morphed into one of the most quintessentially perfect pop bands in music history.

Produced so well it was scary in its attention to sonic detail, Buckingham's Brian Wilson–like vibes merged with the supernatural twinning of the Nicks and McVie feminine voices, churned relentlessly forward by the suddenly even more obviously brilliant bass and drum lines of the rejuvenated Fleetwood and McVie engine. Buckingham's guitar work made us understand and acknowledge what Fleetwood, ever the electricity-drenched road hound, heard and felt in his playing. More nervous than the visionary Green feeling, more angry than the spooky Welch touch, Buckingham exploded into a perfectly realized role as technically clever producer and resident guitar genius. His soft playing in a gentle McVie song like "Warm Ways" and his fierce playing in a rocker like "Rhiannon" made us appreciate that, in relative terms, this "debut" record of a reincarnated eight-year-old British blues band was every bit as good in its way, as *Rubber Soul* was for The Beatles, or *Pet Sounds* was for the Beach Boys. And of course, these early feelings of, "Oh my God, this guy can really play!" would only be multiplied many times over two years later with their follow up of *Rumours.* He forced us to like him in spite of ourselves—he is that good.

The record opens and closes with Buckingham and Nicks songs, and in many ways, the Lindsey-Stevie sandwich that chef Fleetwood had concocted was inherently their own follow up record, on the heels of their own debut two years earlier. So it would pretty much remain for the entire rest of the Fleetwood Mac saga: John and Mick producing the rhythmic tidal waves on which Stevie, Lindsey and Christine would surf. Once a formula is found to be so winning, only a fool would ever mess with it. Except, of course, when Buckingham was handed the reins later on and was allowed to make an experimental Mac record that is still exotic to this day. But that was not a fool messing around; it was a seriously gifted talent with too much money, time, and drugs, and too much fear of the hot young breath of punk music breathing down his neck.

From the vantage point of 1975, the self-titled *Fleetwood Mac* was a bull in the china shop. "Monday Morning," the album's opening number, can easily be imagined as one of the follow-up Buckingham songs he conceived for their second solo record. In it, he conducts his usual survey of all the possible reasons his peace of mind is disturbed by his girlfriend: "First you love me then you fade away, I can't go on believing this way, I got nothing but love for you, so tell me what you really wanna do. But I don't mind, I don't mind, I'll be there if you want me to, no one else that could ever do. Got to get some peace in my mind."

But it is when the husky tones of Christine McVie, supported by the suddenly stunning harmonies between herself and the new members, that we know a new Fleetwood Mac has arrived fully formed. "Warm Ways" is so gentle, it is shocking, with her trademark muskiness hovering perfectly above the softly swirling rhythms beneath it: "Sleep easy by my side, into gentle slumber you can hide. You made me a woman tonight, sleep until the morning light. I, I'm waiting for the sun to come up, I can't sleep with your warm ways." Something tells me she may not exactly have been referring to the tempestuous ex-husband in this regard. In "Blue Letter," an otherwise customary love-song-rocker, Buckingham abruptly seems to announce his guitar prowess with the long sinewy and jagged lines of passive-aggressive energy which has since become his own trademark.

But then the surprise arrives. "Rhiannon," a Nicks song she had penned as a kind of feminist goddess–channeled ode to the Celtic witch-healer-lover of the same name, declares with equal ferocity her own maturity, both as a singer and a songwriter. She steps out of Buckingham's shadow in this one, and realizes that she never has to be sheltered there again. She can manufacture her own poetic shelter. Plus, the audiences went wild over her personal delivery style, a paradoxical mixture of saintly mysticism and slutty rockchick that somehow worked perfectly for the time.

This is the track that made us all realize that Mac was newly reconstituted and meant business. Buckingham's guitar in this one almost forgets itself and swings into a kind of high gear that almost competes with the singer's message. In this one, everybody's is playing flat out. Fleetwood's drumming has a new sense of urgency, pumped along by McVie's incredibly articulate bass lines, shaped into a slippery beat that makes him feel like a lead guitarist too. "All your life," Nicks snarls, "you've never seen, a woman—taken by the wind—would you stay if she promised you heaven, will you ever win?" And one of her most telling and prophetic lines, "Dreams unwind, love's a state of mind."

"Over My Head" is another classic Christine song, rightly adored by the public as the nearly perfect pop song it is. It also serves as the perfect emblem for the new band's personal intimacy and emotional intensity. They were all in over their heads by this point. Side One closes with Nicks's "Crystal," a song that seems to sum up everything about her that the public finds so endearing, a mixture of outlandish vulnerability, childlike worship, and romantic doom. "How the faces of love have changed, turning the pages. And I have changed, but you, you remain ageless. Drove me through the mountains, through the crystal like and clear water fountain. Drove me like a magnet, to the seas, to the sea."

Three of the first five songs on the new and improved debut Mac album were by this precocious young duo, pulled by strong accidental forces into the crazy orbit of Mick Fleetwood. Their private relationship and public disputes would form the fuel for some of the contemporary Mac mythology, stirred as it was into the already boiling cauldron of marital and professional madness already underway. They became the emblem for doomed lovers everywhere, couples who supposedly stayed together in the name of something bigger than themselves.

With "Say You Love Me," the conflicted love dirge by Christine that jumps onto the bandwagon of partnership dissolution set in motion by the other obsessive themes explored by the new turbocharged Mac. "Baby baby, hope you're going to stay away, cause I'm getting weaker, weaker, weaker everyday. I guess I'm not as strong as I used to be, and if you use me again, it'll be the end of me." But of course, she is now twice as strong as she used to be, since detaching herself, at least personally, from the self-destructive syndrome she and her former husband had become. Professionally, it was another story: the Mac machine required bodies and souls to continually add to the soup of dreams and nightmares their careers had become. She was only too happy, and sad, to comply, providing the kind of mellow and co-dependent celebration of the death of intimacy which eventually became one of her own stylistic devices.

One of the great strengths of the record was its constantly shifting emotional landscape, an alternating current from Buckingham, to Nicks, to McVie, which echoes the call and response format of early blues music, but without the structure holding it up. Now their blues was being wrapped in a shiny new package. "Landslide" is the best example of this. "Oh mirror in the sky, what is love? Can the child within my heart rise above? Can I sail through the changing ocean tides? Can I handle the seasons of my life?" One of the most incredible things about a great Nicks song, apart from how long and convoluted some of them can be and still succeed, is how much perfect sense they can make, even if we do not have the slightest idea what she is talking about sometimes. Hers was the most completely evolved form of confessional singing; she was utterly unafraid of courting the near disaster of cliché in order to fully express her feelings. And those feeling resonated powerfully with the new age disillusionment of the mid-1970s.

"World Turning" is a clever Mac revision of the 1968 Peter Green classic, "The World Keeps on Turning." In his version, he declares that he does not have to look for worries, since worries and trouble find him all by themselves; that he has got to keep his feet on the ground, all the while accompanying himself brilliantly on an acoustic guitar. In the Mac version, a kind of silent tribute to their long lost grail-boy, they swing into that special high gear they keep reserved for special occasions like this one. Christine McVie and Buckingham take writing credits, with Christine belting out a gentle lament about the world getting her down, while Lindsey does some dexterous picking that does not mimic so much as evoke the lost salad days of their early blues roots. But the song is now covered in the crisp gift wrap of an expensive pop song. It starts to drift away just at the point where Peter Green would have been gearing up the guns to really get the thing underway. It is an oddly elegiac piece, for reasons that remain unclear. "Maybe I'm wrong, but who's to say what's right? I need somebody to help me through the night."

Switching channels swiftly, one of the key secrets to their record's success, Christine McVie sings a soft and gentle ode to the fantasy of having a permanent protector. "Sugar Daddy," ostensibly about everyone's favorite dream of someone to look after them, makes its plaintive plea very clear, "I'm not asking for love, just a little sympathy." The album ends with one of Buckingham's finest monuments to self-doubt, "I'm So Afraid," a harrowing confession about the seemingly inevitable slide into depression as a result of unchecked feelings and too deep an allegiance to our own personal perspective. "I've been alone all the years, so many ways to count the tears. I never change, I never will. I'm so afraid of the way I feel. Days when the rain and the sun are gone, black as night. Agony's torn at my heart too long. So afraid, slip and I fall, and I die." Shades of the kind of angst in which Green, Spencer, and Kirwan all specialized, it is Buckingham's blues, but covered in a blanket of pop sparkles that only barely conceal the horrors underneath. It is blues that cuts so deep it becomes purple.

With this remarkable debut, the new crew was fully fledged and ready to reach for the ring. This was an almost perfect pop record. Their shimmering follow-up to it would actually become just that, a perfect pop record, of the sort that only they could have made in quite they way they made it. It would be their manifestation of what The Beatles did with their album *Revolver*—not stylistically of course, but even more importantly, a masterpiece in terms of making something as perfect as it could possibly be, and something only they could make.

Other significant releases of 1975: Physical Graffiti by Led Zeppelin; *Blood on the Tracks* by Bob Dylan; *Tonight's the Night* by Neil Young; *There's No Place Like America Today* by Curtis Mayfield; *Another Green World* by Brian Eno; *Rhinestone Cowboy* by Glen Campbell; *Born to Be with You* by Dion; *Al Green Is Love* by Al Green; *Waves* by Jade Warrior; *Still Crazy After All These Years* by Paul Simon; *A Night at the Opera* by Queen; *Hissing Of Summer Lawns* by Joni Mitchell; *Horses* by Patti Smith; *Koln Concert* by Keith Jarrett.

The *Rumours* Are True: Arrival of the Blockbuster

6

Sometimes it seems that anyone who did not own a copy of this mid-seventies monument to middle-of-the-road musical mayhem must have been living in the Sahara Desert. People who did not otherwise own or even listen to records owned and listened to this one. It has become the brand name for love affairs in which the love is conspicuously missing but the affair somehow drags on (and on, and on). But the perfect pop record they were all apparently born to make, the record that *made* them, was almost never made at all. As the almost-never-quoted John McVie put it, "The energy level within the band slumped each time there was a personnel change—but we got over each successive hump, and our optimism was re-achieved. There was never a sustained period of depression or else we'd have split up. The highest points were the original band and the current line-up."[1] The brilliant bassist seems not to want to count the quiet but superb four years and five albums that Bob Welch created out of the morbid gloom of their post-Green phase. That is however, his prerogative.

Of course, the members of Fleetwood Mac were not the only rock musicians to sacrifice their personal lives to the insatiable god of the road and its church, the buying marketplace. But they did do it on a grand scale so operatic, so soap-opera drenched, that the public began to appreciate the fact that they were more important than the very inner lives of the artists they loved. Sacrificing your sanity in the name of your work and its public—now *that's* an accomplishment of the highest and most compulsive order. Few people, apart from the great melancholics such as Brian Wilson, John Lennon, or

Bob Dylan, ever went as far as to compromise their consciousness in the pursuit of their muse and its material reality.

"The divorce," Fleetwood remarked, "didn't really hit me too hard at first because I just kept working on the band." He continued:

> The McVies' marriage cracked up for good while we were living in a rented house in Florida, having taken some time off from touring. We decided to use the vacation to rehearse and write for the next album. "Go Your Own Way" and a couple of other songs were written there. That was our attitude, no matter how awful things became, the band had to come first. John and I became very close to each other again because our marriages were both failing. We rode around the USA in our station wagons and talked and talked. That's how we got through.[2]

It was becoming clear that, to put it as mildly as Bob Brunning does, the interpersonal problems plaguing the band members began to affect the atmosphere surrounding Fleetwood Mac. The founding father, Fleetwood, though himself mired in his own difficulties, was still seen as both the psychic glue holding the group together through all trials, and as even the in-house marriage counselor, despite the fact that he was among the least talented of marital partners on earth. "When we started recording the follow up album to *Fleetwood Mac* in early 1976 we were all in an emotional ditch. Everybody knew everything about everyone. But I was definitely piggie-in-the-middle, though in actual fact my marriage was going down the tubes too. But I was spared the in house up front situation. I didn't have to actually *work* with my ex-spouse!"[3]

On that score, McVie has noted that though rocky, his relationship had certainly started off well enough. "Yes, it was wonderful, because we didn't know any different. Maybe in retrospect our problems might not have happened if Chris hadn't joined the band...We just reached the point where we couldn't be in the same room together. We've probably spent more time with each other than most couples who have lived together for twenty-five years. We had no individuality, no separation."[4] McVie's legendary drinking problems, dating back to the days when he first joined John Mayall at the impressionable age of 17, certainly did not help matters. Brunning has characterized him as affable, witty, gentle, and amenable when sober, but extremely difficult and belligerent when drunk.

Once again, there was some degree of cursory discussion about whether the pair would leave Fleetwood Mac to ease the tension, but of course that never happened. As Brunning has also pointed out in explanation, "There seemed to be a kind of corporate loyalty to the band from all its members which apparently superseded the personal traumas they were experiencing."[5] Indeed, if the couple had left, there would never have been an album called *Rumours,* simply because the rumors would not have been *about* anything. The same traumatic truth applies if anyone else had left, for that matter, such as the third angle of the tortured emotional triangle, the newest members of the group. Though not technically married, they were in many ways more married than any average couple, to the point of being two sides of the same creative coin. And though they had been partners since 1970, their unraveling relationship (actually already coming apart when they first joined the group) provided more than enough emotional entanglements to fuel the fire. But they were also as steadfast as the others, and like the McVies, their personal problems would never ever permit them to abandon the entity called Fleetwood Mac.

Nicks has a suitably straightforward explanation for the phenomenon of their all sticking together:

> Because basically we really like each other and once we go on stage, all those problems, the fights, the arguments, the disagreements, they all disappear. That two hours on stage is beautiful, and always was, even when things were at their worst. Really, each one of is way too proud and way too stubborn to walk away from it. I wasn't going to leave. Lindsey wasn't going to leave. What would we have done? Sat around LA and tried to start new bands? Nobody wanted to do that. We liked touring. We liked making money, and we liked being a band. It was just, grit your teeth and bear it![6]

You have to admire her candid nature.

The band was passing through something—not something new, but something all too customary for their own good. McVie was seen in the company of Peter Green's ex-girlfriend and also fantasized about Linda Ronstadt. Stevie started a relationship with Don Henley of the Eagles, the only other band as big as hers, and Christine began an affair with the group's lighting director, Curry Grant. (This last one is a favorite of mine, falling into the arms of the man who controls your spotlight and makes sure you were properly illuminated.) As Christine put it so well,

> After ten years of struggling, it would have been silly to throw it all away. We proved to each other that we had a pretty strong character as a band, that we could cope with the problems and surmount them, which we did. The bonds were just too great to sever just because there was an emotional ruckus going on. Everyone cared about everyone else. There might have been problems between John and me but that didn't mean we didn't care about Mick, Stevie and Lindsey, and vice versa. There was a certain responsibility not only to the band but to the whole unit. There were a lot of people on the payroll. And then there was the fact that we were *good*. Whatever happened, that was the overriding factor. The band was at the pinnacle of their career, and we had a responsibility not to break that up for anything as trivial as a divorce.[7]

"Resilience in the face of adversity" may as well be the middle name of the group itself. Even though the obvious, deeply human emotional strains could well have demolished the group, Buckingham, Nicks, and the McVies decided to take the only creative course open to them as truly committed and chaotic artists and performers: they turned it *all* into their art. Their album would eventually come to be a mirrored receptacle for everything they were feeling. Who knew that so many members of the listening public would hear the heartache and imagine that the group was so effectively voicing *their own* intimate insecurities. That oddity, plus how remarkable it sounded at the time, made the record the hit it was.

Christine, always the coolest and most grounded member of the wrecking crew, recalls that "The outcomes of the various separations and upheavals in the band that caused so many *rumours* are in the songs. We weren't aware of it at the time, but when we listened to the songs together, we realized they were telling little stories. We were looking for a good name for the album that would encompass all that, plus the rumor that they band had given up, the most active rumor flying about. And I believe it was John one day, who said we should call it *Rumours*.[8]

Fleetwood still expresses some confusion about the whole circus, especially how it began to affect the newest members of the group so dramatically. That, even though he would eventually himself succumb to Nicks's charm and launch into a mesmerizing two-year affair off to the side of all the other madness around him.

> I remember that Stevie went into the sessions for the new album as a single lady, as did Chris. At the time, she said something in a joking way about Lindsey being more interested in his guitar than he was in her, and she got tired of it and left. There was some conflict, I recall, about the "cracking up, shacking up" line in "Go Your Own Way," which Stevie felt was unfair and which Lindsey felt strongly about. Stevie has also said that the relationship between her and Lindsey was already a bit rocky when they joined the band. As Stevie began to express herself more, as she became a star, things didn't get any better....These were the less than ideal conditions under which Fleetwood Mac began to record our next album.[9]

Once again, if the new couple had divulged that they were splitting up upon joining, *Rumours* may never have been made; and Fleetwood, though remembering the details correctly, is forgetting the amazing fact that such conditions were actually, on the contrary, "more than ideal" for the making of an album as idiosyncratic and intimately harrowing as *Rumours* was, and still is.

* * * * * * * * * *

While it was clear that their yesterday may have been gone, it was also equally obvious that their today was dreadfully threatened with extinction. Their fearless, and occasionally mindless, leader booked them into a Sausalito, California, studio for nine weeks, where they all repaired with family, friends, and "assorted helpers" to begin work. Fleetwood comments that in Sausalito was "where the real Fleetwood Mac craziness really started."

Fleetwood Mac had been recorded in a quick three months. The new album would take us almost a year, during which we spoke to each other in clipped, civil tones while sitting in small airless rooms listening to each other's songs about our own shattered relationships. I mean, it was heavy. We all felt so fragmented and fragile. These sessions were almost indescribably difficult.[10]

The gifted producer Richard Dashut, who deserves considerable credit as an audio master for guiding this insane flock towards success instead of dissolution, has his own take on the dynamics.

The band had brought some great songs with them, but they needed arrangements and a unified sound. All I can say is that it was trial-by-ordeal, and the craziest period of our lives. We went four or five weeks without sleep, doing a lot of drugs. I'm talking about cocaine in such quantities that at one point I thought I was really going insane. The whole atmosphere was really tense, with arguments all the time and people storming in and out. To relieve the tension we'd look for sexual release, but even that didn't help much. The only refuge was in the music. Music was the only release we could find. And yet, I turn on the radio today, and they're *still* playing that album. It took a long time, but our system worked for us. Our attitude is—if that's what it took, so be it![11]

Creating that "unified sound" out of all the harrowing raw material in those songs fell largely to the new wunderkind member of the band, Lindsey Buckingham. Some people feel that considering his pivotal role in retuning the Mac engine, the apparent neglect he received from the public and critics was probably extremely irritating to a man of his consummate technical confidence. He once clarified his role to Timothy White for *Rock Lives* as not necessarily that of a guitarist, a writer, or a singer, though he was superb at all three (with the possible exception of his shaky staccato voice); but rather as someone who knows how to take raw material from Christine McVie or Stevie Nicks and "forge" that into something. And that is indeed one of his superlative gifts—as a producer and arranger, he is, like his early mentor Brian Wilson, unparalleled.

But producers, no matter how brilliant, and even though he was also quite an extravagant stage presence, seldom get the standing ovations and fan mail. Those little treats were tossed toward Nicks, the swirling little blonde tornado that bounced around the stage and gave the whole unit one of its most durable personas. Still, this goddess of vinyl emotions has always been more than ready to attribute her own success in large portion to Buckingham's intelligence as a producer/arranger, even if her own star power eclipsed his crucial prowess and further strained their already cracked partnership. "I write my songs, but Lindsey puts the magic in. If I were to play you a song the way I wrote it and gave it to them, and then play it the way it is on the album, you would see what Lindsey did."[12] Luckily, she has always been smart enough to avoid that particular pitfall, and happy to prance on the stage that his clever production and complex arrangements built for her.

Leah Furman hit the target precisely when she said that as the competitive working relationship between them swallowed up everything that had once made their coupling viable, their personal relationship was left in a state of "terminal dysfunction." And yet that was the blueprint with which the entire band proceeded from that point on. "We're your everyday soap opera." Christine once told *Newsweek* magazine.

Fleetwood recalls with amazement that they are all still around at all. After nine weeks of this routine, they were all ready for the asylum—conveniently forgetting, of course, that from its inception in 1967, Fleetwood Mac has always been an asylum of sorts. Yet he also recalls a peculiar premonition he had back then, the kind his innate intuition often whispered to him over the years.

> Just before we left the Record Plant...we were all sitting around the studio, listening to the rough cassettes of the work we'd done. *Fleetwood Mac* (their 1975 debut album) had just gone platinum, and there was the usual concern and fear about whether this follow up would do as well. I said that this new album was going to do much better, that it could even sell as many as eight or nine million copies if our momentum held. The others laughed, and someone touched wood. The strange thing is that this turned out to be a conservative guess.[13]

But the really strange thing is that now, after some 30 years have passed, the album is approaching 30 million copies! No one laughs at Fleetwood anymore, no matter what he says.

Back then, no one was really laughing much, period. One of my favorite descriptions comes from Leah Furman's observations: "Once again, the inaudible sound of breaking hearts filled the psychic air." The incredibly odd manner in which the personal and professional lines can be blurred together when the stakes are high enough is plain to see and hear in the evidence provided by the record itself, with the three singer-songwriters, Chris McVie, Nicks, and Buckingham, "communicating" with each other, but only through their songs.

John McVie, a very vulnerable and insecure man despite his boisterous behavioral problems, confided that it was "very clumsy sometimes, I'd be sitting there in the studio while they were mixing 'Don't Stop,' and I'd listen to the words, which were mostly about me, and I'd get a lump in my throat. I'd turn around, and the writer's sitting right there."[14] And since poor McVie didn't write songs with which to communicate back, to, or at the others, he drank on, dissolving slowly in his own repressed rage.

At this point in the making of their follow-up record—a kind of creative nadir that few ever reach, let alone sustain—the crew had to halt recording the new one and go back on the road to commercially support the last one. They toured and supported it the best way they knew how, by staring into the whites of their live audience's eyes. (Well, maybe the audience's eyes were almost as bloodshot as the band's at that point.) And when Fleetwood remembers gazing out into the huge crowds that packed the stadiums and fields they played in, he also knew something even bigger than he imagined in his most dazed days was happening. "I beheld hundreds, no thousands of girls dressed exactly like Stevie in black chiffon dresses and top hats—Stevie's stage costume. At one point in our set, when Lindsey began to play the guitar intro to 'Rhiannon,' and Stevie walked out and intoned, 'This is a song about a Welsh witch,' these girls went mad, swaying and singing and giving themselves to the music, to Stevie, and to the spirit of the ancient Celtic goddess."[15]

It was the beginning of something like Mac-mania—perhaps not yet as global as their British peers and his brother-in-law George Harrison's band, but equally wild, equally heady, and equally self-destructive. Harrison had once quipped that their fans had given them their screams but his group had given them their nervous systems. In the case of Mac, they threw in their personal lives, families, lovers, friends, and, of course, their sanity and physical health, for good measure. Their circus lifestyle became the stuff of legend, excessive even by the already self-indulgent standards of the rock industry, and the volatile mix of personal hubris with professional acclaim both made and maimed them. *Uncut* magazine did a fine profile of the indestructible members in which they ruminated about how they managed to survive it all.

Nigel Williamson offered an excellent précis in his piece "Five Go Mad," in which he described them perfectly as "rock's greatest living soap opera" and tried to follow the wavering course of their astonishing history and longevity. "Fleetwood Mac went to hell and back to bring the world some of the most popular, and most perfect, hard-centred easy listening music of all time. But it nearly cost them their sanity, and their lives."[16]

Williamson had a great take on their merry-go-round and seemed to relish encapsulating it in terms as dramatic as the scenario seemed to require. He points out that we could have been forgiven for believing that the pinnacle of Fleetwood Mac's "convoluted, incestuous, drug-fuelled, trash novel insanity had been reached in 1976 when they were recording *Rumours,* when in reality, this period was only the beginning of their apparently endless public-private opera." Williamson explained that, "apart from being in the same band and writing songs about each other that detailed every jealousy and betrayal in the emotional maelstrom they had created, the only thing they now had in common was the huge velvet bag of cocaine that engineer Ken Calliat kept under his mixing board, and that the band demanded at regular intervals in order to 'refresh themselves.'"[17]

Now part of both their own personal mythology and our pop culture dreams, what the band did with their "traumatically troubled and tangled web" is something hard to imagine these days. Their amazing achievement was primarily, apart from surviving at all, largely founded on attaining the level of success and creative freedom only fantasized about by most artists, especially since they originated in the heady blur of 1960s acidic blues. But the price they paid is what makes their tale both fascinating and distressing at the same time. The tale of how the "Famous Five" went somewhat dotty, with lifestyles, as classified by Williamson, that would not have been out of place on the set of the television shows *Dallas* or *Dynasty,* and the most outrageous touring circus this side of Led Zeppelin, and which caused them to descend into a "collective drink and drugs hell."[18]

One of the most precious comments in the *Uncut* profile comes from silent wild man John McVie: "About the only people in the band who haven't had an affair are me and Lindsey!" Maybe that is a testament to some tiny shred of rare restraint that at least saved them from *that* particular excess.

* * * * * * * * * *

But they were game for every other form of self-destruction that creative people have ever devised to distract themselves from pain with huge dollops of pleasure. The rest of the summer of 1976, which to many of us felt exactly like the reverse of the summer of 1967, they were where they loved to be, on the road. Fleetwood admits that while mostly "things were great, we had a hot record, the audiences were wonderful and we had a big winner in the can," the perils of the band's hold on their reality were getting hefty. "I do remember that the tensions between Stevie and Lindsey were very real. They were still re-negotiating their personal adjustments to each other while touring in a band and making a record. Oh, the sparks, and how they did fly!"[19]

The band's nominal leader believes, probably correctly, that it all boiled down to Buckingham's sorrow that Nicks had left him, while Nicks feared that her music would lose its appeal without Buckingham's guiding hand. In addition, Buckingham felt jealous, since new men were being drawn to the now-single Nicks "like honeybees to a gorgeous, pollen-laden blossom."[20] While he seems to reveal perhaps a tad too much of his own feelings for his lead singer, he nonetheless captures the essence of some of the burdens that were being borne by the band at its peak.

During the ascent to this peak, one day in October 1976, while taking some time off from recording to visit Europe and meet the music press there, Fleetwood was stunned by the appearance of a ghost from his past. As he tells it, they were entering London's Montcalm Hotel when a "scruffy and unattractive character with wild long hair" approached them carrying a big portable cassette player blaring disco at top volume. It was the ghost of Peter Green. Fleetwood recalled the meeting this way:

> We were shocked, no one had seen him in six years. The onetime Green God had turned into a flabby ex-hippie, dissolute and disheveled. Aren't you embarrassed? Chris asked him. "Naw," Pete said. "I mean, fuck it. What the hell!" We couldn't believe it. We didn't know quite what to do. So he stayed at the hotel with us for a few nights. He'd knock on your door, sit on your bed, and not say anything. We were so brought down by this, and appalled that in our time

of triumph we should be so terribly reminded of the fragility of life as we were living it. There but for fortune...[21]

But they were not so appalled that they could prevent themselves from courting a similar fate, and only barely escape falling into that same dark place themselves. Money was the only thing that separated that lost creature from these new lords. It was a stark and scary border line. And notice what he did not say—there but for the grace of God, go I, he said, there but for *fortune*. Once again, "chance is the fool's name for fate."

* * * * * * * * * *

Meanwhile, their collective lucky stars were beginning to assume that rare alignment necessary for overwhelming success. In late 1976, Mac's career path took a sudden surge forward and began to accelerate so dramatically it made their heads spin. In November, their three-year-old record *Mystery To Me* was awarded a gold album, likely due to the extra airplay the song "Hypnotized" was getting. Their eponymously titled first outing with the new lineup was still climbing the charts and firmly establishing their new style and sound in the public's imagination. The public, it seems, has been just waiting for something like this, something resembling the mania of the sixties but with a new twist: corporate validity.

By early 1977, American radio was going to town with the record, playing it almost constantly, as it became the soundtrack to nearly everyone's lives (whether they liked it or not) during this intense period. Over 800,000 copies of the record were shipped out to retailers in February 1977, at that time the largest advance order in Warner Brothers history. Within a month, as a direct result of the new and softer format of the fledgling FM stations, not only did the record start its dramatic rise on the charts, but the media also began to zero in on the "traumas and travails" they had been experiencing. It could not have been more perfect as a product for the new radio dimension: FM radio may as well have been named after Fleetwood Mac at that point.

By the end of March, *Rumours* went platinum, having sold a million copies during its first hysterical month after release. Then, as Fleetwood puts it, "We were off again, to France, Holland, Germany, and Sweden, places where the name Fleetwood Mac still meant the blues. It was our pleasant duty to show them our new tricks and change their minds."[22] New tricks, indeed. But old habits die hard, and when Mac achieved their first really spectacular global success, naturally they brought along with them all their personal histories of dysfunction, wrapped in shiny new paper—a seemingly endless flow of money. As Fleetwood recalled:

> Suddenly, as the manager of the band, I found myself described in the press as the sullen and and menacing Svengali of Fleetwood Mac. I tried to explain to interviewers that nothing could be further from the truth. Fleetwood Mac, I'd

explain, was more a way of life than a business. To us, success came as a pleasant surprise, not a vindication after years of worry over low sales figures. We never cared about how many records we sold, we just wanted to get out and play. I'd explain that it was just like going to the office for us, and that our job, our duty had always been to play through all the ups and downs. That's how I felt in 1977, and that's how I still feel today.[23]

Besides, if anyone in the press or the public had been paying attention properly, it would have been perfectly obvious that Buckingham was the most appropriate figure for that Svengali tag. Of course, by the time his group gave him the creative authority to produce the follow-up record to *Rumours* (and he created an arcane, nearly solo masterpiece, *Tusk*, in response) everyone would know that *he* was largely the creative fuel, and Nicks the engine, behind the new lineup. As the Svengali Buckingham put it, "Not everything was totally fabulous, as I recall. There were dark moments when the tremendous tensions and the inability to separate personal and business lives erupted into fierce battles, but the band never once let it affect the live shows. Perhaps as a result, our cocaine intake skyrocketed."[24]

They continued ever forward, sales of the record pushing them ever higher. Twenty-three shows with hardly a day off. Chemical enhancements practically for breakfast. More money than they could even count. In the wild and wacky world of Fleetwood Mac, and in the mysterious recesses of the mind of Mick Fleetwood, it must have seemed like the perfect time to start a love affair with Stevie Nicks.

Fleetwood is incredibly candid and honest about all his own foibles, just as he is with the many public perceptions about his ongoing soap opera of a band. He has commented that it seemed like everyone in the music business in California thought they had the exclusive inside information on their comings and goings, and that no one ever hesitated to circulate the most scurrilous tall tales. They said that Stevie was sleeping with him; that Christine had run off with Lindsey; that Stevie was seeing both John and him on alternate Wednesdays; that violent fistfights were commonplace in the studio; that Stevie was definitely leaving the band next Friday; that Stevie had left them months ago and this was the reason the album was delayed; that they were all crippled with massive quantities of alcohol and cocaine; that Stevie practiced black magic and led a coven of witches in the Hollywood Hills; that Fleetwood Mac was a burnt-out case. As he put it, tales of flamboyant infidelity and dementia circulated like polluted air. The rumors about *Rumours* were stunning, and the band itself was mostly stunned, period.

Luckily, on April Fools Day, when they flew to England for a series of shows, they were pleasantly surprised to have their expectations, that they had largely been forgotten by British rock fans, to be turned around entirely. Instead, they found many enthusiastic old fans who were joined by enthusiastic new fans. They were all naturally thrilled, as the three phases of their wild career seemed to be synchronizing almost beyond their most extravagant fantasies.

Unfortunately, they also learned in England that the near-ghost of Peter Green had been committed to a mental hospital due to a heavily publicized event the previous year. Green apparently wanted all the money that was still flowing to him as a result of his great youthful work to be halted post haste. So he took a pump-action rifle and went to visit the band's management to demand that it did. The police were called, and a judge was persuaded to send him to the mental hospital rather than back to prison. Fleetwood was saddened. "All we could do was shake our heads, having already spilled enough tears over Pete. We felt we'd done our share of crying."[25] Alas, while it was true that they had cried enough over Green, there still remained many new and upcoming reasons for fresh tears aplenty. That is the amazing thing about this group: they always seem to be at a new and hopeful beginning, no matter where in their long career you might choose to look.

* * * * * * * * * *

From the perspective of 1978, while raking in the spoils and rewards of all their hard work for a full decade, they were both sitting on top of the world and falling off of it at the same time, as per usual. Everything after 1977 must seem like a blur to the members of Fleetwood Mac, and it is little wonder, considering the roller coaster ride they have been on ever since.

Nicks gave a gala New Years Eve party to ring in 1978 and to celebrate the astonishing victories they had collectively experienced in the past year. Fleetwood attended it accompanied by Jenny Boyd, and together with a trillion friends, they partied in the style only they can manage. Triumph was in the air.

Fleetwood has indicated that though they were all agog and somewhat dazed by this "sudden" success, they were also prepared for it, especially he and McVie, who both clearly remembered being big in England but losing it all so tragically. Acid, cults and mental breakdowns had robbed the youthful unit of their chance at reaping the whirlwind, but paradoxically, their bad fortune back then was now being replaced by good fortune on a nearly unimaginable scale. You couldn't have one without the other, and they knew it. Especially Fleetwood: "At that time, we knew what we were doing. The best part for us was that we still felt good as a band. Through everything, Fleetwood Mac was still a road band, and the trappings and trimmings didn't affect us that much because we didn't have much time to think about it. We just carried on and played."[26]

Nicks concurs completely:

I didn't care that everybody knows me and Chris and John and Lindsey and Mick all broke up...because we *did*. So that's fact. We were all trying to hold the foundations of Fleetwood Mac together, and trying to speak to each other in a civil tone, while sitting in a tiny room listening to each other's songs about our shattered relationships. It was very, very tense—a room full of divorced people who didn't dare bring anybody new into the same room, because nobody was gonna be nice to anybody brought into the circle.[27]

In Furman's study of this period, *Rumours Exposed*, she summed it up quite nicely:

Of course, the greatest counterbalance to the members' personal distress was provided by the musical triumphs that sprang from these pressure-cooker recording sessions. The manner in which a few of Stevie's cryptic verse from the Buckingham-Nicks period were turned into one of the band's best songs exemplifies the overall success of these sessions.[28]

The song Furman refers to is "The Chain." Although I cannot quite agree that this is one of the band's finest compositions, it is certainly the only one created by the band in a collaborative and mutual mode, and it does firmly state the titanic efforts they made, and the extreme lengths they would go, to remain together. One thing for certain is that the song has become, as Furman put it, "An emblem of their resolve never to break the chain binding their artistic union."[29] So throughout 1978, before, during and after their tours, and even to this day, they celebrate that union in the only way they know, by dragging themselves forward no matter how rusty that chain might become.

They had climbed these dizzy heights before, in England, but the big difference this time was "we were millionaires." Their sales figures were "validated" for them by both the music media and their own professional peers. The band ruled the American Music Awards in January 1978. At the Grammy Awards in February, *Rumours* was named album of the year, as well as receiving the *Rolling Stone* magazine reader's awards for artists of the year, band of the year, and best single for "Dreams." They used to be the band on the brink; now, they were the band at the bank.

While Fleetwood is very candid about the flaws and foibles of his long-suffering but long-lasting group, he is equally up front and forthcoming about what makes his band a great one. Few rock titans are as clued in to what makes them titanic:

Many theories again appeared in the press to explain Fleetwood Mac's enormous new audience. One held that our three singer-songwriters and their different voices kept the public from getting bored with a monolithic big Mac sound. Another postulated that the group fulfilled various deeply ingrained Anglo-American archetypes, with myself as the public school aristocrat, McVie as the British cloth-cap working-class type, Christine as an English Rose from the Midlands, Stevie as the Californian Girl, and Lindsey as Byronic rock star.[30]

Again, as Fleetwood recalls it: "Along these lines, I remember Stevie remarking, as she looked at the motley Mac about to take the stage at some stadium in various costumes comprising bits of Dodgers uniforms, chiffon outfits, waistcoats and breeches, silks and bell bottoms: "This is weird. We all look like we're going to a different place." And, Fleetwood continued, "Most critics agreed that our writers were producing hits songs that fit into the modern romantic tradition established by The Beatles. But my favourite theory was that we were one of the first white groups since The Mamas and the Papas to successfully bring female voices into the context of rock music. We didn't sound like anyone else."[31] They still do not.

RUMOURS:
RELEASED 1977, WARNER BROTHERS

Yes, in answer to the recent question of a confused friend, it is indeed possible for music to be both a superb work of art as well as shameless kitsch at the same time. This is one of the greatest examples of that strange phenomenon. In fact, once the listener realizes the core content of this famous album, and that it feels like we are sneaking peeks into private diary entries or personal letters between conflicted lovers, the guilty pleasure of celebrating the bouncing forward thrust of the music only increases.

Rumours opens, like the eponymous *Fleetwood Mac* of 1975, with a Buckingham lamentation containing his usual cutting edge. Even a cursory listening to both the first Buckingham-led Mac album and this amazing follow-up achievement, will reveal that these are *blues* songs, albeit covered with the shiny varnish of pop logistics.

Just as Buckingham had with the opener of the 1975 debut, the *Rumours* opener presents his own classic dilemma: "I don't trust my lover, I can't live with her, but I can't live without her, I'm just her 'second hand news.'" Of course, the irony-drenched fact that he still has to harmonize, write, and sing songs and perform concerts with that same reluctant lover is what gives this song—indeed, the whole album—its paradoxical edginess in the first place.

Buckingham is often fond of stating the obvious: there is nothing to say, but he will say it anyway, since someone has taken his place (just as someone did in the earlier album's opening song, "Monday Morning"). He knows he has nothing on his lover, and that there is nothing to be done about it. "One thing I think you should know. I ain't gonna miss you when you go." Ironically, this is oddly similar to that old joke punch line: "How can I miss you if you won't go away?" Indeed, he and his lover can never separate, at least not psychologically and certainly not artistically, since they actually do not really exist as separate and independent entities, but rather as conflicting portions of the same single essence. Buckingham further laments: "I know you're hoping to find, someone who's gonna give you piece of mind [*sic*]. Won't you lay me down in tall grass and let me do my stuff. I'm just second hand news. I'm just second hand news."

The infamous partner in question, Stevie Nicks, answered this petulant call with her own unique brand of response, and in the process she crafted one of the most enduring song-myths of Mac's big years. In "Dreams," Nicks immediately grabs Buckingham by the horns: "Now here you go again, you say you want your freedom. Well who am I to keep you down? But listen carefully to the sound of your loneliness...like a heartbeat, drives you mad. In the stillness of remembering what you had, and what you lost, and what you lost, and what you lost." Just in case either her partner, or the dazzled listener, is not quite sure that it is she whom he has lost. Except, of course, that just like in her partner's songs of separation, she is never really lost to him in her own, either. After all, 15 years after *Rumours*, they would be reunited, with the entire group blasting out Bill Clinton's chosen campaign and inauguration song; and incredibly, 20 years afterward, they would be reunited yet again, as if doomed to forever relive their adolescence in public.

One cannot help toying with the famous Peaches & Herb song: "Re-united, and it feels so baaaaad!...Re-united, and I've been haaaad!" But Nicks seems to anticipate even that irony when in her uniquely nasal wail she famously intones, "Thunder only happens when its raining, players only love you when they're playing. Say, women they will come and they will go. When the rain washes you clean, you'll know."

Naturally Buckingham bounces back with his retort in the next song, "Never Going Back Again," in which after first pleading his earlier case as second hand news ("Been down so long, I've been tossed around enough.") he now boldly declares, "Been down one time, been down two times, I'm never going back again."

It is left to the wistful wiles of Christine McVie to interrupt this emotional slugfest with her own personal message to hubby John about the past being past, in "Don't Stop," the song that became Clinton's anthem and one of Mac's biggest hits ever. "Open your eyes and look at the day, you'll see things in a different way. Don't stop, thinking about tomorrow, don't stop, it'll soon be here. It'll be, better than before, yesterday's gone, yesterday's gone." But, of course, it was not better, and their yesterdays would never be gone, not as long as audiences required or demanded more Mac music that could only be made by these particular people, with their particular problems. That plus, of course, their remarkable talent for transmuting the lead of love lost into the gold of music sold.

Side one of the album continues with Buckingham's most vicious but also most entertaining rouser, "Go Your Own Way": "Loving you, isn't the right thing to do. How can I ever change things that I feel? You can go your own way, go your own way, you can call it, another lonely day. Tell me why, every-thing turned around, packing up, shacking up is all you wanna do." And he punctuates his command to basically "go away" by making sure she and the audience knows the reasons why: "If I could, maybe I'd give you my world, how can I, when you won't take it from me?...You can go your own way, go your own way..." Never has a declaration to get the hell out of one's life ever sounded so positively ecstatic in its pounding beat and relentless rhythm, with Fleetwood and McVie thrashing away in all their former British-blues glory while their frontline performers drag their personal lives through the mud, and through the money hidden under the mud.

Then once again, it is left to the surprisingly sweet Christine to round out the album's first side, and to soften the vitriol with her lovely "Songbird": "For you, there'll be no more crying, for you, the sun will be shining. And I wish you all the love in the world, but most of all, I wish it from myself... And the songbirds keep on singing, like they know the score, and I love you, I love you, I love you, like never before."

But side two is all about being back to the basics. Suddenly you are slammed into the nervous wall of "The Chain," the only song ever composed jointly by all the members—which means, of course, that it originated as an extended jam that was subsequently stitched together from several different sources. Its message contains in a nutshell the entire operating method for survival that the band had managed to develop over the years, and that was especially crucial to allowing them to go forward with an album all about disintegration, loss, and abandonment. McVie's bass lines are particularly sinister on this track, though it is hard to identify why. He was always a gracefully articulate player, if not as a person; but in this song he soars somewhere new, and the band summons all their apparently limitless capacity for celebrating chaos and plunge fully into the abyss along with him.

The second song on side two is once again a lovely and remedial piece by Christine McVie, "You Make Loving Fun," which we knowingly suspect could not possibly be directed at her ex-husband and current bass player. More likely it was about the lighting technician who fixed her spotlight, the ironic partner with whom she sought solace from the mercurial madness generated by John McVie. It intones, in the most cheerful possible terms, a declaration about "sweet wonderful you, you make me happy with the things you do" She goes on to croon that though she never did believe in miracles before, it might be time to start believing now. Why not?

But the next song is back to the angst of Nicks in full flight. In "I Don't Want to Know," she uses a similar term as that used by Buckingham in their first Mac album together, when he growls in "Monday Morning" that "I got nothing but love for you, so tell me what you really wanna do. First you love me, then you move on down the line..." In her response song, Nicks pronounces, "I don't want to know the reasons why, love keeps right on walking down the line...Trying to believe, you say you love me, but you don't know, you got me rocking and a'reeling...oh."

The two final songs on *Rumours* are classic polar opposites. "Oh Daddy" is a tender and painful ode to an unknown loved one in which Christine purrs about being wrong and her loved one being right, "And I can't walk away from you baby, if I tried." By then it was perfectly obvious that she could not walk away; in fact, none of them could. That was the whole point of *Rumours,* after all: they could not live with, or without, each other.

One of the most harrowing Nicks songs is also one of the most honest, direct, and confessional. In "Gold Dust Woman," Nicks begins to cast her glance into her own future as a serious cocaine addict, but from the early stages of her dependency and its softer vantage point. Ten years later, she would be a certified zombie, ensconced in the Betty Ford Clinic, where she eventually substituted one addition for another and plunged into a nightmare relationship with prescription tranquilizers, which robbed her of her sparkling consciousness and caused her lithe little frame to balloon up drastically, almost as if she needed extra armor for self-protection. But by all means, at this point the group's primary obsessions and compulsions were with the psychic character armor required to allow them to work together and continue reaping the benefits of not giving up, not breaking up, not living another life but the one that had secured their place in the spotlight— though what a shaky and nerve-racking spotlight it was.

Fleetwood Mac, of course, was not the first or only group to soldier on through mayhem and madness of various kinds, only perhaps the most famous, and with the most popular album as a documentary soundtrack of their personal and professional distress.

Uncut magazine, along with *Mojo,* offers the most insightful access to popular music in general, and often to the outer edges of its soap opera in particular. They have entertainingly outlined a grand scale of indulgence in exactly the same gold mine being dug out by Mac. In one recent *Uncut* issue chronicling the band's incendiary personalities, they astutely placed them in a wider context that helps us get a better perspective, albeit perhaps still chilling.

They called their coverage, "M.O.R. Madness," as in middle of the road, and referred to "those other unexpected easy-listening debauchees." Among these were the Monkees, the world's first manufactured boy's band—acid heads a-go-go, every zany one of them; the Beach Boys: clean-cut Californian surfing kids—and fear, loathing, drugs, and madness in the bosom of America's most dysfunctional family; David Cassidy, bubblegum to his airbrushed core, but underneath the Clearasil was all groupie action and druggie despair; Patsy Cline, the queen of redneck country conservatism who lived a life of hard-drinking promiscuity and depravity, brought to a premature end in an air crash at 30; Frankie Lymon, the boy wonder who recorded "Why Do Fools Fall in Love?" at 13, was a heroin addict by 15, and dead on a bathroom floor at 25; the Carpenters, the wholesome brother and sister on top of the world for most of the 1970s, yet by the 1980s, the Quaalude-addicted Richard was in rehab and Karen was dead from anorexia; and the Mamas and the Papas, who may have been "California dreamin'" but set the gold standard for Fleetwood Mac with their own divorces and addictions.

By 1977 and 1978, when Mac was in touring frenzy, they had eclipsed all these other self-destructors and given new meaning to the notion of suffering for one's art. They were at the top of the bottom.

Other significant releases of 1977: Boston by Boston; *Low* by David Bowie; *The Clash* by the Clash; *Trans-Europe Express* by Kraftwerk; *Live at the Hollywood Bowl* by The Beatles; *Small Change* by Tom Waits; *Hard Again* by Muddy Waters; *In Colour* by Cheap Trick; *Pacific Ocean Blue* by Dennis Wilson; *Lust for Life* by Iggy Pop; *Aja* by Steely Dan; *Never Mind the Bollocks, Here's The Sex Pistols* by the Sex Pistols; *Brel* by Jacques Brel; *The Stranger* by Billy Joel.

Tusk: Buckingham Takes Command

7

Lindsey Buckingham is one of those genuinely strange and authentically gifted talents that comes along at just the right time, in the right place, and for exactly the right reason. Like most wildly successful bands, Fleetwood Mac needed a supremely confident follow-up record to their massive hit, *Rumours.* Unlike more pedestrian bands, however, they decided to move sideways artistically, with what *Mojo* magazine once called "one of the greatest career sabotage albums of all time." So, for two years they toiled under the experimental muse of Lindsey Buckingham as he took creative control of the band's sound, stretched it into a different dimension and plunged them into a frenzy of low-fidelity, high-concept excursions away from their mainstream Mac sound.

Through it all, the creative collaborators at the heart of the band's brilliance, Mick Fleetwood, John McVie, and Christine Perfect proved they were the quintessential masters of surfing the roiling waves of creative chaos. Once again, they just pulled it together, as they were falling apart, and launched themselves into an utterly unknown stratosphere: something as different from the now iconic Mac sound as the first blues phase was from the second progressive rock phase. But there was no name to use to call the place that Buckingham took them. It was as hermetic a place as that explored with such idiosyncratic distinction by his musical mentor Brian Wilson on his legendary 1967 *Smile* album. This was the stuff of dreams, but also of waking nightmares.

Looking back now from this vantage point almost 20 years since its release, in many ways it can be considered a concept album, much in the manner of

Jethro Tull's ethereal and strange, *Thick As A Brick,* perhaps. Except that in this case it would need to be qualified as "smart as a tack." If it was Buckingham's notion of a concept album, one which seems far more in tune with today's world than it did with the scene in 1979, the concept was a simple one: "This is not Fleetwood Mac!" Or at least not the one everyone so sorely desired to have delivered as a sequel to *Rumours.*

* * * * * * * * * *

During the band's touring, performing, and promoting of their latest outing, *Uncut* magazine interviewed Buckingham on the subject of *Tusk* as both a travesty and a triumph, that rare combination of success and failure simultaneously. His personal take on the direction the band swerved into as a sequel to their blockbuster is very informative, especially in terms of how he perceived the creative dynamics as work within the group.

When asked about the kind of impact or influence that punk and post-punk had on the way he felt Mac's music should going, Buckingham commented that, "Although punk had a fairly huge impact on me, its influence on *Tusk* wasn't so much on the music but more that it gave me a little room to deprogram and reaffirm things—to retrieve my own style, which I had when I joined the band in 1974, but which I had then given up to the situation of the group's collective femaleness. I was inspired by the honesty, integrity and sensibility of bands like The Clash and Gang of Four."[1] The natural follow-up question was how the rest of the band felt about this intended new approach. "It started out as a shouting match at Mick's house but they gradually came to accept my ideas about re-defining the band's style. I was very intent that we shouldn't just reproduce the *Rumours* formula. I was very aware of punk shaking up the status quo."[2]

Buckingham also responded to questions about the "homemade" approach to his *Tusk* songs and some of the strange recording techniques he used.

> I wanted to work on my songs alone with a tape machine and then bring them to the group. More eclectic ideas came out as a result. It's the difference between a one-on-one canvas painting, where the artist takes off in a more meditative, subconscious direction, and movie-making, which always carries a political aspect because a bunch of other people become involved, which I find counterproductive. So I went ahead and ran the status quo into the ground! The Kleenex boxes as drums, the mics taped to the bathroom floor—these were all just experiments in the mode of Brian Wilson. There was no great plan behind it. Only after this did *Tusk* become a "band thing"—although I also worked hard to make sure Stevie and Christine's songs were produced and arranged as well as they could be.[3]

And the fact that *Tusk* sold only an unfortunate fraction of what *Rumours* had sold. "Only three million in the States. After that we had a band meeting and agreed that we had to return to functioning on a more realistic level.

Maybe there was, to an extent, sand in my eyes insofar as getting songs done the way I wanted, though I feel, with *Say You Will* we've become a lot more focused as a group, even if I did originally intend it to be another solo album!"[4] Technically, *Tusk* was a solo album, much in the same vein as Brian Wilson's experimental *Smile* was a similarly solipsistic exercise in private creativity versus a collaborative dynamic.

But exactly what was, and what is *Tusk* really? First and foremost, it was a gentle poke in the eye (and ear) of critics and public alike, designed to disrupt expectations and elude any delivery of dreams as hoped for by the public's appetite for Fleetwood Mac's menu of themes and emotional flavors. One of his oddest comments was his perceived need to retreat from the band's "collective femaleness." After all, with Fleetwood and McVie, two of the most vibrant monuments to testosterone in rock music, plus the kinetic spirit of barely concealed machopoetic posturing for which Buckingham is best known, we have three living advertisements for male attitude. It is hard to imagine how he could have felt constrained by the tiny tunesmith Nicks, or the mellowly maternal Christine. Some of that collective femaleness simply must have been the product of his own feverish imagination and insecurities, and especially was a reflection of the immense star status which Nicks had accrued by then, as well as the fact that Christine was so effective at materializing the warm humanity of her songs as a counterpoint to the ongoing angst of the Buckingham-Nicks brand.

Tusk, named rather blatantly after the erect male member, was a complete surprise, given what the Mac menu had by then come to represent. Almost 30 years after its initial release as a double vinyl package, it is still a surprise, still avant-garde in the most off-the-wall possible antipop sense. In his excellent profile of the period for *Mojo* magazine in 2003, Phil Sutcliffe "journeyed back to a time of diaphanous beauty, marching bands and very confusing inter-band relationships."[5]

This was a profound, almost blatant attempt by the band, at that time under the edgy command of Lindsey Buckingham, to totally subvert their "brand." In the process, they almost sank the group under the weight of both their own lunacy, and the public's collective disdain for that degree of anticommercial rebranding. "God knows all our lives are unimaginable without each other," commented Mick Fleetwood, who by 1979 had, along with his boyhood crony McVie, seen so many ups and downs for their legendary group that they had come to expect the unexpected and to embrace the sheer chaos of their unique creative working method together. Sutcliffe delightfully and accurately referred to them as "the longest running soap opera in rock and roll history."[6]

When if first appeared, amidst an astronomical amount of hype surrounding its sequel status, record moguls sarcastically dubbed it "Lindsey's Folly." Yet after nearly three decades, *Tusk* is often named as a major influence on young bands such as the Strokes, Air, and the Webb Brothers. It has even been recently lauded as a "landmark of radical MOR" by the *Guardian,* even though it is hard to comprehend what can be both radical and middle of the road at the same time. Yet if anything can perform that schizoid double role, *Tusk* can.

Among the lone voices applauding its 1979 release was Greil Marcus, always an astute observer of pop culture on the edge, and over it. He in fact called it a record that allowed Fleetwood Mac to subvert their own art form from the inside out, almost like a mole within an organization who slowly and invisibly sabotages the whole operation. That term fits Buckingham to a T: he became the mole within Fleetwood Mac, struggling to legitimize and validate what he felt had become too tangled up in money and success. Ironically, in order to do so it was necessary for him to ignore the fact that it was largely his own abilities, talents, and production brilliance which created that vast success in the first place.

It has been said that *Tusk* evolved out of lives in a tornado of turmoil. Apparently, when Buckingham dropped into Fleetwood's Bel Air home to discuss strategy in 1978, it took three entire days to broach the single subject characterized later by Fleetwood as basically, "What the fuck do we do now?" Buckingham declared that he could not and would not tolerate any "laurel-flaunting" for their sequel, and once again he tried to explain to the nominal leader how he had tried to adapt to the band's format but was "losing a great deal of myself" in the process. He announced that he wanted to record his songs at home, a classic Brian Wilson scenario, then bring them to "the band," once they were finished, for them to record together. This obviously eliminated one of the cherished notions of the utopian Mac concept: we are a collaborative machine, we create together and perform together.

Begrudging agreement was finally won by the persuasive guitarist, and he was off to his own races. Ken Caillat was the coproducer of *Tusk* and one of those who valiantly attempted to follow the new intuitive direction spearheaded by the band's sound savant. "He was a maniac. The first day, I set up the studio as usual, then he said to turn every knob 180 degrees from where it was now and see what happens. He'd tape microphones to the studio floor and then get into a sort of push-up position to sing. Early on he came in and he'd freaked out in the shower and cut off all his hair with nail scissors. He was stressed. And into sound destruction."[7]

But what at first appeared to be sound destruction was really much more like sound sculpture, with the results only assuming their proper context once a little time had passed between the frenzy of creation and the calmness of history. In fact, these days, without stretching the comparison too far into the incredible, some people feel that if The Beatles had achieved a zenith with their *Sgt. Pepper* album and then started a slow slide into entropy with their double white album one year later, Mac had accomplished something similar (not stylistically of course, but in their own language) by achieving the

Rumours plateau and then gleefully jumping off the creative cliff that it had represented for them.

Like The Beatles before them, Fleetwood Mac had begun the arduous task of making three solo records and trying to pretend they were still a unified band. And they did not have a Yoko Ono to blame for their splintering, nor did they need one—their level of dysfunction was so grand that they imploded all by themselves, bludgeoned by their own global success and the joy ride that it allowed. But unlike The Beatles, who could no longer sustain the illusions they helped manufacture or continue performing live music that could never approximate their studio genius, Mac went off on their usual ragged world tour, the longest ever, and for 13 months they went where few musicians had gone before. It was a precipice of self-indulgence and addiction so profound that most musicians who approached it are no longer with us. How Mac survived at all is yet another testament to some supernatural dynamics at work within the unique creative chaos they chose to call collaboration.

Fresh friction abounded, McVie was alarmed at Buckingham's interference with his precious (and perfect) bass lines, culminating in his fleeing on board his yacht for parts unknown. He was only in the *Tusk* video in the form of a cardboard cutout, carried around by his ex-wife in a classic moment of irony. She would soon add to her own personal sense of ironic loss and bad instincts by starting a liaison with the doomed Beach Boy Dennis Wilson, a man so bent on self-destruction that he made John McVie look like an altar boy by comparison.

By June 1979, somehow *Tusk* had been completed, including the band's spare-no-expense indulgence of recording the title track brass section in Dodger Stadium with a 100-piece marching band from the University of Southern California. Their management was not amused. Mo Ostin remarked that their product, 20 songs on a double vinyl record costing more than a million dollars, was "insane." "The business is fucked," Ostin remarked. "We're dying the death, we can't sell records, and this will have to retail at twice the normal price. It's suicide. You've got to stop them!"[8]

Naturally enough, once the artists heard the management's side of the story, they went right ahead and veered even closer to the cliff's edge. They had earned the financial power to do what they wanted, even if it did amount to career suicide. The sales figures would reveal that only a quarter of the buyers for *Rumours* showed up at the counter carrying *Tusk*, although to be fair, its "failure" still amounted to some nine million copies—hardly a bust entirely, but certainly nowhere near the tall shadow cast by the eventual 30 million mark achieved by *Rumours*. Relativity is fun, is it not?

* * * * * * * * * *

In 1979, the year that *Tusk* descended on an unsuspecting audience, the ever prescient Greil Marcus wrote a review that was more of an appreciation championing the creative direction that Fleetwood Mac had swerved into under the command of Buckingham. It was later collected in his anthology *Ranters and Crowd Pleasers*, a crystal-clear assessment of the inherent conflict between entertainment and artistry that the fresh anger of punk music had unleashed on the record industry. In the ironic case of Fleetwood Mac and Lindsey Buckingham, however, it was not a case of either-or, since they obviously wanted to be both crowd pleasers *and* ranters, trying as usual to have their cake and eat it too—or in this case, to smash it too. Marcus was a bit of a lone voice in the wilderness back then, and has only recently been proven correct, and nearly prophetic, in his personal and critical take on *Tusk*.

For his delightful judgment of recording reality called "Fear In The Marketplace," Marcus was able to cast an insightful glance into the dynamics of success and failure at the top.

> There is no stronger proof of the growing conservatism of the rock and roll mainstream—by which I mean the audience that puts records on the charts and the radio stations that play them—than the reception received by Fleetwood Mac's double LP *Tusk*. The appearance of this album should have been an event. The band's two previous LPs, *Fleetwood Mac* and *Rumours*, had sold close to twenty million copies worldwide, and were still on the air. Huge numbers of people were eager to find out what the group would come up with. In the past decade, even as a noisy but small minority had pledged allegiance to the willful outcasts and obscurities of popular culture, the vast majority has taken extreme pleasure in consciously associating with success, or, as it is now called, money.[9]

Tusk almost accidentally succeeded as a result of audience expectations: they ran out to buy it sound unheard and sight unseen, only to be stunned into silence by the double-headed monster that the band had finally released after sinking into a veritable abyss of drugs, alcohol, capitalist angst, and sheer commercial bravado. It climbed the charts in spite of itself. But radio suddenly abandoned the group like a disease, passing a dollar-and-sense judgment in what amounted to a blackout.

Radio can be cruel when it has to be. They withdrew their support entirely from the massive hit-makers and literally punished them for their audacity in attempting to experiment with what they considered a near-perfect formula. Fleetwood Mac had been the ultimate mainstream music machine, and now here was *Tusk*, radically refusing to acknowledge any and all of the mainstream's constricting creative limitations. The word radical is an intriguing one, especially since its own root meaning is "roots." Thus, ironically, to the educated ear Mac really was further exploring their own roots, and rock music's roots, as deep as they could go. But the audience would have none of it. This does not mean the audience itself is uneducated, only that it has certain appetites for the menu of their choice. When they go to the Fleetwood Mac restaurant, they want to order the Fleetwood Mac sirloin steak, not Buckingham's macrobiotic swirl of slick answers to punk's rude questions. Defeat was heralded early on by releasing the strange anthem *Tusk* as a single. Today it strikes many of us as a masterpiece, but back then, hot on the heels of "Go Your Own Way," it seemed a bit psychotic, even though it is the direct inheritor of the brilliant hubris of "Don't Stop." Indeed, its subtitle could have been, "Don't Stop Thinking, Period."

* * * * * * * * * *

Meanwhile, Mick Fleetwood, it seems, was passionately engaged in a personal campaign to expunge almost all thought, and most consciousness, from his life in general and from the institution he had founded in particular.

> My life was appropriately chaotic for that of the proprietor of what one London paper called far and away the most commercially successful rock band since The Beatles. Running the group, managing Bob Welch, husband and father in ever decreasing frequency, secret lover, budding real estate mogul, the son of a dying father, friend and sideman to many musician friends, interviewee and spokesman for the group—all of these roles began to jangle in my head. Add to this my contracting a thoroughly unamusing case of severe hypoglycemia and a neo-Falstaffian intake of alcohol and cocaine, and what do you have? Someone often described in the press as "gruff", "soft spoken", "unapproachable", "heavily bearded" Such was my image in this era. Looking back now, I think it was my reality as well. All I can say is I was trying to live many different lives, and sometimes it worked and sometimes it didn't. Even my memories of this time, post-*Rumours,* are hazy, as if the borders between what I experienced and what I dreamed are indistinct.[10]

This "life without borders" brings to mind the oft-quoted remark of the artist Goya that the sleep of reason produces monsters. It certainly produced a monster of a record in the breakaway mystery sequel of *Tusk*. By the way, lest the word monster be misinterpreted, I still believe that *Tusk,* and especially the immediate following release of their live concert recording of its maniacal tour, are the best Fleetwood Mac albums produced since the early English blues and the mid-1970s Bob Welch era. Strangely enough, in retrospect, Fleetwood himself also believes that *Tusk* was their major achievement, though he sincerely doubted it at the time.

However, one of the almost lone voices in the wilderness back in 1979, the always astute Greil Marcus, firmly believed it to be a masterpiece, albeit an off-the-wall masterpiece.

> The band tipped its hand early on, issuing the LP's title track as a 45. More a set of fragments than a song, *Tusk* was as unlikely a prospective hit single as a major group had offered in years—a Bronx cheer to radio programmers—and it died a quick death. The album itself seemed more palatable, but only at first, and only if you sat down and played the two discs all the way through.
>
> Jarring, disorienting accents emerged from the sound and then took it over; the vocals, especially Lindsey Buckingham's, retreated, came shouting back,

and then faded again. The fragmentation evident on the single defined the album: the most striking tracks were not quite songs, and they didn't make their claim as tracks. Programmers looked for The Cut, the one tune that hooks an album onto the air, the single number that would make programming rational, and programmers couldn't find it, because Fleetwood Mac had left it off. Instead, programmers just kept playing *Rumours*. One can assume that many listeners, more than anything, were relieved.[11]

So true, because after all, "relief" is what most listeners want and wanted, not new and fresh distress to digest. And yet that distress is the very essence of what great artists always do. Indeed, some alert listeners have even credited Mac with the same kind of creative bravery that Bob Dylan demonstrated when he released the blissfully acoustic and poetic *John Wesley Harding* after having already electrified his audience with his earlier experiments at self-reinvention. As Marcus wrote, "*Tusk* is, in its lyrics, about romance out of reach, which means that you have to make a certain effort to get hold of it."[12]

This brings us close to the crux of the issue, in my opinion. Both of the debut albums of Mac's third phase, *Fleetwood Mac* (1975) and *Rumours* (1977), were essentially about the band's personal and professional relationships falling apart. But once those relationships had fallen apart, there was no longer any actual content for the strange dynamics of their creative chaos that could assume a form suitable to their now famous brand. They were left adrift, without anything to sing about.

The question of how to surpass former excellence is, of course, something that plagued all creative artists, from Mozart to The Beatles, but seldom has it seemed so definitive as in the case of Mac. "How do you follow, let alone top, the best work you've ever done in your life, work that almost killed you to complete?"[13] The answer is that you do not, but not necessarily that you cannot. Hence, in handing over the command of his motley army to Buckingham, Fleetwood was excruciatingly aware that one's time in the spotlight is forever threatened by newer and younger faces and voices, and that competition is not only fierce, it is brutal and often deadly.

> We had to contend with cultural backlash within our industry. In England the punks, and in America the New Wavers, were trying to build careers and gouge a niche for themselves by declaring that all the old bands—The Stones, Led Zeppelin, Elton John, David Bowie, Fleetwood Mac—to be a bunch of decadent and boring old farts, completely out of touch with their audience and the real world. We of course knew that this was just a big wank, but it did make us think about what we were doing and how we were presenting ourselves.[14]

"Gouge" is the appropriate word here: how do you respond when the new and upcoming sound was breathing down your successful but rapidly aging neck? And then, naturally, because this *was* Fleetwood Mac, after all, there was an internal cultural backlash within the ranks of their own band that Fleetwood and McVie simply had to address.

Lindsey Buckingham was especially perturbed: he felt that with the success of *Rumours*,"the work" was being being ignored in favour of "the phenomenon". This was important because Lindsey was our chief architect and creator. He was totally dedicated to the art of it, and driven by pure intentions. He lived for his art the way Brian Wilson did, with few outside interests and a dislike of distractions. Lindsey wasn't even in it for the money anymore. He just wanted it to be good.[15]

And it was good, but it was also drastically different. So different, in fact, that after the debacle of the *Tusk* experiment, he plunged into a despair groove, especially when Warner Brothers decided to outsource the advertising and marketing of the record in an attempt to recoup anticipated losses. The band rejected a publicity campaign that they felt tried to sell them "like chewing gum." They forgot, of course, that they *were* chewing gum as well as being incredibly talented creative artists, and naturally enough the listening public did not want to chew on *Tusk*. Its flavors were too exotic and unusual, almost unrecognizable as either gum or music at all. "Of course, he was right," Fleetwood was the first to agree. "The old twelve bar blues of Fleetwood Mac had now completely mutated into the *Rumours* groove, but that *wasn't* what we were about either. That was just one epoch in a long history."[16]

By now it should be abundantly clear that what they were really *about* was the perpetual change associated with surfing the waves of creative chaos, so brilliantly and effectively that at each stage they peeled off their skin like snakes and left their own audience scratching its collective head and ears. But perhaps even more importantly, at least in my humble opinion, is the primary fact that this was one of the best live performing bands in history. So, naturally enough, they hit the road once again, in a tour that this time quite nearly killed them all. This is also one of the key reasons that the follow-up to *Tusk*, the 1980 live double concert album, is possibly their single best effort, for the simple reason that *there*, on stage and staring into their audience's glazed eyes, was the creative fire that consumed them so utterly.

According to Fleetwood, he fully understood what Buckingham was going through and where he wanted to go artistically with the music, but neither McVie or Christine particularly appreciated his methods. So, as usual, the tensions of sharing space within a band continued to be the very bedrock of what made the group great in the first place. That, and also having a remarkable succession of superb guitarists fronting the mayhem, from Green, through Kirwan and Welch, and up to Buckingham. But Buckingham was also a superb producer whose voice thus carried additional weight, since it was obvious to all that it was *his* magical ability to weave it all together technically, and especially to form and shape the sometimes gooey lyrics of his ex-girlfriend into a magnificent whole, that manufactured a magic carpet indeed. And in the midst of all this maniacal musical mayhem, with Fleetwood's marriage burnt out and his starting a new and equally shaky relationship with Sara Recor, and with Christine making the absolutely bizarre relationship choice of Beach Boy Dennis Wilson (even more of a self-destructive binger than her ex-husband), this was naturally the worst possible time, but for the best possible reasons, for Mac's original founding genius Peter Green to reenter the wilding spinning orbit of his former blues disciples.

The formerly godly Green had arrived in Los Angeles in 1977, apparently looking for a "new life" and coincidentally choosing the very city in which his old bandmates had actually constructed a new life for themselves without him, having hit the big time in the biggest way. It was ironic, or perhaps synchronistic, that Green chose Los Angeles, since he had declared it so long ago to be the capital of sin on earth. But Green was never that logical to begin with. His legend contains the following salient details: after his acid meltdown, he had worked as a grave digger and a hospital orderly. He also spent time in prison as well as various mental hospitals and private clinics, where he had injested many pharmaceutical therapies that were nearly as devastating as his own experimentation had been in the first place. After marrying his girlfriend in 1978, in a ceremony at Fleetwood's home, it was hoped by all that his life would get back on a more even keel. Oh, how the mighty have fallen, as the saying goes.

Fleetwood, ever the altruistic good friend despite his own incipient madness, signed Green on as a client of his own management firm, appropriately called Seedy Management. Fleetwood tried to get him a recording deal as a solo artist, only to hear the obvious response of, "Wait, didn't this cat go haywire on you once upon a time?" But Fleetwood, now likely the most powerful musical performer on earth in commercial terms, was insistent if not consistent, declaiming that Peter Green was one of the greats. "Ask Eric Clapton," he pleaded, "Ask B.B. King! This guy is a legend!" But the operative word was still "was."

Fleetwood arranged what he called a "sweetheart deal" with his own label, Warner Brothers, a company at least smart enough to know that Green had invented Fleetwood Mac wholly out of his incendiary brilliance, way back when. But when Fleetwood arranged a meeting in his office, elated and delighted that he could help resurrect one of the greats, and hoping to show the world that Fleetwood Mac took care of its own, as a family even more than a business, his hopes were dashed.Fleetwood reports that as soon as he saw Peter Green step forward toward Mo Ostin, the man with the money who was ready to hand it over to the man who had once been the best blues/rock guitarist in the world, he "felt sick": "Disheveled, his deportment gone slack, Pete had that desperate look in his eyes, a desperate look that cried out that Pete had flashed back to the bad old days. I tried to cheer him up, showing him the contract, at which he looked with undisguised loathing. 'This is *evil*,' he said, 'I'm not doing it. I feel very close to the devil right now, Mick, and it scares me.' In any case, Pete freaked out, he wouldn't sign, I looked like a total idiot, and that was the end of that."[17] Unfortunately, the wrong Peter Green had shown up for the meeting.

Weirdly, the following year Green went back to England, a country he perhaps should never have left, and released a fascinating and haunting record called *In the Skies,* one of my favorites. But it was still only a ghostly shadow of his former musical greatness. The most arresting aspect of it was that it hit the market the same year as *Tusk,* and was all but lost in the huge wave of critical reaction toward Mac's new direction. By that time, few members of the listening public, apart from cult fetishists like my friends, even knew that there ever even *was* a British psychedelic blues-rock origin to Fleetwood Mac, let alone had any awareness of the second great progressive phase of the five-album-long Bob Welch era. History is often unkind to the visionaries, they all but get gobbled up by the lurid success stories of those who deliver the goods in a more palatable manner, on a more accessible menu. People like Green get stuck in their own private sky.

By the early summer of 1979, the band had finished recording its magnum opus, though as Fleetwood has often pointed out, "finish" is a relative term. "Like the proverbial poem that's never complete, but only abandoned in despair,"[18] the recording process just finally stopped in its own tracks. But still, even though exhausted, enervated, and seemingly at the end of a rich emotional gold mine, they still all considered *Tusk* to be the crowning jewel of Fleetwood Mac's recorded work. So even though they had too many tracks, and even though they were all quite eccentric in a "new wavy style," Mac decided they could get away with releasing *all* of the music on what Fleetwood later called a "left-field double album." Who was going to tell them that they could not?

Thus a whole new set of *rumors* about the band's follow up to *Rumours* ensued—chiefly that they were going to go down in the history books as spending the most money in history on recording an album. Mac certainly understood these economic concerns; they just did not care about them. The company wanted them to carry on as usual, making a ton of money for everyone around them. The band understood that this was the company's, indeed the whole industry's, measure of success. But Fleetwood Mac's only measure, they declared, was the art of making and performing music, especially performing it. This is why they nearly died trying to support the record with a decadent tour to end all tours, and to try and salvage some integrity later by releasing a live record of that. And that live record, released in 1980, the last real year that Fleetwood Mac existed in its own spectacularly creative and chaotic stratosphere, was one of the best records in their long and winding history.

* * * * * * * * * *

It turned out that Fleetwood Mac, like most bands who have reached a dizzying pinnacle and then, almost against their will, allowed entropy to creep into their earlier amazing creativity flow, embarked on a dizzying descent into the solo-album phase of their career. It happened most obviously to The Beatles, the group that first established the pinnacle for everyone else; it happened to the Beach Boys, once the creativity of their leader had melted down into a sibling catfight with his own family over control and direction. So it was that 1979–1980, a pivotal turning point for one of the most successful pop groups in the world, saw the sudden release of a spate of solo efforts, both from former burnt out alumni, from the founding fathers, and from the twisted romantic team that had sparked their greatest hits.

Mac archivist Mark Trauernicht called this pivotal period the "return of the triumvirate," with the apparent return to music of the group's original guitar triumvirate, after a few years in the wilderness of madness, drugs, religious cults, and just general existential ennui. Jeremy Spencer, Danny Kirwan, and Peter Green all tried to stage comebacks, perhaps even as a result of their former band's rise to the Mount Olympus of the music world, as well as their own descent into the bog of personal problems and obsessions. After an initial attempt from both Kirwan and Spencer, music whose arteries were clogged by their own personal compulsions, neither ever really managed to approach the mountain again. As for Green, his story is still ongoing. He was so gifted that even his lamest and most confused gestures still had sparks to spare.

Bob Welch, the great master of the spooky transition, also released his second solo effort, *Three Hearts*—more or less a retread of his first, *French Kiss*. Although I still believe Welch was and is one of the most talented musicians on the planet, nothing he did after his magical collaboration with Fleetwood Mac ever even hinted at that level of sheer melodic, compositional, and lyrical intelligence. His records with Mac are as preciously unique as Brian Wilson's own perpetual genius machine.

Kirwan continued a long slide into both obscurity and incipient madness, which continues to this day, and sadly, the latest reports have him incarcerated, probably forever, in a mental institution. As early as 1976–77, most likely stirred by the grandiose shadow of his former bandmates, he released a record originally called *Midnight in San Juan* in the UK, for no apparent reason. It was later released stateside as *Danny Kirwan*, with a prominent label on the cover declaring him to be the "former" lead guitarist, vocalist, and writer for Fleetwood Mac. His is indeed one of the saddest and most melancholy-inducing efforts for me personally, since I had always extolled his brilliant virtues as one of the driving forces behind what I believe are the two most accomplished Fleetwood Mac recordings of the post-Green era, *Future Games* and *Bare Trees*. Several tracks hint at his former greatness, among them "Windy Autumn Day" and the tear-producing instrumental "Castaway," the latter of which echoes the sheer profundity of his old mentor's "Albatross." But suffice it to say that he also included a truly bizarre interpretation of The Beatles' "Let it Be," delivered in an inexplicable reggae beat version. Go in peace, Danny: we will always remember your soulful playing on the 1970 Mac masterpiece *Kiln House,* such jewels as "Station Man" and "Earl Gray." You will always have a place in our hearts and ears, even if your own self-loathing and insecurity caused you to compete in that category with the Olympian pains of Peter Green.

It is difficult and painful to discuss Jeremy Spencer, the sad little figure who had so much fun in the early days, until his own volatility found a dark outlet in the "religious" cult known first as the Children of God and later as the Family. Moses David, its founder, was later revealed to be only the leader of a ring of child molesters, scooping up acid-wrecked kids from the drowning streets of San Francisco, just as they had scooped Spencer up. His abysmal album, *Jeremy Spencer and the Children of God,* is best left alone. Cults and disco sounds seldom achieve much artistry when blurred together. But he too, starting in 1977—again the year his former bandmates struck it big with *Rumours*—returned to the air, if not the airwaves, to release *Flee,* a record with several moments of bliss-coated sadness. *Flee* was Spencer's final recording for almost two decades. Lately however, apparently slowly distancing himself from his "faith," he has made tentative steps back towards humanity. You too, Jeremy, have a special place in our memories, especially due to the ribald and wacky antics you were able to inject into the otherwise heavy blues oriented oceans which consumed the early band. Your place in blues history is also assured, even though it was so regrettable that you had to actually *live* the blues rather than merely performing it.

Archivist Trauernicht quite rightly points out that all this solo activity—including, I would add, even some of the upcoming solo efforts from Nicks, Buckingham, and the McVies—was dramatically overshadowed by the reemergence of Peter Green. I prefer to call this his "reemergency," however, since Green was never far from the edge, simply due to his own constitution. Green's gifted pathology, it should be remembered, is precisely the same personality profile of other demolished great ones, such as Brian Jones, Syd Barrett, Keith Moon, Jimi Hendrix, Jim Morrison, Janis Joplin, Brian Wilson, and saddest of all, John Lennon. My own copy of *In the Skies,* Green's 1979 return to the light, hardly has any grooves left on it. I highly recommend it to anyone who wonders if it is possible to still remain extremely creative even after losing most of your mental marbles.

Mick Fleetwood simply has one of the biggest hearts in show business, bar none, and most people in the know can agree with this regardless of what the rest of his antics might provoke. He has even gone on record as feeling it must be a kind of calling of some sort.

> I was determined, in a low key kind of way, to try to help everyone who'd been connected with Fleetwood Mac. We'd tried and succeeded with Bob Welch. We'd tried with Peter Green, to no avail. Jeremy had written to me from Sri

Lanka. That left Danny. While we were in London, I got his number, and in due course he showed up at the hotel. I was having breakfast in the suite when he appeared, looking grubby and very unwashed. It was heartbreaking. He'd lived with us at Benifols, the kids loved him, and he'd been a good looking chap. Now he looked like a derelict. I still hadn't been able to elicit what he'd been up to, or how we could help. Then we had to go downstairs to catch the transportation to Wembley. Danny refused to go and got quite paranoid. The buses pulled up to the curb and I tried to give him a hug. "No," he said, "Don't do that. I don't want to be touched." I got on the bus, and I never saw him again.[19]

Fleetwood had found Danny's number, but it was too numb to matter.

Meanwhile, the monstrous *Tusk* tour continued to roll around the world. Its anthems were certainly innovative, but they were also jagged, self-indulgent, and, as one observer noted, "borderline weird." It was, in short, just what a great rock record should be—impossible to define, and yet impossible to escape. How do you market something like that? The answer is, you cannot—especially if one of the marketing gimmicks to publicize it was a complete playing of the record on FM radio to celebrate its release, a move that made purchase after taping both redundant and academic. It also alerted the loyal listening audience that something fishy was happening to their favorite group.

TUSK:
RELEASED 1979, WARNER BROTHERS

In reality, something the Mac family has never paid much attention to, there were two records in this album package—not just because it was a double album, but more so because one album is a Fleetwood Mac record and the other is a solo Buckingham record. The difficulty for listeners was that those records were mixed together into a compelling but challenging dream stew. As a matter of fact, if traditional Mac fans shuffled the tracks and taped their own versions, it would have been easy to establish the borderline where Mac ended and Buckingham began.

The title track, "Tusk" itself, also to be insanely released as the most unlikely single since "Oh Well Parts One and Two," was and still is a peculiar anthem. Recorded in the empty Dodger Stadium with the 112-member University of Southern California Trojan Marching Band, it was a creative but strange attempt to recreate the feeling of a village brass band that Fleetwood had once encountered while hung over one morning in Normandy. As mentioned, *Tusk* was Fleetwood's "jocular term of affection for the male member," a title that made Stevie Nicks angry and almost quit in revulsion. She did not, of course—no one ever quit Fleetwood Mac on purpose, at least no one in their right mind.

The song "Sara" is a meaningful one for both Nicks's fans and for Fleetwood himself, in which Nicks sings in tribute to her muse, in her classically opulent manner. One of the best ways to appreciate the unusually innovative material wrapped around the usual Mac formulae is to play the record in its entirety, which today's CDs make easier than yesterday's four sides flipped, and hear the splendor of their madness stretch out in its full true eccentric and schizoid glory.

But, as Cath Carroll points out in her study of *Rumours* and afterward,

> With the gruelling years of non-stop touring, the success, the excess, and the need to get on and create, it would have been difficult to keep a sensible perspective. That they all *made* another album together is really the big story, for ever since the success of 1975's *Fleetwood Mac,* the band had been plagued with constant quizzing about exactly when they were splitting up. Stevie Nicks was happy to go on record about how much she disliked the packaging of *Tusk,* and that, although she loved the *spirit* of the album, she was not about to repeat the experience. Mick Fleetwood experienced similar ambivalence when the album was released, although he has insisted that *Tusk,* in retrospect, is his all time favourite album.[20]

The music press was equally undecided, not especially liking the Buckingham contributions and his overall concept, and not certain that the songs with the more classic Mac feel were as good as they should or could have been. Mitchell Cohen, writing in *Creem* magazine, described Nicks's songs as "fruit suspended in jello," but he did single out *Tusk* itself as a "blessed out image risk, but not a commercial one."[21] The album's length, he believed, made it all the more obvious that by this time, Fleetwood Mac was really three separate bands, a phenomenon we have seen played out before in harrowing emotion by The Beatles. Stephen Holden, writing in *Rolling Stone* magazine, called *Tusk* a "mosaic of pop-rock fragments," which is why I myself so often compare it to Brian Wilson's doomed *Smile.* He also said that this record ushered out the 1970s "with a long melancholy sigh."[22] Visionary Greil Marcus, of course, called it "subversive middle of the road, a change to The System from within."[23]

All genres have their own following, and artists generally would rest easy with that fact. But still, Buckingham has had to carry on for nearly three decades with the constant criticisms from the public, the press, even the band itself, that he had not just deconstructed but destroyed the band's heritage. But lately, the world seems to have caught up with his contrary visions, acknowledging it as a creative island waiting to be discovered by future musicians.

FLEETWOOD MAC LIVE:
RELEASED 1980, WARNER BROTHERS

Recorded during the *Tusk* tour, this is the ultimate statement about what this band means, wants, needs, and does best. A hundred years from now, *this* will be the most effective way to experience what made Fleetwood Mac so special. It certainly has to be counted among the best live recordings in pop history, a list than also includes the Who's *Live at Leeds,* the Doors' *Absolutely Live,* and the Rolling Stones' *Get Yer Ya-Ya's Out.*

As expected, *Tusk* had proven to be a severe kind of borderline between their shared musical history and their burgeoning careers as solo artists. Nicks had even declared that after *Tusk,* she was never going to do another Buckingham record on Fleetwood Mac time again. And they did not. The live record is a pure celebration of what it means to sweat in public and deliver the goods, yet again, with perfect precision and with pop majesty. By 1980, the band sought a "divorce" from Mick Fleetwood by firing him as their manager, after realizing that he had squandered and snorted a massive amount of their revenues.

Fleetwood had to convince his bandmates that now was the time for a live album, still their only live album except for the late great return of *The Dance* in 1996—one of their best ever, period. However the album did not do as well as anticipated, possibly as a consequence of audience shock after the wild detour of *Tusk,* but more so as a result of accidentally bad timing, a financial downturn in the general economy, and sudden cultural shift in taste and style that we now recognize as "the eighties."

By this stage, the band had both run out of the time needed to reinvent themselves yet again or to rejuvenate and renovate their 1970s persona, as well as run out of the personal and creative steam required to do so. In Bob Brunning's excellent study *Fleetwood Mac: Behind the Masks,* Fleetwood explained that after so many years of being the hardest working band in show business, it was time to deliver live evidence of that fact. They had never done a live release in their long history, so it seemed that the time was just right.[24]

And this one was a masterpiece, even if it is a collage. Friends of mine who saw the three Canadian shows in Vancouver and Edmonton tell me that it was the greatest rock concert they have ever seen, even though Mac was not their favorite band. Performing live always was the secret of their success and longevity. It opens with the classic sneer of Buckingham's first song on the 1975 debut of the new group, the angry and defensive "Monday Morning"—sounding even more suspicious and sarcastic live then it did n the studio, perhaps because everyone could plainly see Buckingham and Nicks avoiding each other's gaze, but collaborating to produce great music. Remarkably, even tracks culled from hundreds of different concerts still sound like they belong to one single, impossible sequence that summed up their modus operandi perfectly.

Each well-known cut is revived by being done in a slightly different live version. All demonstrate the incendiary guitar skills of Buckingham, even rougher and tougher live than in the studio, and carrying on a great electric lava tradition stretching back all the way to Peter Green. His swooping edge and raw cutting swirls manage to convince us that there really was a unique reason that Mick heard the future one day when he first heard "Frozen Love" from Buckingham and Nicks's only other record release.

"Say You Love Me," the classic Christine song about loving the wrong person, follows quickly and she does it great justice live, as she is falling, falling, falling, back and forth between woo and wicked. Nicks's "Dreams" is delivered next, with a fiery rage seldom contained in any pop songs since Lennon, declaring once again, by this time probably for the millionth performance, that "players only love you when they're playing." All the while, she stands on stage next to the ultimate player in her life, her ex-boyfriend yet paradoxically current collaborator, who still somehow manages to turn her dour songs about him into scintillating little pop gems.

But the biggest surprise on the double live record comes next, Buckingham's touching and insane rendition of Peter Green's timeless "Oh Well," the song he listened to as a teenager in order to teach himself how to play the guitar. Suffice it to say he learned his lessons very well. He plunges into the mad muck of Green's hysterical hatred of stardom and delivers an exquisitely tortured reincarnation of Green's breathtaking guitar runs and jagged stops and starts. Fleetwood in particular shines on this one, since he is called upon to race wildly to keep up with Buckingham's lava flow, as he cranks up the screaming solos while the crowd goes nuts with unrequited adoration for their absent electrical hero. Buckingham may not be Green, but he is the next best thing.

After reaching far back into the past for their playlist, the band quickly rushes into the real reason for the concert tour, selling *Tusk* to an unprepared audience. They launch into "Over and Over," the *Tusk* opener, which sets the tone for the rest of the concert—especially since they play it in a stripped and slowed-down version that almost approximates classic Mac vibes. The live version of *Over and Over,* followed by "Sara" and "Not That Funny," softer and mellowed out slightly, somehow manage to convince the fans, at least the ones sitting in that concert, that, maybe this *is* the same group they loved after all. Those paying attention would have clearly noticed that Buckingham, far from hijacking and holding the Mac sound hostage to his own experimental whims, was actually revealing what was inherently radical and experimental about Mac in the first place: the ironic fact that they still played the blues, but in a new and postmodern form that left behind not only the 12-bar style, but all bars and all styles.

As if they had been waiting for a century, the crowd explodes when the band finally delivers some *Rumours* material, "Never Going Back Again," only to be further teased and seduced by "Landslide" from *Fleetwood Mac,* and "Fireflies," a Nicks song of little consequence. But then finally Christine's addictive "Over My Head" and the always tasty Nicks logo, "Rhiannon" send the concert spinning into overdrive. That momentum carries them all away on a cloud of sheer frenzy, over the top entirely, once "Go Your Own Way" and "Don't Stop" kick out the stops.

Inexplicably, but then again may not so much, the live album careens to a peculiar ending with its monument to embodied fear, Buckingham's "I'm So Afraid": "I've been alone all the years, so many ways to count the tears. I never change, I never will. I'm so afraid the way I feel." It is his own private "Surf's Up." This song alone is worth the price of admission. It is harrowing, its guitar lines are astonishing, and I firmly believe it is Lindsey Buckingham's personal "Green Manalishi." If this is not the blues, then for God's sake, what color is it? By this, I mean it is his dark night of the soul, his hour of the wolf. There is more of a continuum between Peter Green, Brian Wilson, and Lindsey Buckingham than first meets the ear. Listen again to that guitar! Talk about a stairway to hell.

But this was only to be capped off by perhaps the oddest song they have ever performed, one composed in the dark ages by Buckingham's idol, Brian Wilson. With "Farmer's Daughter," the band appears to reach back to the very roots of their craft, to stroke those roots fondly, before disappearing from public view as a group for a long, lonely two years.

During this two-year vacation from their creative chaos, they experimented with several different solo projects, with varying degrees of success, until finally admitting that what they had together was special, and that breaking up was hard to do. Their marriage made in hell together was saved by the therapist who runs the big cash register. After two years of waiting, the public finally received what they always wanted and craved from the band, the "real and actual" sequel to *Rumours*. The album was appropriately entitled, *Mirage*, which is exactly what it was.

Other record releases of significance in 1979–80: Music for Airports by Brian Eno; *Slow Train Coming* by Bob Dylan; *Broken English* by Marianne Faithful; *London Calling* by the Clash; *The Wall* by Pink Floyd; *Get Happy!* by Elvis Costello; *Remain in Light* by Talking Heads; *Ace of Spades* by Motorhead; *Fresh Fruit* by Dead Kennedys; *Underwater Moonlight* by the Soft Boys; *Crocodiles* by Echo and the Bunnymen; *Back in Black* by AC/DC; *Peter Gabriel III* by Peter Gabriel; *Warm Thoughts* by Smokey Robinson; and last, but certainly not least, the weirdly wonderful *In the Skies* by Peter Green.

Then Play On, Again: The Last 27 Years

8

From today's vantage point in 2007, one might have expected Fleetwood Mac to have had relatively quiet times as they all slid into middle age and beyond. The last 27 years, however, have been punctuated by several surprising ups and downs, as per usual for this group. In fact, one could almost quote a famous song by their British peers, "they've been going in and out of style but they're guaranteed to raise a smile"—except that they still raise a difference of opinion, even an argument, as well as an occasional smile. No arguments any more from Lindsey Buckingham about how best to control his own creative muse and the music it produces: just do it all by yourself, they way you always wanted to, but always hold on to the possibility of there being yet another Mac reunion.

In the fall of 2006, Buckingham released another opus, *Under the Skin*, and was downright philosophical about how mature he had finally become, after all those incendiary years of mutual infighting. That new record has not only proven his durable longevity as a singer-songwriter but has also clearly highlighted how powerful and dynamic his role as the central sound alchemist for the Fleetwood Mac spirit. He was not just crucial, he was indispensable.

Writing in the *New York Times* after a successful concert of new solo material by Buckingham in October 2006, Ben Ratliff commented that there are some "difficult to like aspects" of his work, but that he was daring enough to put the most difficult up front in his live solo show, while performing his first solo record in 14 years. Ratliff focused on a certain degree of self-pity that has always hounded Buckingham, even during his most acclaimed period of bonanza record sales. In short, this perspective amounts to the burden of growing older as an artist and "being tensely aware that even if you are great at what you do, you may not receive proper recognition, and this may make you feel aimless."[1]

Clearly, Lindsey Buckingham is still toiling in the shadows, not only of his visionary but underappreciated *Tusk* experiment, but also of the entire empire of pop acclaim he helped create for Fleetwood Mac. It is as if guilt over his success makes him perpetually run towards ever more daring and original musical territories. For Ratliff, and for anyone else who knows the background story and subtext of Buckingham's self-aggrandizement, it was obvious that the brilliant singer-songwriter-guitarist-producer was stacking the deck against himself. But it was also obvious that his talent always pulls him through, no matter how maudlin his complaints about fame might become. As Ratliff phrased it in the *Times,* the day after Buckingham's Town Hall solo show: "But everything was all right in the end, the strength of his songs, his singing and his guitar playing, and his strange intensity as a performer, allowed him to carry the evening."[2]

As always, for Buckingham, and even for Fleetwood Mac, everything turns out all right in the end. Despite the customary paranoia and dissatisfaction in his songs that have become his stock in trade—evident from the very beginning with his debut in 1973 with a practically adolescent Stevie Nicks under his Svengali-like tutelage—he still manages to speak for his audience, and to articulate on their behalf half-formed feelings and fears that everyone shares beneath the surface.

It was telling that no matter how far away Buckingham tries to run from the shadow of the Mac monster, his audience will still demand its blood-payment of at least some of those famous songs. So, true to form, at Town Hall last year, while attempting to debut at least half of his new solo effort, *Under the Skin,* he was also compelled to pull out some of his extraordinary Mac anthems, among them "Second Hand News," "Go Your Own Way," and, of course, "Tusk."

Other observes of his return to the spotlight have shared in the same queasy feeling that we simply like this guy's music no matter how neurotic or self-absorbed he may be or become. One entertainment report in the *Toronto Star* newspaper tried to project the surprise of an unexpectedly content man, calm now after years of madness on the road with his famous mates. "Sudden Maturity Strikes Guitar Whiz," they cutely named the piece. Perhaps that maturity has something to do with being suddenly 57 years old, with a stable marriage and three young children to take care of, rather than only trying to care for his own genius, and to shepherd the volatile lyrics, emotions, and ego of Stevie Nicks. In the *Star* piece, Buckingham noted that "It gets into a more bare-bones look at what's going on with me after all this time. I've finally gotten married and am slowly shedding the dysfunctional thing everyone in the band seemed to have emotionally. Its something I've been interested in for a long time: trying to distill down the essence of that certain thing I do. I want to still have it sound like a record, but very much in the spirit of someone just sitting and playing guitar."[3]

Of course, the inevitable question hovered above the crowd, the way smoke used to hover above them in the old days: What about Fleetwood Mac? Incredibly, given the history, Buckingham says that he and the other members of the band, made so infamous through emotional conflict and confrontation in the service of creativity, are all up for future touring, but unsure if future recordings are a likely reality. Ironically, his latest album features two tracks with the old brilliant rhythm section of Fleetwood and McVie, a surprise to no one. "Despite what has gone on," Buckingham readily admitted in the *Star* piece, "This is a group of people I'll know as well as ever know except my family. I've been through more with them than I've ever been through with my own family!"[4] But still, that second-family feeling can produce some cutting and incisive lyrical content, such as the opening cut from the album, a confessional tune in which he opines: "Reading the papers, saw a review, said I was a visionary but nobody knew. Now that's been a problem, feeling unseen, just like I'm living somebody's dream." Well, yes you are, Lindsey; you are living *our* dream.

In another appreciation of his new record and his New York debut of the new material, Anthony DeCurtis pointed out correctly that "in rock critic circles, the term 'visionary' clings to Mr. Buckingham the way 'fleet-footed' define Achilles in Homer's *Iliad*. He garnered much of the credit for *Rumours,* the 1977 pop masterpiece that sold close to 20 million copies in the U.S. alone. Even that album's more daring follow up, *Tusk,* widely regarded as a commercial failure, won Mr. Buckingham critical admiration for his willingness to ditch the hit-making formula in favor of daring sonic experimentation."[5] Once more Buckingham—who I suppose is living proof that if you survive long enough they start calling you Mister—was able to varnish his favorite piece of mental furniture: "Much of Fleetwood Mac was a double edged sword. Band politics can be joyous and supportive, or competitive and sinister. For me, things tended to fall into the latter category. Maybe that's because I was the glue, the one putting the songs together, and yet I wasn't necessarily the one with the political power in the group. That's a strange place to be, but you know, that's my paranoid side."[6]

DeCurtis also perfectly captured the essence of what a Buckingham record both sounds and feels like: "The result is a kind of intensely modern folk music, candidly personal, seemingly directly songs that flirt with soul-baring and then retreat into a cocoon of sound." This insight is supported by Buckingham's own surprisingly modest summary: "Those are probably my strong points (production skills and eloquent acoustic guitar playing) I'm not the best singer, and I don't even think of myself as a writer per se. I'm a stylist. But you can get a long way on style, so I'll take it. I'll work with what I got!"[7]

And after the tour for his newest 2007 vintage Lindsey record is done? "Well..." Buckingham begins to intone the obvious, "There's Fleetwood Mac. I suppose I don't have to, but they'd like to do something. And why wouldn't I want to do that?" he told the *Times*. Why not, indeed?

* * * * * * * * * *

It must be difficult to walk away from something so grand, so decadent, so huge, so global, as the music machine Mac had become by 1980. That year, the various members of the always fractured and occasionally splintering group were each exploring their own solo directions. This is always a sure sign that the life expectancy of a group is limited, once they are more absorbed in their own personal hubris and private creativity at the expense of the communal consciousness required for effective collaborations.

And so, as one chronicler adroitly put it, "it's come to distances." The decade of the 1980s served as one of the biggest booms in our popular cultural history and, on the surface at least, seemingly diametrically opposed to the 1960s fervor that had given birth to Fleetwood Mac. The decade began and continued with each member taking some time to live their own lives for a change, instead of literally being in each other's pockets figuratively, creatively, financially, and emotionally. It must have seemed like a vacation from entropy for all of them.

For Mick Fleetwood, of course, all vacations still involved making music, the one thing in his life he never left behind. So he went far away, to Ghana, and began to record a relaxing little record with local indigenous musicians, especially drummers. This led to his own first solo effort, almost synonymous with the double live Fleetwood Mac album, *The Visitor*. This was the phenomenon of rock royalty meeting the roots musicians in a big way, one that Buckingham could not help but gently satirize in his wonderful "Bwana" song, released on his own solo record of 1981, *Law and Order*. While some people may have rested after a decade of excess, after *Tusk* and the exhausting double *Live* record, Fleetwood's idea of taking it easy was to drag two complete portable recording consoles across Africa, as if to unwind a bit after surviving the 1970s. He even invited his old idol Peter Green, the founder of Fleetwood Mac, to sing with the African musicians on their version of his own old "Rattlesnake Shake" opus from *Then Play On*. It was pricelessly strange.

Stevie Nicks would also release her *Bella Donna* solo effort in the same year as Buckingham's, and it is considered by many people to be the true sequel to *Rumours*. True, in some ways it is, but not in any of the substantial ways that would have made it a Mac artifact. In fact, it is extremely similar to having a bowl of hot chili sauce but without any meat on which to pour the spicy mixture. And it was, of course, more fabulously successful than any other solo effort by a Fleetwood Mac member.

No, the true Fleetwood Mac sequel and follow-up to *Rumours* would have to wait until 1982, when after being coaxed back into the feverish fold, and perhaps aware that *Law and Order* may have been pure Lindsey but the public wanted impure Mac, Buckingham agreed to return and collaborate on *Mirage*. This record is exactly what the title suggests it is, a shimmering phantom masquerading as a living entity. Buckingham was sorely displeased with the results of *Mirage,* even though the public ate it up, since the public's appetites were never high on his list of creative priorities. He would linger on the Mac threshold for a few more years until producing a more suitable departure for himself, or so he thought. *Tango in the Night,* their triumphant 1987 return to form of sorts, was not really a comeback but more of a come again.

The origins of this magical return, in keeping with Mac's usual standard of creative chaos, was almost entirely accidental, or at least circumstantial. Christine McVie was recording something in the studio and invited long-time producer Richard Dashut along for the ride. Naturally enough, Buckingham also somehow arrived, followed shortly afterward by both Fleetwood and McVie, apparently always ready for another party, and all together appearing like predators who have caught a whiff of some new prey. The resulting tango together seemed to ease past pains and apply at least a little ointment to their collective wounds. Starting as a solo Buckingham record, just as so many other Mac productions had, he eventually allowed it to morph into a collaborative group album release. By this time he had no doubt drawn the obvious parallels between himself and the Godfather character portrayed by Al Pacino in one of Francis Ford Coppola's sequels, most notably in the revealing line about trying to escape from the clutches of his notorious mafia family: "Just when I thought I was out, they keep pulling me back in!"

It is not an exaggeration to liken the musical institution known as Fleetwood Mac to an intricate mafia-like family where no amount of infighting can sever the bond, or in Mac's case, "The Chain." And the band would be the first to readily admit that it often felt that way to all of them. Yet it was not the usual capitalist desire for "more, please" that kept them running on their wheels, since they already had all the money they ever needed. They had all won and lost fortunes several times in fact.

"It would be naïve to say that we were oblivious to the money," Fleetwood has remarked, "but the music came first. *Then* maybe you make some money. We didn't want to approach our lives with the understanding that '-soft rock' is the sort of music we have to do to make money. I shit on that whole concept, because the point of the music is lost. It becomes nothing more than another business. We had to please ourselves first, that was the point of what being an artist was all about. If you didn't keep your integrity in the face of hard commercial decisions, you were lost. Your soul was dead.''[8] And Fleetwood applied the same vital creative credo to his own solo work as well. "We finished *The Visitor* toward the end of April 1980. George Harrison came over and put some slide guitar on "Walk a Thin Line" for me. Other English musicians added a guitar part here, a synthesizer there. When the whole project was done, we'd spent a half a million dollars. The album was released soon after and didn't make one fucking dime! But I had learned and experienced more than money can buy.''[9]

Upon Fleetwood's return from his little vacation from reality, reality was waiting patiently for him to start the process all over again. He called them "rumblings" back home: "Looks like the end for Fleetwood Mac!" boomed the headline from the *New York Times* in March 1981, surely not the most encouraging publicity for rock royalty, but certainly something he and they were well accustomed to. "There's big trouble among members of rock's hottest group," the story declared, to no one's surprise, "and some highly placed musical sources are saying the band is swiftly heading for the rocks." The media cited creative differences and a major loss of income from their last tour to support the unsupportable *Tusk* as prime indicators. The article implied, as the media always liked to do, that their internal troubles were heading the band for the rocks, in an anticipated breakup unmatched since The Beatles.

Heading for the rocks? But they were born on the rocks! Untimely? But they had been breaking up since 1969! One way or the other, the band decided, yet again, to prove their critics wrong. The only real way to do that was to release another *real* Fleetwood Mac record, and post haste. So, as Fleetwood recalls it, they launched into an attempt to get into the *Rumours* groove again, perhaps conveniently forgetting that *Rumours* had been the fluky result of their crumbling relationships being held together with the creative glue of music and performance, and that without that strange and exotic tension (having now all gone their own ways with other lovers and partners), they were in fact bereft of raw material.

Their idea, which was not really a bad one, was to somehow "update" that *Rumours* groove, but exactly how does one do that? It amounts after all, to reprising youthful indiscretions without either the youth or the discretion involved to support the creative claims of the new music. Fleetwood has distinct impressions of the nearly impossible expectations that were once more piled onto the group's collective shoulders. "I remember some semi-tense conversations about musical direction in this era, as Lindsey felt that I still blamed him for the relatively weak sales of *Tusk*. I thought that we should do what we do best, and insisted on doing this album *as a band*. This time the entire band played on almost every track; then Chris, Lindsey and I spent months in the studio, overdubbing in typical Fleetwood Mac fashion.''[10]

Mirage was released in mid-1982, an artistic and financial success. At this stage, Nicks's persona of the resident "wicca girl" had enlarged itself to be the primary face and voice the band, at least in the public's imagination, with *Rolling Stone* magazine dubbing Nicks, "The Reigning Queen of Rock and Roll." Also helping out the public image and the market sales of the group, just as FM radio formats had lifted them up in the 1970s, was the new cable television format called MTV, which broadcast such Nicks anthems as "Gypsy" into the ears of North America's suburbs on a 24-hour basis. As usual with this long-lasting band, they happened to be in the right place at the right time. *Mirage* went to number one, though it was a pale shadow of both the *Fleetwood Mac* and *Rumours* albums in terms of its emotional weight, form, and content.

That record also marked the first time that Fleetwood Mac did not automatically launch itself into the mad stratosphere of touring to support a record, largely due to the fact that Stevie Nicks now had a billowing solo career almost as huge as the band in which she was famous for singing. Naturally enough, without the extensive touring that allowed the band to demonstrate its remarkable live prowess, the album "died" after about five weeks on the charts, replaced by the newest new thing in an endless chain of new things.

After a succession of well-intentioned, occasionally interesting but generally mediocre solo attempts by all concerned (with the exception of Buckingham's, which were always exemplary), Fleetwood finally watched the financial foundation disappear beneath his feet in 1984, having been forced into facing the reality of a massive bankruptcy petition. "Mick's Missing Millions," the papers chided and opined, always ready to kick someone when they are down, especially if that someone is a Rabelaisian decadent rock star who personally put acres of Colombian product up his nose in a maniacal way not seen since the days of Charlie Parker's binges. I love the laconic and understated manner in which Fleetwood himself describes the hiatus period: "Time passed. It took another three years to get the next Fleetwood Mac album made, and the band back on the road."[11]

The road always was the only place that many any sense at all to both McVie and his boyhood mate, no matter how senseless that road really was in actuality. The road needed sacrificial victims, and Mac was always ready to comply and prostrate themselves before the idols at the altar of commerce. But by this time, the gang was clearly getting a little tired, a little past it all, and a little jaded. The only member of the group who may have actually experienced a little fun during this 1982 *Mirage* period, was the still-superb bassist John McVie, a man not at all known for ever having much of a personal relationship with fun for its own sake. But by reaching back into his own musical and personal roots and joining John Mayall for a record and tour reunion of past Bluesbreakers, he must have been feeling the fire that got him started in the first place. It was a welcome break from being on top of the world but feeling like he was buried under his own hubris. A blues-break in fact, one that celebrated the kind of music that had first inspired him almost 40 years earlier, when Mayall had launched his career by introducing him to Peter Green.

MIRAGE:
RELEASED 1982, WARNER BROTHERS

The album is just what its title suggests—not quite an illusion, but not quite the real thing, either. A mirage is technically not a dream or a fantasy, but rather the image of something real which cannot possibly be mistaken for the original thing itself. This release quite simply had "I'm sorry, mea culpa, please forgive me for *Tusk*" written all over it, with Buckingham making a valiant but miserable attempt to reprise and repeat the band's brand flavor and temperature.

In the middle of a dizzying blizzard of solo projects from a group continuing to operate on the edge of extinction, *Mirage* floated serenely onto the plates of their hungry Mac fans, satisfied that this one was just what the menu ordered. Nicks's "Gypsy," in particular, was what the madding crowd wanted, and she delivered with her usual gauzy aplomb. In "Straight Back," she also seems to sum up the entire Mac enterprise from a particularly wistful perspective: "The dream is not over, the dream is just away...the dream was never over, the dream was just lost." That, indeed, is the subtext and unconscious message of this record.

Christine McVie, in her own erstwhile and dependably quiet manner, succeeds in injecting a few lighter moments of romance into the mix, with such songs as "Love in Store," "Hold Me," and "Wish You Were Here": "Each moment is a memory, time is so unkind. Every hour, filled with an emptiness I can't hide." Accidentally, her song offers itself as an emblem of the energy at the heart of their collective collaboration, and of the feeling when something formerly full recedes into a state of lacking. Though fantastically successful for Fleetwood Mac, *Mirage* was also a terrible struggle for its long suffering members, especially Buckingham in his attempt at self-redemption. Only Mac could end up celebrating a state of mind where life can be *filled* with emptiness, thus managing to illustrate how most of our lives are ironically full and empty at the same time.

* * * * * * * * * *

To Christine McVie, and her mates, Fleetwood Mac was like a living thing, and a source stronger than its various members. Even Fleetwood Mac sees Fleetwood Mac this way, as if it were a behemoth risen from the depths of the sea to swallow them all up individually, but also to strengthen them all collectively. Weirdly, it seems that a monster had indeed been born and continued to trudge forward, but it had risen from the depths of the very real personalities and problems of its various members. It may not, in fact, have any existence at all apart from those parameters, no matter what the rest of us may choose to project upon the screen they offer us for precisely that purpose.

By 1983, the entire band and its extended family were due for a break, and they took a hiatus that lasted four years, an eternity in the world of pop music. Their voracious need for outlets for their creative chaos and its phenomenal by-products however was stoked with still more solo projects.

In addition to his *Law and Order* release, pretty much the only Mac alumni effort to amount to a solid piece of independent work, Buckingham also performed on other musicians' outings. Several of his songs, including the minor but cheerily up-tempo "Holiday Road," were featured in the movie *National Lampoon's Vacation*. He also appeared on Randy Newman's *Trouble in Paradise,* a title that might just as well have been the subtitle to all of Fleetwood Mac's output, as well as Walter Egan's *Wild Exhibitions.*

Christine McVie also sang on Egan's record while preparing her own solo album, the first solo effort from her in 14 years. She was always less obsessed with her own solo career than the others, partly due to her own laid-back nature, and partly due to the principal obsession in her life, as indicated by her quote above. Stevie Nicks, the most commercially successful of the solo Mac alumni, if not the most artistically advanced, was busy readying her *Bella Donna* follow-up, *The Wild Heart*. Meanwhile, true to the basic nature of the record industry, that of selling product wherever there was a suitable demand for it, even the past of Mac was being mined for future releases. This category contained a delightfully nostalgic 10" EP of the original Shotgun Express band, featuring an impossibly young Mick Fleetwood and Peter Green.

Never one to linger over the past, however, Fleetwood also formed a temporary unit called "Zoo" in order to harness his excess energies, releasing the aptly titled "I'm Not Me" and featuring, to no one's surprise, Lindsey Buckingham and Christine McVie, as well as a video appearance by Stevie Nicks. The family that plays (or rages) together, stays together.

Peter Green was still toiling on the most lamentable aspects of his character, yet somehow managed to produce a collection called *Kolors,* a lackluster expedition to nowhere fast and a pale shadow of his former greatness. His continued efforts to make music despite his legendary psychological problems adds even more sorrow to his long sad story, since it reveals the core and crushing ambivalence of his original meltdown back in 1969 over the evils of the industry.

But this was an industry that was ever willing to embrace the talents of the great or formerly great, as long as there was profit to be made for the company. That explains most accurately the ongoing rise and fall of Fleetwood Mac: the artists cannot live without making music, and the managers cannot live without cashing in on it. And so, Mac itself was poised for yet another ascent of the mountain.

One could not call it a comeback, since they never really went way; but Fleetwood does call it that in his own autobiography, even if he meant it largely tongue in cheek. By 1985, he was mostly engulfed in trying to reassemble the shattered parts of his reckless life, personally, professionally, and financially, after his catastrophic bankruptcy and ouster as the band's manager. The way he puts it, in his typically lovelorn fashion over his lifelong baby, "My main concern was the revivification of Fleetwood Mac. The problem was how to make it happen. I was the only member of the band desperate to see it back together."[12] The others had no such desperation; indeed, they were beginning to savor the feeling of being free agents, and free of the personal relationships that had so burdened them throughout a magnificent success. Nicks's album *Wild Heart* was selling in the millions, and she was busy on the next one, *Rock a Little*. Buckingham was working on a third solo project, and Christine had a big hit with *Got a Hold On Me*, perhaps another veiled reference to her primary creative affiliations. John McVie was more than pleased to drink away his semiretirement years, occasionally gigging with old friends such as the Mayall Bluesbreakers alumni, something he did not need to take too seriously and actually enjoyed playing on, unlike his Mac labors.

"The reformation process started somewhat inauspiciously," Fleetwood recalls, "when the rest of the band visited Stevie Nicks backstage at a benefit she was playing. It was the first time Fleetwood Mac had been together since the end of the *Mirage* tour, three years earlier, and the tension was so thick you could choke on it."[13] It turned out that Christine McVie would be the driving force for a reunion. She was asked to record a version of the Elvis Presley song "Can't Help Falling In Love" for a film soundtrack, and she requested the production services of Richard Dashut, who in turn suggested some involvement from big Elvis fan Lindsey Buckingham. Then Christine's manager John Courage called Fleetwood and McVie, and suddenly in August 1985, four-fifths of Fleetwood Mac were trapped together in the studio cutting a record, almost by accident. But by now we all know that there are no accidents when it comes to this band, and we especially realize that "chance is the fool's name for fate," once again.

Tango in the Night, a sterling success for the band from every perspective, gave their hungry 1987 audience the menu they had paid for, were used to, and just wanted—pure, plain, and simple. Well, simple, at least, if not plain or pure, since by this time Stevie Nicks's cocaine addiction had escalated to astronomical proportions, and in 1986, during most of the actual preparation of the record, she entered the Betty Ford Clinic for rehabilitation. And, of course, it was down to Buckingham's brilliant technical mastery to simulate her presence on an album for which she was little more than a tiny blonde ghost.

Buckingham by this time was too fed up with the whole dynamic he had partly created to want yet another road trip and tour to support the record. He was feeling far too fulfilled creatively working on his own to desire a reprise of what by then must have felt like an adolescent obsession. He walked out, and they balked. Fleetwood, constantly on the verge of seeing his institution and corporation fade into history, decided to enlist the aid of Rick Vito and Bill Burnette. Absolutely nothing of any consequence can be said about these two imposters, even though they helped the band make *Tango* a number one hit by playing their hearts out on a European tour, in the gaping absence of the turbocharged Buckingham vibration.

That same year, the BBC showed a documentary on Fleetwood Mac, which it called "the epitome of adult rock music," and one of the producers had sought out Peter Green to get some foundational material and footage. As Fleetwood remembers it with heartbreaking sadness, Green was unrecognizable at this point, with long matted hair, four-inch-long fingernails that seemed to scream "I'll never play guitar again!" and a confused and confusing pallor suffusing his very being. Green declared on camera that he did not even own a guitar anymore, and even more distressingly announced that he was "recuperating from taking drugs," even though his meltdown took place almost a decade before. "I only took LSD eight or nine times, but it lasted so long. That was my failing I guess." When questioned about whether he might rejoin the band under any circumstances, he responded: "If Mick called and said he needed me, I'd be tempted to cut them...(referring to his nails)...but I'd probably let it pass." Had he ever regretted leaving Fleetwood Mac, he was asked? "Yeah, I've regretted it," he answered aimlessly. "But then I also regret joining them as well."[14] Joining them? He invented them. There but for the grace of grace, go many other rock stars.

For Fleetwood, apart from losing a great and close friend and inspiring genius, the Green legacy is another cautionary tale: "His fate haunts a generation of successful English musicians, all now entering middle age, who saw one of the authentic geniuses among them withdraw from the lists, refusing to sell out or play the fool. He not only started Fleetwood Mac and gave the rest of us a career; he also taught me something about my playing that's very important to me. He gave me the feeling he understood who I was as a person. Most of all he gave us that magical, ongoing gift of a name—Fleetwood Mac."[15] If only any one of us had been able to understand who *he* was, as a person, but that was difficult, if not impossible, since he stopped being one so long ago, so tragically young in his creative demise.

TANGO IN THE NIGHT:
RELEASED 1987, WARNER BROTHERS

Dissatisfied with the results of *Mirage*, it would take Buckingham five years to be convinced to try again. The results, a decade after *Rumours*, were astronomically better, and managed to garner the band the number one spot yet again. But the wear and tear of supporting a living institution with a brand the size of Mac was beginning to be evident. Once again, *Tango in the Night* was wildly popular with Mac fans globally; but once again, it seemed a pale shadow of the kind of work they were producing when they were all disintegrating personally and professionally. It is quite a lamentable curse in a way: the best music they can ever produce is forged out of the fire of their own dysfunction and confusion in and out of love.

This was the Lindsey Buckingham solo record that got away from him and somehow morphed into yet another Fleetwood Mac record—with his full compliance, of course, and yet somehow also against his will. "Big Love" is the big booming hit song material that kicks it all off. *Tango in the Night,* the title track, makes it quite clear exactly to what dance Buckingham was referring: "Then I remember when the moon was full and bright, I would take you in the darkness and do the tango in the night." And with "Mystified," Lindsey and Christine seem to be reaching far back into the memory vaults, possible even without realizing it, and producing a veritable clone of Bob Welch's "Hypnotized" from the halcyon *Mystery to Me* days of 1973.

Christine again saves the day with one of her husky ballads, "Everywhere," and Nicks is up to her usual tricks, except that she was barely functioning during this period due to her drug, alcohol, and later tranquilizer addictions. Ever the trooper, however, and ever able to convert her own suffering into a product that millions would want to share in, her brilliant and harrowing "Welcome to The Room Sara" is a magnificent tour de force about her own voluntary incarceration in the "help me survive" clinic for overindulgent goddesses and stars. Luckily, Nicks came through her private hell, though her voice has never been the same after a decade of abuse and the ravages of cocaine addiction finally took their toll. Phil Sutcliffe summed it up best in his *Mojo* profile: Buckingham resentfully drops a solo project and then leaves pre-tour; Nicks is semidetached by Klonoptin, the tranquilizer that helped her beat cocaine addiction; and the routinely inebriated Anglos soldier on, retrieving some mid-1970s enchantment.

* * * * * * * * * *

Lindsey , you walked out on Fleetwood Mac to pursue the love of your life, music, all on your very own. No matter what was sometimes said or done, your mark on Fleetwood Mac will forever stand the test of time...

Love, Mick[16]

And indeed, it has. The test of time has in fact proven not only that Buckingham was a central creative core for the group throughout its third incarnation, but also that he was a truly visionary producer and performer who consistently pushed and pulled at the "brand" of Fleetwood Mac, making it largely his own. It was also a brand he shared with the most publicly high-profile person of the group, his former girlfriend Stevie Nicks, who of course became a huge solo star right in the middle of the spotlight she shared with the rest of the group.

Subsequent to their reaching the pinnacle of creative and commercial success, the band still had to cope with the intimations of mortality that face us all. Few people process the awareness of our impermanence as passionately as rock music stars, since they know better than anyone else just how fragile and impermanent their own careers and heights of power really are in reality.

Fleetwood has often quoted one of Nicks's own principal preoccupations ever since she joined the band in 1975: "What does happen after the glitter fades?" In the case of Fleetwood Mac, a legendary monster of creative chaos and commercial rebirth more times than most fans even know about, it was a question of launching a new military offensive as solo performers, with the occasional big-bang reunion, as if they hoped they could simply scoop up some of the mountains of glitter that had fallen to the floor of their careers and fling it back up into the air on themselves, hoping that shiny shower would continue forever. In this respect, they are no different than any other aging baby boomer rock celebrities such as The Rolling Stones, The Who, or Crosby, Stills, Nash, and Young: it is so very hard to give up that unique view from the top. So hard in fact, that some of them just cannot and do not, or will not give it up. But few titans are as titanic as Fleetwood Mac in the ongoing desire for that lofty view.

"After the making of *Tusk*," Fleetwood has stated, "and a seemingly endless year of touring which finished at the Hollywood Bowl, we were left with a sensation that the roller coaster ride might very well have come to a permanent end." As usual, the media had a good nose for decline and entropy, and was continuing to ask in press conference whether the band was breaking up. It is an odd question, really, since from the vantage point of this 40-ear history, we can all plainly see that the band was *always* breaking up, and writing and singing about it; but also that *breaking up was hard to do,* as the old Neil Sedaka pop song warned us. But by then, Fleetwood had his stock answer that still persists to this day: the band is definitely concentrating each on their own solo projects and careers, but that there will *always* be a Fleetwood Mac, in *some* form or other. But that despite these persistent rumors (no pun intended) the band would not break up.

On Nicks's solo effort *Bella Donna,* she was clever enough to include her own plea to the gods of fame written way back in 1975 by actually intoning those horrifying words: "the feeling remains even after the glitter fades"— as if in answer to critics questioning either her or their right to keep on keeping on.

Meanwhile Buckingham's *Law and Order,* possibly the most stable and secure work of the post-Mac period, was proceeding to deconstruct everything he had helped to build up within the group format. Cath Carroll called him "one of rock's great pop brains who just can't keep still, these recordings defy fashion." In *Never Break The Chain,* she observed that "Those who found his *Rumours* vocals to be reverb-heavy would have been scandalized by the veritable burlesque show of echo and delay on *Law and Order,* all of it very tongue in cheek. Maybe."[17]

But the band quickly realized that no matter how successful their solo projects were—and several of Nicks's outing almost rivaled Mac's own popularity —they each lacked the integral ingredients of the other's input and collaboration, even if it did mean they had to admit that need despite such monumental personality clashes. So the already grizzled road warriors assembled yet again in the Chateau D'Herouville in France, to chart the course that would eventually become the disappointingly delayed *Mirage* of 1982. This was a record that Buckingham really disliked but apparently felt enough guilt over *Tusk* to agree to participate in making. He would be devastated by the process and remained unable to consider another Mac project until the equally flaccid, yet still wildly successful *Tango in the Night* of 1987, a record that typically began as his own solo project but morphed organically into a Mac effort. After that, it was all over for Buckingham, or so he thought.

As they say in sports vernacular, "it's never over till it's over." Following Buckingham's unceremonious and acrimonious departure, Fleetwood Mac added two more guitarists to the group, as if forever attempting to fill the impossibly empty void left by Peter Green, Danny Kirwan, Bob Welch, and Lindsey Buckingham. But Billy Burnette and Rick Vito, while assuming the task valiantly, were not up to the challenge of standing in those particularly gifted shadows. They filled in on the band's tour in support of *Tango,* and that same pale imitation contributed to the sorry 1990 outing *Behind The Mask*—which, according to one ironic account, "only went gold."

BEHIND THE MASK:
RELEASED 1990, WARNER BROTHERS

Behind one mask, there is yet another mask; but that one too is not the real face. The second mask has eaten into the face, the way all celebrity masks do, to the point where the face and the mask are indistinguishable. An ironic parallel to "Make Me a Mask," this outing proved nearly fatal for the resilient band, only to be followed by an even more questionable effort that proved that time and tide wait for no band.

"Love is Dangerous" is an almost comical assessment of the raw material that had formerly fueled the band's massive momentum, and "In the Back of My Mind" is a truly scary anthem about being haunted, or obsessed by a lover who refuses to leave your memory alone. "In the back of my mind, you live all the time" is intoned over and over until one almost wishes for a little ego-shattering "Go Your Own Way" if only to wake us all up a bit.

After yet another housecleaning by McVie and Fleetwood, by that time downright Paleolithic in terms of their blues-rock music pedigree, Burnette and Vito's brief incarnation in the revolving door band membership was over—as was, it appeared, the group's claim to having any authentic musical message left to impart, let alone sell.

Surprisingly, in 1993 the members of Fleetwood Mac heard a voice from on high compelling them to reunite one more time: it was the drawling voice of the president-elect of the United States no less, as if personifying the whole nation's peculiar craving for this remarkable group's antics. Bill Clinton "asked" them to perform together at his first Inaugural Ball, having famously used "Don't Stop" as his campaign theme song, a brilliant tactic that may have cemented his image in the public's mind as a forward thinker fixed on that perpetual "tomorrow" that makes the song so catchy. They followed his orders, but were none too happy about sharing their lives yet again with the same people who had nearly torn them to emotional shreds for two decades.

By 1995, the low point in the band's glorious history inevitably arrived with another album attempt, this time using the historically important perhaps but by then creatively bereft talents of Dave Mason, founder of Traffic along with Steve Winwood in the mid-sixties; and Bonnie Bramlett, founder of nothing, but the daughter of Bonnie Bramlett, of Delanie and Bonnie and Friends, the core unit of Clapton's own Derek and the Dominos, back in their heyday. Unfortunately, this amounted to marketing themselves as a nostalgia/rival band, something along the lines of, and on the same bill with, REO Speedwagon and Pat Benatar, performing at a local casino. The musical results were expectedly dismal, and, of course, the record went nowhere fast.

TIME:
RELEASED 1995 BY WARNER BROTHERS

One of the worst albums of all time, period. There is one truly remarkable effort by Mick Fleetwood, which one critic friend has suggested to me was literally tacked on to the end of the record in order to spruce and juice it up a little, so different is it from the tired and quotidian rants that precede it.

"These Strange Times," with a rare vocal by Fleetwood, is a majestic hymn to his former mentor Peter Green, is one of the most harrowing personal statements of love and loss ever committed to record. "My friend, I do wish that I was in love. I wished I was in love. I love you, I love you" But not even the historic presence of Traffic founder Dave Mason could save *Time* from itself, or from the naturally occurring ills to which all time and energy is eventually subject: entropy. This album is so full of emptiness it can barely contain its own weariness.

But just when it seemed everything had pretty well ground to a halt, after three decades in the spotlight ignited by Peter Green, the music industry, and indeed the rest of the real world, was taken off guard by a 1997 reunion that actually yielded serious musical results. Once again, the group had been assembled in order to contribute elements of another solo Buckingham record. This chance encounter together led inexplicably to a full *Rumours*-era lineup reunion for a live "concert in the studio" recording, entitled *The Dance* and filmed for MTV.

THE DANCE:
RELEASED 1998, WARNER BROTHERS

The Dance is a truly mersmerizing live concert of greatest hits, performed by a reunited band that clearly could still seriously rock. Fleetwood and McVie are powerhouses of rhythm, while Buckingham's guitar solos are worthy of him and of any of the great guitarists in rock music. For oldsters, this outing had more real and raw performance juice than many other groups a third of their ages. This was really the last hurrah of sorts. They were all on the road together touring to support *The Dance*, a remarkably entertaining and well-performed concert that made for a tantalizing film and record package. Finally, Fleetwood Mac was inducted into the Rock and Roll Hall of Fame in 1998, and they performed live at the Grammy Awards that year to celebrate the fact.

Unfortunately, as mentioned earlier, only the two bookends of the Mac legend were recognized, namely the first Peter Green lineup with Jeremy Spencer and Danny Kirwan, and the last blockbuster lineup with Buckingham and Nicks. The glorious middle period, led by the multitalented singer, songwriter, and guitarist Bob Welch, was utterly ignored, even though he was responsible for five of their most innovative and progressive recordings from 1971 to 1975. The music industry, as always, remains a puzzling and maddening affair.

By 1998, after more than 30 years with Fleetwood Mac, and after her own stellar career as a genuine blueswoman with the illustrious Chicken Shack, Christine McVie had finally had enough and threw in the towel, retiring back to England for some well earned peace and quiet. Buckingham and Nicks however, ever the erstwhile troopers (or is it just an addiction to celebrity?) reunited yet again to do vocals, instrumentation, and production on Fleetwood Mac's latest record, *Say You Will*, released in 2003.

SAY YOU WILL:
RELEASED 2003, WARNER BROTHERS

This swan-song record debuted at number three on the Billboard charts and was supported by a successful, if largely nostalgic, world arena tour through 2004. Mick Fleetwood and John McVie now remain the only original members of Fleetwood Mac still choosing to call themselves by the name Peter Green had first bestowed in his favorite rhythm section while his then boss John Mayall was out of the room.

Say You Will harkens back to the debut Buckingham-Nicks album from 1973, and appears to retread some of those intense stories from a retrospective point of view. Whereas the first record looked forward to a dream, the last record looks backward at a dream, with predictable results. In some ways, it is the best real Fleetwood Mac record in years, even with Nicks's shattered voice and monotone nasal renderings. It captures what the fuss was all about in the first place. Yet another solo Buckingham record that got away from him, *Say You Will* is a perfect climax to a perfect career path, unless there is yet another swift kick left in the old brood yet. Unfortunately, Christine McVie was missing from this last one, peacefully retired from the fray.

"What's The World Coming To?" starts the coaster rolling in fine style. Buckingham laments in fine fierce form, "I don't say what they want, I don't do what they say. So I'm on their list, so I'm gone I guess...what's the world coming to?" He follows this existential query with a remarkably strange and sinister song, one of his best in that flavor, "Murrow turning over in his grave, Ed Murrow had a child, the damn thing went wild, Murrow turning over in his grave." It is one of the best indictments of popular television, and the media in general, ever encapsulated within the soft shell of a shiny pop song.

Nicks does her usual diva turn with "Illume" and "Thrown Down" but manages to reach a true emotional clarity with the title track, "Say You Will": "Say you will say you will, give me one more chance, at least give me time to change your mind. That always seems to heal the wounds, if I can get you to dance." And her "Silver Girl," directed toward some of her songstress offspring such as Sheryl Crow, offers cautionary tales to any young girl who thinks rock and roll might be a suitable lifestyle. Her grand "Destiny Rules" also serves as a synopsis of why the group has been through so much together and what the glue might be that links the chains that bind them. "It appears to me that destiny rules, that the spirits are ruthless with the paths that they choose, its not being together, its just following the rules, nobody's a fool."

But as if saving the best for last, the two closing numbers, Buckingham's "Say Goodbye" and Nicks's "Goodbye Baby," summarize their own frayed bond together as both lovers and collaborating artists:

> Buckingham: "Once you said goodbye to me, now I say goodbye to you."
> Nicks: "Goodbye baby, I hope your heart's not broken, don't forget me, yes I was outspoken. You were with me all the time, I'll be with you one day."

But some goodbyes are not just *long* goodbyes, some goodbyes go on forever. Several quotes from the band members prior to their last big reunion seem to summarize their personal and professional trajectories perfectly. They come from Bob Brunning's book on the band, and they focus squarely on the main question asked most often by anyone who knows the soap opera history of this group and the gargantuan amounts of creative angst that always awaits them whenever they enter the same musical room.

From founder Fleetwood: "We've been asked many times over the years to reform, but the time was never right. I think we were all still in the process of growing up and discovering that the things that had once pulled us apart didn't seem nearly as important anymore. The level of success we had together was, quite simply, overwhelming. We've had the opportunity to step back and get some perspective, to realize that what was important all along was the music."[18] Now why could not The Beatles have stepped back and obtained a similar perspective on *their* music?

From founder John McVie: "The 20th anniversary of *Rumours* gave us a vantage point to look back and forward. We realized that we had created this tremendous body of work and that we wanted to celebrate that accomplishment. 1997 marked the 30th Anniversary of the founding of Fleetwood Mac, so the occasion seemed especially auspicious for that reason as well."[19] Does this sound like voice of a man who does not want to do something special this and next year, for the 40th anniversary edition of his dream?

From resident earth mother Christine McVie: "It was an odd feeling, being back together, but it was obvious we were having fun. I was very content with my life, but I must admit...I felt the pull."[20] This is the husky-voiced echo of a woman who kept up and was on equal terms with some of the most crazed and talented musicians in England before joining Mac and living out her marriage on stage.

And from the majestic interlopers, Lindsey Buckingham and Stevie Nicks, a tortured duo of undeniable talents guided by a technical production wizard of prodigious gifts, there is obviously more blood left in this very smooth stone, polished from years of mutual creative caressing. Even if sometimes with a clenched fist, caressed smooth nonetheless.

What Mick Fleetwood and John McVie will do next is anybody's guess. Some people still hold out hope that somehow a miracle will occur and the original 1960s Mac lineup will resurface around a triumphantly resurrected Peter Green. But miracles like that do not happen more than once. One thing is certain, however—if anything is, this group may be poised for another kick at our can sometime soon, either in 2007 or 2008, the 40th year since they first plugged in and took us all on the ride of a lifetime—their lifetime, and our lifetime. For a life lived in the incredibly unforgiving and hypertemporary world of popular music and culture, theirs has been a very long, if not necessarily healthy, life span indeed.

Conclusion
Unplugged: Say You Might as Well

This particular group of talented musicians, singers, and songwriters gives new meaning to that popular song, "still crazy, after all these years." The megapop behemoth known as Fleetwood Mac is practically a golden metaphor for the entire creative partnership phenomenon, both its magic and its mayhem. They are the principal evidence for the argument that a certain personal chemistry can be neither copied nor duplicated. One author, Douglas Wolk, has even suggested that they might be the least influential great band ever, simply because they are impossible to imitate. No one can accurately identify just what it is they play in order to copy it. But how, after all that angst merged with bliss, do they just keep on keeping on? Two things: allegiance and obedience to their successful brand, and because nobody does it better, as evidenced by the group's surprise hit of 2003, *Say You Will* (or as I like to call it, "Say You Might as Well").

And as Phil Sutcliffe points out so well in his *Mojo* profile of their latest reunion, "When Nicks rejoined Fleetwood Mac for the intriguingly Tusk-like *Say You Will,* Buckingham found her ready to forgive, not to forget, but to laugh about" all their shared travails. "Now, on the road, we have many good talks," he says, "We've known each other most of our lives and we're still trying to figure out what's going on....It's significant that someone can end up...you know...not having killed you!" Says Nicks, "Now I just adore him," with ravishing candor. "He is my love, my first love and my love for all time. But we can't ever be together. He has a lovely wife, Kirsten, who I really like, and three children. The way he is with his children just knocks me out....I look at him now and just go, 'Oh Stevie, you made a mistake!' But then when we go on stage together we are able to experience our love affair again, and again, and again."[1]

Mick Fleetwood clarifies it all surprisingly well: "It's a forever story with them, as it is with all of us! Loyalty. Musically, we've done it together for so long that anything else is shallow, compared to McVie. Long ago, playing the blues, we learnt that a rhythm section needs to be *gracious*. We don't have any *musical* egos at all."[2]

And as if to further prove some of the observations on the glue that holds creative artists together, during last year's tour to support his newest solo record, *Under the Skin*, Lindsey Buckingham finally relented and gave his live audience a taste of what they really wanted. He delivered his classic *Rumours*-era Mac opus, "Go Your Own Way," but he naturally spiced up the flavor of that now 30-year-old pop song by tearing its melody to shreds with his angriest guitar solos in years, mangling our memories at the same time as preserving them.

Is it strange for a book on a massively successful pop group to open with a quote from the somewhat obscure seventeenth-century philosopher Francis Bacon? Not really. This British thinker seems to have spookily captured the very heart and soul of this group's strange combination of creative collaboration dynamics and their uncanny ability to understand in their blood and bones just exactly what will sell and what will not. The surprise is that they never really "sold out." So that should not be any more surprising than Fleetwood Mac's own choice of another English poet, William Shakespeare, to partially title their third (and last) early lineup record. "If Music be the Food of Love," Shakespeare remarked in Twelfth Night, "Play On..."

And in "The Chain," one of the only songs actually credited to the entire group as its composers rather than to one or more of the dynamic writing duos in tow, the band said it in a way that maybe even Shakespeare could have envied : "I can still hear you saying you would never break the chain... the chain holds us together."

Make no mistake about it. There are three Fleetwood Macs, and all of them are equally brilliant bands. Somehow, Mac celebrates 40 unlikely years in 2007. Do not be surprised if yet another event, performance, or release appears on the pop horizon to memorialize this astounding achievement. Surely someone is currently cooking up a 30th-anniversary celebration staging of *Rumours,* delivered in its entirety, perhaps accompanied by a symphony orchestra? Equally certain will be a public spectacle of some sort staged to celebrate the 40th-anniversary release of their first English recording, *Peter Green's Fleetwood Mac* in 1968, so long before they became living emblems of the Californian ethos constructed from their personal and professional relationships.

Our overview of the remarkable creative arc of this band focused on their unique ability to adapt to both internal and external changes and perpetually reinvent themselves. One of the key elements of their success, apart from the catchy quality of their well-produced and distinctly delivered sound, is also the rare quality of its two male leaders to allow their formerly gritty macho blues sound to be softened and enhanced with the addition of not one, but two lead female singers and songwriters. And they took the blues, painted it with the glistening varnish of perfectly crafted pop music, made the world jump up and down to its freshly sharpened and shiny edges, and made themselves legends in the process.

What becomes a legend most? Never giving up, apparently. As if to celebrate his own 40th anniversary as the leader of this remarkable band, Mick Fleetwood continues to do what he loves best—perform live in front of an audience, even a small audience, where he can almost see the whites of their eyes. In January 2007, in fact, Fleetwood went on the road again, performing in Niagara Falls at the Avalon Ballroom, in front of a mere 1,500 fans. But at least they were 1,500 happy fans, with a long memory perhaps, myself among them. Apparently Fleetwood celebrates by going back out on the road yet again. "Can't stop thinking about tomorrow," indeed!

Instead of the brilliant John McVie, possibly the only bass player in rock music at the same level of mastery as McCartney, Bruce, Entwistle, or Wyman, Fleetwood was joined in rhythm by George Hawkins Jr., who as an alumni of multiple Californian bands (including Fleetwood's own 1980 solo effort *The Visitor*) will manage to channel McVie spookily well. But there is still no one like McVie, ever and anywhere.

On lead guitar, still stranded in the long shadow cast by early band founder Peter Green's youthful flare-out, the grizzled veteran road warrior was joined by guitarists Rick Vito and Billy Burnette, both of whom tried to replace the incomparable Lindsey Buckingham in the early 1990s version of Fleetwood Mac. And for a couple of nights in Niagara Falls, they attempted the impossible yet again. Of course, no one could ever attempt to replace the sultry, smoky tones of either Christine McVie, my personal candidate for best female blues vocalist of all time, or Stevie Nicks, not quite my cup of tea but still an extraordinary talent, which is why even Fleetwood knows enough to leave those two spaces vacant.

One keen observer of that *other* famous British pop band once commented that you cannot be in people's past and also in their future. But as in so many other things, Fleetwood has proven logic wrong yet again, especially since his group has lasted a full five times as long as John Lennon's. Those early Mac records were all the evidence anyone needed that this group was well worth listening to, wherever they chose to go stylistically. And history has proven this to be true, three times over. Theirs is pure creative chaos at its finest and most impressive, not to mention occasionally depressive, with a working method not recommended for average musicians; yet it worked supremely well for Fleetwood Mac. The link of their musical continuum is still the same:

the joys and sorrows of being in love. "Don't Stop" and "Go Your Own Way" are essentially still blues songs, but varnished, expanded, and inflated until they practically become purple.

In the year 2007, we can still see and hear the 40-year-old chain that keeps Fleetwood Mac together, because Fleetwood himself is rattling it right in front of us. Four decades atop the pop music mountain means that Fleetwood Mac has *always* been a part of our past, present, *and* our future, does it not? After all these years, the core of this group—a majestically indulgent drummer gifted with a perfect sense of rhythm and an even better ability to pick the right new band members at just the right moment—continues to feel the pulse of live music. Whether or not the classic lineups of all three Fleetwood Mac's ever record again together, as a historic creative ensemble they have given us three successive phases of sheer musical muscle flexed like no one else but them could ever have flexed. They have also proven the often suspected truth: that all the biggest and best dreams need to be paid for in blood, sweat and tears. If this music is the result, then long live creative chaos.

Notes

INTRODUCTION: PLUGGING IN

1. Vera John-Steiner, *Creative Collaboration* (New York: Oxford University Press, 2000), 32.
2. Ibid.
3. Vicente Todoli, *Collaborations* (Edition Mayer, 2003) 6.

CHAPTER 1

1. Bob Brunning, *Fleetwood Mac: The First Thirty Years* (London: Omnibus Press, 1998), 22.
2. Bob Brunning, *Blues: The British Connection,* paperback ed. (London: Helter Skelter Publishing, 2002), 10.
3. Marilyn Stasio, "In Postwar Britain, Mysteries to Solve," *New York Times,* April 29, 2006.
4. Ibid.
5. Ibid.
6. Ibid.
7. Greil Marcus, *Lipstick Traces: A Secret History of the Twentieth Century* (Cambridge, MA: Harvard University Press, 1989), 9.
8. Marcus, 21.
9. Brunning, *Fleetwood Mac: The First Thirty Years,* 13.
10. Ian Macdonald, *Revolution in the Head: The Beatles' Records and the Sixties* (Pimlico Publishers, 1998), xv.
11. Macdonald, *Revolution in the Head,* xix.
12. Brunning, *Blues: The British Connection,* 11.
13. Ibid.

14. Ibid., 13.

15. Macdonald, *Revolution in the Head* (Pimlico Publishers, 1998), preface.

16. Ibid.

17. Macdonald, *Revolution in the Head*, xv.

18. Macdonald, *Revolution in the Head*, 2.

19. Raymond Williams, *Keywords* (Oxford: Oxford University Press, 1983), 87.

20. Jon Savage, "The Simple Things," in *The Faber Book of Pop*, ed. Hanif Kureishi and Jon Savage (Faber and Faber, 1995), xxix.

21. Rodney Garland, *The Heart in Exile* (Millivres Books, 1996).

22. George Melly, *Revolt into Style* (Oxford: Oxford University Press, 1989).

23. Macdonald, *Revolution in the Head*, 13.

24. Ibid.

25. Steve Clarke, *Fleetwood Mac* (Proteus Books, 1984), 10.

26. Brunning, *Blues: The British Connection*, 10.

27. *The Mojo Collection* (Canongate Books, 2000), 180.

28. Ibid.

29. Ibid.

30. Liner notes for John Mayall with Peter Green, *A Hard Road* (Decca Records, 1967).

CHAPTER 2

1. Mick Fleetwood, *My Twenty-five Years with Fleetwood Mac*, with Stephen Davis (New York: Hyperion Press, 1992), 27.

2. Mick Fleetwood, *Fleetwood: My Life and Adventures in Fleetwood Mac* (New York: William Morrow and Co., 1990), 29.

3. Liner notes for Mayall, *A Hard Road*.

4. Quoted in Peter Lewry, *Fleetwood Mac: The Complete Recording Sessions, 1967–1992* (London: Blandford Press, 1998), 15.

5. Quoted in Lewry, *Fleetwood Mac: The Complete Recording Sessions*, 16.

6. Quoted in Lewry, *Fleetwood Mac: The Complete Recording Sessions*, 17.

7. Mick Fleetwood, *My Twenty-five Years with Fleetwood Mac*, with Stephen Davis (New York: Hyperion Press, 1992), 3.

8. Ibid.

9. Quoted in Lewry, *Fleetwood Mac: The Complete Recording Sessions*, 20.

10. Leah Furman, *Rumours Exposed: The Unauthorized Biography of Fleetwood Mac* (New York: Citadel Press, 2000), 25.

11. Fleetwood, *My Twenty-five Years*, 1.

12. Fleetwood, *Fleetwood: My Life and Adventures*, 37.

13. Martin Celmins, *Peter Green: Founder of Fleetwood Mac* (Surrey, UK: Castle Communications, 1995), 13.

14. Clarke, *Fleetwood Mac*, 22.

15. Lewry, *Fleetwood Mac: The Complete Recording Sessions*, 33.

16. Celmins, *Peter Green*, 19.

17. Quoted in Fleetwood, *My Twenty-five Years*, 55.

18. Samuel Graham, *Fleetwood Mac: The Authorized History* (Washington, DC: Warner Bros. Publications, 1978), 35.

19. Graham, *Fleetwood Mac: The Authorized History,* 37.

20. Ibid.

21. Ibid.

22. Fleetwood, *My Twenty-five Years,* 27.

23. Brunning, *Fleetwood Mac: The First Thirty Years,* 24.

24. Ibid.

25. Furman, *Rumours Exposed,* 25.

26. Brunning, *Fleetwood Mac: The First Thirty Years,* 28.

27. Graham, *Fleetwood Mac: The Authorized History,* 115.

28. *The Mojo Collection,* 176.

29. Lewry, *Fleetwood Mac: The Complete Recording Sessions,* 20.

30. Lewry, *Fleetwood Mac: The Complete Recording Sessions,* 21.

31. Mike Vernon, liner notes to *Complete Blue Horizon Sessions* (Blue Horizon Records, 1999).

32. Ibid.

33. Quoted in *The Mojo Collection,* 176.

34. *The Mojo Collection,* 176.

CHAPTER 3

1. Quoted in Lewry, *Fleetwood Mac: The Complete Recording Sessions,* 42, 43.

2. Quoted in Lewry, *Fleetwood Mac: The Complete Recording Sessions,* 47.

3. Lewry, *Fleetwood Mac: The Complete Recording Sessions,* 42.

4. Brunning, *Fleetwood Mac: The First Thirty Years,* 32.

5. Quoted in Lewry, *Fleetwood Mac: The Complete Recording Sessions,* 49.

6. Macdonald, *Revolution in the Head* (1998), 30.

7. Macdonald, *Revolution in the Head* (1998), 32.

8. Macdonald, *Revolution in the Head* (1998), 24.

9. Fleetwood, *Fleetwood: My Life and Adventures,* 65.

10. Aldous Huxley, *Heaven and Hell* (London: Chatto and Windus, 1956).

11. Brunning, *Fleetwood Mac: The First Thirty Years,* 30.

12. Ibid.

13. Ibid.

14. Ibid.

15. Charles Baudelaire, "Artificial Paradise," in *Zig Zag Zen,* ed. Alan Badiner (San Francisco: Chronicle Books, 2002), 104.

16. Christine Kenneally, *New York Times Book Review,* September 29, 2002.

17. Ibid.

18. Timothy White, *Rock Lives* (New York: Henry Holt and Co., 1990), 604.

19. Ibid.

20. Ibid.

21. Ibid.

22. Ibid.

23. Brunning, *Blues: The British Connection,* 138.

24. Ibid.

25. Francis Bacon, *Essays* (1625; repr., Renaissance Editions, University of Oregon, 1998).

CHAPTER 4

1. Fleetwood, *My Twenty-five Years*, 40.

2. Fleetwood, *Fleetwood: My Life and Adventures*, 83.

3. Fleetwood, *Fleetwood: My Life and Adventures*, 25.

4. Fleetwood, *Fleetwood: My Life and Adventures*, 88.

5. Ellen Willis, Preface, in *Trouble Girls: The Rolling Stone Book of Women In Rock*, ed. Barbara O'Dair (New York: Random House, 1997), xvi.

6. Ibid.

7. O'Dair, ed., *Trouble Girls*, xxv.

8. Ariel Swartley, "Little Mama, Wild Women," in *Trouble Girls*, 8.

9. Swartley, in *Trouble Girls*, 9.

10. Clarke, *Fleetwood Mac*, 66.

11. Clarke, *Fleetwood Mac*, 56.

12. Ibid.

13. Fleetwood, *Fleetwood: My Life and Adventures*, 90.

14. Clarke, *Fleetwood Mac*, 66.

15. Quoted in Clarke, *Fleetwood Mac*, 67.

16. Quoted in Brunning, *Fleetwood Mac: The First Thirty Years*, 38.

17. Quoted in Brunning, *Fleetwood Mac: The First Thirty Years*, 39.

18. Ibid.

19. Quoted in Brunning, *Fleetwood Mac: The First Thirty Years*, 40.

20. Ibid.

21. Fleetwood, *Fleetwood: My Life and Adventures*, 118.

22. Quoted in Graham, *Fleetwood Mac: The Authorized History*, 60.

23. Graham, *Fleetwood Mac: The Authorized History*, 100.

24. Fleetwood, *My Twenty-five Years*, 55.

25. Nigel Williamson, "Five Go Mad," *Uncut*, May 2003, 43.

26. Graham, *Fleetwood Mac: The Authorized History*, 115.

27. Williamson, "Five Go Mad," 47.

28. Mark Trauernicht, "'One Together' at the Penguin: An Early History of Fleetwood Mac (2000), http://www.fleetwoodmac.net/penguin/onetogether/index.html (accessed July 16, 2007).

29. Fleetwood, *Fleetwood: My Life and Adventures*, 128.

30. Trauernicht, "'One Together' at the Penguin."

31. Cath Carroll, *Never Break the Chain; Fleetwood Mac and the Making of Rumours* (Chicago: Chicago Review Press, 2004), 44.

32. Carroll, *Never Break The Chain*, 56.

CHAPTER 5

1. Fleetwood, *My Twenty-five Years*, 63.

2. Lewry, *Fleetwood Mac: The Complete Recording Sessions*, 58.

3. Fleetwood, *Fleetwood: My Life and Adventures*, 141.

4. Fleetwood, *Fleetwood: My Life and Adventures*, 153.

5. Quoted in Fleetwood, *Fleetwood: My Life and Adventures*, 153.

6. Furman, *Rumours Exposed*, 79.

7. Fleetwood, *Fleetwood: My Life and Adventures,* 154.
8. Fleetwood, *Fleetwood: My Life and Adventures,* 155.
9. Fleetwood, *Fleetwood: My Life and Adventures,* 159.
10. Ibid.
11. Furman, *Rumours Exposed,* 84.
12. Furman, *Rumours Exposed,* 85.
13. Ibid.
14. Fleetwood, *Fleetwood: My Life and Adventures,* 160.
15. Ibid.
16. Fleetwood, *Fleetwood: My Life and Adventures,* 165.
17. Brunning, *Fleetwood Mac: The First Thirty Years,* 88.
18. Furman, *Rumours Exposed,* 88.
19. Furman, *Rumours Exposed,* 91.

CHAPTER 6

1. Lewry, *Fleetwood Mac: The Complete Recording Sessions,* 63.
2. Fleetwood, *Fleetwood: My Life and Adventures,* 170.
3. Brunning, *Fleetwood Mac: The First Thirty Years,* 90.
4. Ibid.
5. Brunning, *Fleetwood Mac: The First Thirty Years,* 91.
6. Ibid.
7. Ibid.
8. Brunning, *Fleetwood Mac: The First Thirty Years,* 93.
9. Ibid.
10. Fleetwood, *Fleetwood: My Life and Adventures,* 170.
11. Fleetwood, *Fleetwood: My Life and Adventures,* 171.
12. Furman, *Rumours Exposed,* 95.
13. Fleetwood, *Fleetwood: My Life and Adventures,* 174.
14. Fleetwood, *Fleetwood: My Life and Adventures,* 175.
15. Fleetwood, *Fleetwood: My Life and Adventures,* 177.
16. Williamson, "Five Go Mad," 47.
17. Ibid.
18. Ibid.
19. Fleetwood, *Fleetwood: My Life and Adventures,* 177.
20. Fleetwood, *Fleetwood: My Life and Adventures,* 181.
21. Ibid.
22. Fleetwood, *Fleetwood: My Life and Adventures,* 187.
23. Ibid.
24. Fleetwood, *Fleetwood: My Life and Adventures,* 191.
25. Fleetwood, *Fleetwood: My Life and Adventures,* 187.
26. Fleetwood, *Fleetwood: My Life and Adventures,* 201.
27. Furman, *Rumours Exposed,* 108.
28. Furman, *Rumours Exposed,* 109.
29. Ibid.
30. Fleetwood, *Fleetwood: My Life and Adventures,* 203.
31. Ibid.

CHAPTER 7

1. Williamson, "Five Go Mad," 64.

2. Ibid.

3. Ibid.

4. Phil Sutcliffe, "Taking it to the Limit," *Mojo,* May 2003, 48.

5. Ibid.

6. Ibid.

7. Ibid.

8. Ibid.

9. Greil Marcus, *Ranters and Crowd Pleasers: Punk in Pop Music, 1977–92* (New York: Doubleday, 1993), 82.

10. Fleetwood, *Fleetwood: My Life and Adventures,* 203.

11. Marcus, *Ranters and Crowd Pleasers,* 82.

12. Marcus, *Ranters and Crowd Pleasers,* 83.

13. Fleetwood, *Fleetwood: My Life and Adventures,* 207.

14. Fleetwood, *Fleetwood: My Life and Adventures,* 215.

15. Fleetwood, *Fleetwood: My Life and Adventures,* 216.

16. Fleetwood, *Fleetwood: My Life and Adventures,* 221.

17. Ibid.

18. Fleetwood, *Fleetwood: My Life and Adventures,* 203.

19. Fleetwood, *Fleetwood: My Life and Adventures,* 226.

20. Carroll, *Never Break the Chain,* 226.

21. Mitchell Cohen, "Fleetwood Mac: *Tusk:* From Shining Platinum to Dull Ivory," *Creem,* January 1980.

22. Stephen Holden, *Rolling Stone,* December 13, 1979, 120.

23. Marcus, *Ranters and Crowd Pleasers,* 81.

24. Bob Brunning, *Fleetwood Mac: Behind the Masks* (London: New English Library, 1990).

CHAPTER 8

1. Ben Ratliff, "Playlist," *New York Times,* October 11, 2006.

2. "Buzz" (entertainment section), *Toronto Star,* October 11, 2006.

3. Ibid.

4. Anthony DeCurtis, music section, *New York Times,* October 11, 2006.

5. Ibid.

6. Ibid.

7. Fleetwood, *Fleetwood: My Life and Adventures,* 248.

8. Fleetwood, *Fleetwood: My Life and Adventures,* 249.

9. Fleetwood, *Fleetwood: My Life and Adventures,* 251.

10. Fleetwood, *Fleetwood: My Life and Adventures,* 268.

11. Fleetwood, *Fleetwood: My Life and Adventures,* 250.

12. Fleetwood, *Fleetwood: My Life and Adventures,* 268.

13. Fleetwood, *Fleetwood: My Life and Adventures,* 269.

14. BBC Radio interview, January 1987; quoted in Fleetwood, *Fleetwood: My Life and Adventures,* 88.

15. Fleetwood, *Fleetwood: My Life and Adventures*, 281.
16. Fleetwood, *My Twenty-five Years*, 140.
17. Carroll, *Never Break The Chain*, 213.
18. Brunning, *Fleetwood Mac: The First Thirty Years*, 179.
19. Brunning, *Fleetwood Mac: The First Thirty Years*, 180.
20. Brunning, *Fleetwood Mac: The First Thirty Years*, 179.

Conclusion: Unplugged—Say You Might as Well

1. Sutcliffe, "Taking it to the Limit," 50.
2. Ibid.

Index

About the Author

DONALD BRACKETT is a Toronto-based art and music critic who specializes in contemporary popular culture subjects. He writes regularly for a wide cross section of national media, both in print and broadcast formats, among them: *Globe and Mail, National Post, Canadian Art Magazine* and *Art in America*. He has been the Executive Director of both the Professional Art Dealers Association and the Ontario Association of Art Galleries, and is currently on the faculty of Centennial College in Toronto, where he teaches The History of Art and The Business of Art. His forthcoming book, *Dark Mirror: The Pathology of the Singer-Songwriter*, will be published by Praeger.